GWALI

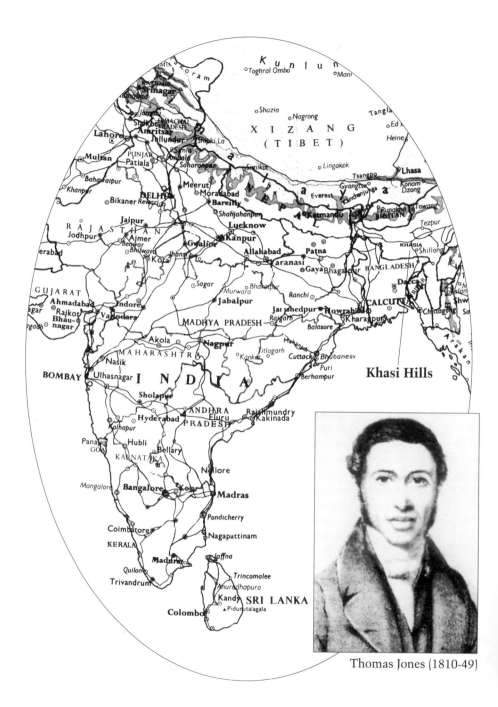

Khasi Hills

Thomas Jones (1810-49)

GWALIA
IN KHASIA

A visit to the site, in India, of
the biggest overseas venture ever
sustained by the Welsh

Nigel Jenkins

First casebound edition – May 1995
First softback edition – October 1995

ISBN 1 85902 412 2

This book is published with the support
of the Arts Council of Wales.

Printed in Wales at
Gomer Press, Llandysul, Ceredigion

1

The Khasis compute their history with stone. Across their hills and lost plains, in their jungle villages and even on the streets of their car-choked capital, long shadows fall from countless thousands of cromlechs and monoliths. Remember, they say, the mother of mothers; remember the dead and venerate their deeds; remember what has been sworn on the blades of swords. The very word for 'remember', *kynmaw*, is megalithic: 'to mark with a stone'. But not a letter of their language is inscribed on these stones: they long ago lost the art of writing, and have had to carry inside themselves their sense of who they are.

Once, though, in a forgotten paradise far to the north, the Khasis were able to read and write. But they were driven away from this original home when a catastrophic deluge descended on the world. One of the few to survive it was a Bengali plainsman. Menaced by the rising waters, he made a bundle of all his sacred scripts, and swam to safety with his book strapped securely to his head. A Khasi hillman also survived, although legend has it that he put his book in his mouth and accidentally swallowed it as he swam through the flood. According to others, this book of all the Khasis' knowledge was swept from the swimmer's mouth by the violence of the current, and was thought to be lost forever.

So the Khasis came to their new home bereft of their book. If their chiefs wanted to keep territorial records or communicate with outsiders they had to make do with the borrowed script of a neighbour – Bengali or Assamese, even Persian or Arabic. For hundreds of years it was only by word of mouth that they were able to pass on, from one generation to the next, dim but persistent recollection of a literate way of life that had once been theirs.

Then a strange new shadow appeared among their stones. It was the shadow of a *phareng* – white foreigner – from a land called Wales far to the west. Tucked beneath the stranger's arm, and pressed between two black boards, was a collection of scripts. The book.

Had it not been for a shipwreck in the Bay of Bengal on the night of January 18, 1837, the Calvinistic Methodists' Mission to the Khasi Hills, the biggest overseas venture ever sustained by the Welsh people, might never have been.

Homeward bound aboard the *Gregson*, "a commodious, and fine new built ship", after more than ten years service in the Far East, was the English Baptist missionary Jacob Tomlin, with his wife and three little girls. Working at first under the auspices of the London Missionary Society and then, being a man of independent means, on his own account, Tomlin had travelled widely, visiting Singapore, Java, Siam and Malacca where he had been a fellow-labourer of the Welsh missionary Josiah Hughes. He left Malacca for Calcutta in 1836, "purposing in the Lord, to proceed thence to the Khassia hills, which form the southern boundary of the valley of Assam"; he would cross from there into China, three hundred miles to the east. But, arriving in Calcutta in the cool season, his family had taken ill, "especially the children, who sunk rapidly, so that we were apprehensive of losing some of them." Friends advised Tomlin to return to England, postponing any further missionary exploits until his family's health had improved.

He took that advice. On January 10 the Tomlins climbed the gangplank of the universally admired *Gregson*, hoping to reach England by May; the Lord, however, "in His mysterious but wise providence", was to disappoint their expectations. In his *Missionary Journals and Letters* the Rev. Tomlin relates how, in spite of a warm send-off and the excellence of their cabins, a feeling of foreboding had depressed his spirits as the *Gregson* cast off and made her way down the Hooghly towards the open sea. The vessel's grounding on a sandbank seemed an ominous portent, but after a day's paralysis she worked free of the obstruction and continued downstream without apparent injury. After a week's sailing, the pilot was dropped off at the river mouth and the *Gregson* spread canvas before the favourable winds of the Bay of Bengal.

By nightfall the following day they had been carried about fifty miles out to sea. "We retired to our cabins to rest, as we thought, in peace and safety, but were suddenly aroused from our beds about eleven o'clock, by a loud call of 'The ship's on fire!'" The passengers crowded hurriedly on deck to find captain, officers and crew struggling with pumps and buckets to quench a fire which had broken out in the steerage, among some bales of India flax, and was now raging beyond control. Soon the order was given to abandon ship. "When, at length, all were forcibly driven from the deck by the devouring flames, we retired to windward, a mile, to contemplate the awful and terrific scene; till the masts, rigging, and hull, of 'the *fine ship Gregson*,' were one blazing mass. A melancholy spirit rested upon all . . . "

For two nights and a day they rowed their lifeboats in the direction of the pilot station at the mouth of the Hooghly, "scorched with heat by day, and pinched with cold by night". At last they were rescued by a ship called the *Cambrian* which, though heading for London, turned around and ferried them back towards Calcutta.

The Rev. Tomlin had not been entirely sure, as he and his family had embarked for England, that he was doing the right thing in deferring his trip to the Khasi Hills. Now, having survived the shipwreck and been delivered safely to Calcutta, he decided that it was undoubtedly God's desire that he should proceed after all with the original plan.

After several days' recuperation in Calcutta, the Tomlins set out by budgerow on a three-week river journey, "safe but tedious", that brought them to the foot of the Khasi Hills. Then, following a six-hour climb up almost sheer mountainsides, they found themselves four thousand feet above the sultry plains of Bengal in a temperate climate of cool and healthy breezes.

This was relatively virgin missionary territory, for British contact with the 'Khassias', as Tomlin called them, had begun only fifteen or twenty years earlier "when their depredations, within the bounds of our territory of Silhet in the plains, called for interference on our part, and brought our troops in conflict with them." The Khasis, with their bows and arrows, had put up a plucky fight against this British 'interference', but eventually

7

they had been "subdued or overawed", and had agreed to the British building a road across their hills and a permanent military station at Cherrapunji, their principal village.

It was at Cherrapunji, on its "lofty and sublime precipice" overlooking the swampy flatlands of what is today Bangladesh, that the Tomlins settled for a nine month stay. They lodged at first with Alexander Lish, a young Baptist missionary who had been working in the hills for three or four years; then they decamped to the home of an invalid ex-army officer, Lieutenant Lewin and his wife, who were staunch enthusiasts of the missionary cause. Tomlin learned much about the Khasis and their way of life, picking up enough of their language to be able to preach the gospel to them on various missionary excursions.

He found them "a bold and independent race of mountaineers, forming a perfect contrast to the timid and crouching natives of Bengal . . . The Khassias are very cheerful, active and enterprising; and when more civilized, and blessed with knowledge of the gospel, they will become a very interesting and noble people; and will, I doubt not, be faithful and able allies to our government."

Among the things that baffled him about the Khasis were their innumerable stone monuments. These structures reminded him not only of Stonehenge but, tantalisingly, of stones raised by the Israelites in Old Testament times – at Gilgal and Bethel and Mizpah. Might not this people, he surmised with awe, be a part of the lost sheep of the house of Israel?

Whatever their origins, their souls were now ripe for God's picking, for "The great foes to Christ and his gospel, the POPE, MAHOMED and BRAHMA, have not yet got upon these mountains, and therefore the Lord's servants may expect to find fewer obstacles in their way than in most parts of the world. But we must proceed quietly, and sow the precious seed plentifully, before these arch enemies come in stealthily, and sow their tares. *Popery*, the most zealous and wary of their foes, is watching the movements of Protestant Missionaries, and following close upon their heels, wherever there is a prospect of success. The Pope's emissaries are coming forth like a cloud of locusts, and settling upon every green spot that has been cultivated by the Lord's faithful servants."

The Tomlins eventually sailed for England in January, 1838, having been obliged by Mrs. Tomlin's poor health and the birth of a fourth child, Joshua Cherra, to forego the onward trek to China.

Soon after arriving home the missionary received from one of the Methodists in north Wales a request for advice as to where an independently constituted Welsh missionary society, should one be formed, might establish a field. The Rev. Tomlin's reply, which represents probably the first mention of the Khasi Hills in connection with the Welsh Calvinistic Methodists, was published in *Y Drysorfa Ysbrydol* (The Spiritual Treasury) in 1839: "It would be good to see two . . . of the Welsh brothers being sent to the Khasia Mountains, a place where you might soon enough gather into Christ's orchard many of the wandering sheep on the distant and until lately unfamiliar mountains, who have at present no shepherd to watch over them, and to feed them. They would have considerable assistance with the language, which can be learned in a year or two."

Tomlin's experience of the Khasi Hills and his subsequent recommendations to the Calvinistic Methodists were to have major repercussions in Wales, and momentous consequences for the Khasis.

3

There is surely no one among the long-dead heroes of Wales who could attract a crowd of a quarter of a million compatriots to a festival of tribute and commemoration – not Glyndŵr, not Dafydd ap Gwilym, not Llywelyn ap Gruffydd, not even, God help us, Dewi Sant himself.

But in 1991 in Shillong, capital of the Indian state of Meghalaya, some 250,000 people, a quarter of all Khasis, walked, drove, rode and scootered from every corner of their land to celebrate the life and work of a Welshman who, unknown in Wales, is a people's hero in the Khasi Hills. The crowd that assembled on Shillong golf course to mark the 150th anniversary of the coming of Thomas Jones, a carpenter's son from Montgomeryshire, numbered thousands more – the Rev Tomlin would have been gratified to note – than even the Pope managed to muster at a similar golf course jamboree in 1986.

Thomas Jones, the first of about 200 Welsh Calvinistic Methodist missionaries to serve in the Hills, is revered by both Presbyterians and Catholics, by non-Christians and even anti-Christians as one of the architects of modern Khasi society, the instigator of literacy and the father of Khasi literature. Not the least of his legacies is the church he founded which, with a growing membership of 300,000, is considerably more vital than the beleaguered 'mother church' in Wales with its dwindling platoon of 55,000 souls.

For these solid reasons Thomas Jones' portrait hangs in schoolrooms and vestries throughout the Hills: the Regency frock coat momentarily unbuttoned to suggest a proper balance between businesslike competence and graceful informality, as he breaks off from reading what might be a letter held in his left hand to fix the viewer directly with those wide and disconcertingly deep dark eyes – eyes that must have rouged the cheeks of many a Welshpool or Cherra lass; and then, as if that cool gaze from between those trim sideburns weren't trouble enough, there are those full and floridly sensuous lips with more than a hint at their corners of the possibility of mischief.

Yes, Thomas Jones, in officialdom's estimation, was capable of being a seriously bad boy, and it is only in recent years that, thanks to belated rehabilitation, his image – based always on the same sketch, sometimes splotched with lurid pastels – has sprouted in so many public places. But in the hearts of the Khasi people Thomas Jones has long held an honoured place beside such Glyndŵr-like champions of the native cause as Tirot Singh and Kiang Nongbah.

No matter that the authorities in distant Liverpool threw Thomas Jones out of the church for "contracting an injudicious marriage" and entering upon "a course of proceedings of a commercial character . . . derogatory to the character and calling of a missionary." He remains for the Khasis a man before his time, a theologian of liberation who worked tirelessly to improve their wretched economic and material conditions, and who defied on their behalf, at the cost ultimately of his own life, the imperialistic excesses of the local capitalist bully-boy.

4

There were Christians in India when the pagans of the Island of Britain were still practising human sacrifice in their sacred groves.

India's first Prime Minister, Jawaharlal Nehru, wearily sensible of the harm that religion had done in the world, insisted on strict observance of his secular state's constitutional commitment to religious freedom for all. Christians, it had been said, were 'the running dogs of imperialism'; it was necessary, therefore, to point out that Christianity had been in India far too long to be regarded as a foreign religion. "Christianity found its roots in India before it went to countries like England, Portugal and Spain," declared Nehru. "Christianity is as much a religion of the Indian soil as any other religion of India."

The first Christian in India was, like the first Presbyterian in the Khasi Hills, a carpenter by the name of Thomas. A third century romance known as the *Acts of Thomas*, one of the apocryphal books of the *New Testament*, describes how the Lord devised a cunning strategy to send a reluctant Thomas the Apostle to India. In Jerusalem at that time there was an Indian merchant seeking a skilled carpenter, and God arranged that Thomas should be sold to him as a slave. Master returned with slave to India where King 'Gundaphorus', who was probably Gundobar, first century ruler of north-western India, was waiting for a craftsman of Thomas's abilities. The King instructed the Apostle to build him a palace, but Thomas had other ideas. He would build King Gundaphorus not a palace on earth but a spiritual home in heaven, by disbursing alms to the sick and needy from the huge provision the King had made for the palace's construction. When in due course the King asked to see the completed palace, the Apostle replied: "Thou canst not see it now, but when thou departest this life, then shalt thou see it." The King, incensed, clapped his insubordinate carpenter in jail, but God intervened to cause a miraculous change in the ruler's heart, and the story ends happily with Gundophorus's conversion.

Nearly two thousand years later, the church that was founded by St. Thomas the Apostle still flourishes in southern India as a significant if somewhat divided branch of Indian Christianity.

Originally a distant outpost of the 'Syrian' or 'Syriac' church of Mesopotamia, it would have maintained fitful contact with the church's Patriarch in Babylon, but there must have been long periods of isolation.

When the Portuguese reached the 'Syrians' in the early sixteenth century, at about the same time as the Muslims were pushing in from Afghanistan to establish Mughal dominion over India, they were astonished to find, in an ocean of Hinduism, 100,000 members of an ancient Christian community confident that they had loyally kept the faith as it had come down to them from their apostolic founder. They had to some extent assimilated culturally with their Hindu neighbours, but they still made liturgical use of the Syriac language which had died out in its homeland three hundred years earlier.

Portuguese delight with the 'Syrians' rapidly gave way to profound unease as it became apparent that there existed between them serious theological differences, the most dismaying of which was that the Thomas Christians of India had never heard of the Pope. This was an apostasy which the Portuguese could neither comprehend nor tolerate. By the end of the century they had succeeded in 'persuading' all Christians in India, including the benighted 'Syrians', to come under the jurisdiction of the Pope's man in Goa, hub of Portuguese power in the subcontinent.

The Portuguese, like the British, have been and gone, but the Keralan Christians of Thomas the carpenter still worship in Syriac, a language not far removed from the Aramaic spoken in Palestine by Jesus Christ.

5

With the Empire long gone and the last of the missionaries expelled from India in the late nineteen-sixties, nearly everyone in Wales seems to have forgotten about *Bryniau Casia a'r Genhadaeth Dramor*, the Khasi Hills and the Overseas Mission of the Welsh Calvinistic Methodists.

Like most contemporaries, I knew nothing of the Khasi Hills until a summer's evening in 1991 when, thirsty after a day spent sanding old paintwork, I sat down with a Guinness to watch a programme called *Monsoon*. In this beautifully made documentary, *The Observer*'s travel editor, Alexander Frater, followed the Indian monsoon from Trivandrum, at India's southern tip, up to Cherrapunji in the shadow of the Himalayas. As the camera swept the sodden greenery and thunderous waterfalls of what viewers were told was the wettest place in the world, a pool-pellucid woman's voice sang hauntingly of the clouds flying upwards from earth to sky. Who were these people? Where was a notepad so I could jot down some particulars and maybe get hold of a tape of this music? As I fumbled for a pen, the presenter went on to explain that the people of this region, the Khasis, were skilled poets, thanks to the presence in their midst, in the nineteenth century, of a Welshman by the name of Thomas Jones, 'the father of Khasi literature'.

Who, I wondered, was Thomas Jones? And what impelled him, 150 years ago, to this remote corner of north-east India? There was nothing on him or the Mission in any of the modern histories of Wales. I found him at last among the three dozen or so Thomas Joneses deemed sufficiently distinguished to be included in *The Dictionary of Welsh Biography*: a miller from Montgomeryshire, the first Calvinistic Methodist missionary on the Khasi Hills, and the first to reduce the Khasi tongue to writing; he had fallen out with his superiors and fellow missionaries, resigned his post and taken to farming; but bad health and ill fortune had blighted his schemes, and he had died in Calcutta, aged 39. It was a sparse enough synopsis but it hinted at quite a story.

With these few leads to go on I asked around – an historian or two, a minister, a couple of chapel-goers – but nobody could tell me anything about Thomas Jones. Might I not have confused him, someone asked, with the renowned John Davies, Tahiti?

In the University library at Swansea I blew the dust off J. H. Morris's *Hanes Cenhadaeth Dramor y Methodistiaid Calfinaidd* and various other long-unread Presbyterian tomes. Gradually the sad drama of Thomas Jones and the remarkable epic of the Overseas Mission began to unfold.

6

"It is a green and mountainous country with record-shattering rainfall. There are abandoned coalmines and iron-workings, and hard-bitten upland farms. In spite of the thousands of cromlechs and monoliths that punctuate the landscape, Christianity is stronger than the old faith, and people still recall the momentous religious revival of 1905. Their overflowing churches resonate every Sunday with the great Welsh hymn tunes – Treforus, Rhosymedre, Abertawe, Capel y Ddôl – and their national anthem is a gutsy native version of 'Hen Wlad Fy Nhadau'.

"Their folk culture, despite the ravages of Nonconformist religion, survives: the people of this land are renowned for the narrative poetry of their traditional songs, in a language that has endured, against all the odds, into modern times.

"Most of its inhabitants suffer from what historians characterise as amnesia about their origins, but they harbour a flickering desire for greater autonomy. Their separatist movements give remote central government cause for concern, though not enough concern, it seems, to improve the country's poor transport links and weak infrastructure.

"The economy is in a mess, and too many of the country's jobs go to pushy outsiders who, pouring over the border in alarming numbers, are threatening to undermine the indigenous

14

culture. In spite of such problems, the women remain as famously beautiful as ever, and the men, though over-fond of their pop, are stocky and industrious. Visitors find them, for the most part, a cheerful, hospitable and open-hearted people, disdainful of caste and class."

Such was the profile of the Khasi Hills that I had constructed when I applied to the Welsh Writers' Trust for a John Morgan Writing Award. I wanted to visit the area in person to see if there were any truth in this implausible picture of a kind of Patagonia of the East.

That I was talking not about Gwalia but Khasia could hardly be believed. "You've forgotten the Welshcakes and Felinfoel Double Dragon," they chaffed. But they gave me the award and sent me on my way, making it clear that they wanted rather more for their money than the Cymmrodorion got for theirs when they sent John Evans, Waun-fawr up the Missouri in 1792 to find the legendary descendants of Madog ab Owain Gwynedd: although Evans spent years exploring the region and lived for long periods with various tribes, his commissioned 'report' on the Welsh-speaking Indians, dismissing them entirely as a myth without substance, ran to no more than a cursory five lines.

Was I too in pursuit of some *fata morgana*? Most of the books I'd read were yellow with age, and written invariably from a missionary point of view. *Bryniau Casia*, these accounts assured me, was a household name throughout the land, but I had encountered only the occasional older Presbyterian with any recollection of those once numinous words. The *Cenhadaeth Dramor* collection boxes, the rousing exhortations of missionaries home on furlough – such things seemed part of a vanished age. Thomas Jones may indeed have been the father of Khasi literature; his fellow missionaries may well have pioneered schools and built hospitals and turned thousands of Khasis into Calvinistic Methodists. But that was all long ago; and besides, fewer than 200 missionaries spread sparsely over a period of 130 years could not, could they, have made that much of an impression? Now, nearly a quarter of a century after the departure of the last missionary, the trumpeted Welsh influence on Khasi society must have worn so thin as to be almost imperceptible.

With a hunch, though, that this might not be the case, I boarded a Bangladesh Airlines 747 one damp October night in 1992 and, like John Evans, Waun-fawr going in the opposite direction two hundred years earlier, took off in search of Welsh Indians.

7

"Missionaries!" Disbelief and contempt had been the tone of Ron's valedictory oration the night before. "We, the Welsh, sent missionaries to India? We should be ashamed of ourselves," he'd frothed over his umpteenth pint. "We should have left them alone, we should be offering the poor sods an apology, not trotting off to write books and make films about how we screwed up their culture. It's a national disgrace."

Altered political fashions had aimed some cruel blows lately at old Ron's habitual Stalinist postures. It was not as easy these days to declare what he was for, apart from another pint, but there were still a few perennials he was heartily against, and Christianity was one of them. Like Wilberforce's cassowary on the plains of Timbuctoo, he would eat a missionary, "Coat and bands and hymn-book, too."

Until that night in the Duke, Ron had never heard of the Khasis, but with the righteous *hwyl* of some irrefutable anti-preacher, he was sure the missionaries had shafted them. It had been a wretched episode best forgotten: I should tear up my ticket and abandon the project.

As the plane banked high over the frenzied orange lamplight of south-east England, I had Ron's sermon clanging in my head.

Ever the extremist sublimely innocent of doubt, he had been his usual absolutist self in his assault on missionaries. But was he, beneath the bombast, so far from the truth? Captain Cook's verdict on British adventures in the South Seas – "It would have been far better for these people never to have known us" – might stand for many today as a suitably chastened epitaph on the entire imperial experiment, an enterprise in which the Bible was seen to tango so compromisingly with the bullet. Indifference, embarrassment, disdain, regret: what people feel in the late twentieth century about the Empire and its agents is invariably couched in negative terms. From the time of Empire and after, there have been enough horror stories about missionaries and their 'ethnocidal' transactions to persuade most of us that they, like the imperialism to which they were handmaidens, are a 'bad thing'. Even the World Council of Churches, according to a 1971 'Declaration of Barbados', is for the cessation of all missionary activity and an end to "the long and shameful history of despotism and intolerance characteristic of missionary work".

Yet if Christians take their bible seriously, is there any escape from the missionary imperative? Perhaps the first missionary call was that of Abraham, who promised that "all nations" would be blessed through him. Then there are the numerous exhortations to missionary endeavour to be found in the *New Testament*, particularly in the Book of Matthew, which was often the first biblical text that the nineteenth-century missionary set out to translate. The message is unequivocal and persistent, and after the resurrection Christ's last words to his disciples leave them in no doubt as to their missionary priorities: "All power is given unto me in heaven and in earth. Go ye therefore, and teach all nations, baptizing them in the name of the Father, and of the Son, and of the Holy Ghost: Teaching them to observe all things whatsoever I have commanded you: and, lo, I am with you always, even unto the end of the world. Amen."

If you reject the missionary principle, say the theologians, you have first to rewrite the *New Testament*. It is, they claim, a universal and permanent obligation that each generation of Christians should make it their business to ensure, as far as it lies within their power, that the Gospel is preached to every non-Christian in that generation.

As the plane reached cruising altitude and the seat-belt signs blinked off, the devout Muslims on board began their evening prayers, taking it in turns to stand barefoot on a plastic bin liner outside the rear toilets where there was just enough room for them to kneel and bow down in the direction of Mecca. The destination of most of them was Dhaka, the capital of Bangladesh; there I would change planes for the short hop over the border to Calcutta.

So would the Indian in the seat beside me, Naval Commander Jyoti Sharma (Ret'd) of Jodhpur Park, Calcutta, as his card announced, with addresses also in New Delhi and Goa. At what time did he reckon we'd touch down in Dhaka? "Time, my dear fellow, time is all you people think about," he said. "In India we have eternity. You should throw your watch out of the window."

He was returning home after his annual visit to his daughter in London, if 'home' was the appropriate word for a man with apartments in three different corners of India and, as he confessed, a seaman's insatiable wanderlust.

Had his travels ever taken him to the Khasi Hills?

"Ah, the Scotland of the East. That's what the British called the place. Lakes, pine trees, hills you'd probably call mountains where you come from. What is your highest peak?"

"Snowdon. About three and a half thousand feet."

"A mere hillock. Shillong Peak can double that. You should go there."

"I intend to. I'm spending about a month there – researching for a book. It's not long, I know, but it's all I'm allowed."

"Long enough. Seven days is long enough for you people to write books about India. Lepers giving birth on the streets. Vultures sailing down the river on dead bodies. Endless amounts of filth. No need to look further than Calcutta for your book about India."

"You don't think much, then, of western attempts to write about your country?"

"Can't be done. Simple as that. But the best of British to you anyway. Why are you writing about the Khasis?"

I started to explain about Thomas Jones and the Calvinistic Methodists . . .

"Missionaries!" he scoffed. I recognised the tone. "I'll tell you about missionaries. Do you know what Francis Xavier did when he wanted to convert Hindus to Christianity? He slaughtered cows, Brahmani bulls, and stuffed their corpses down every well he could find. What could the people do? If they drank the water, polluted with the blood of holy cows, they would commit the greatest sacrilege imaginable. They'd be desperate. Then along would come Xavier and his priests and offer to save them with this new religion. He'd convert thousands at a time. Not that it lasted. They had no idea what they were converting to, and soon went back to their old beliefs. But it must have sounded good back at h.q."

The Welsh, I suggested, had employed somewhat subtler methods. And besides, the cow-down-the-well approach would have meant nothing to the Khasis who ate just about anything, and were notably fond of meats like pork and beef which were taboo in many other parts of India.

"I don't doubt it," he said. "And you had better take care they don't eat you. These tribals, you know, they don't take kindly to outsiders. You won't read about it in your newspapers, but there's been a lot of trouble up there in recent years. And it's getting worse. Riots, stabbings, petrol bombs, the torching of houses. Some of them seem to have decided that they would be better off without the non-tribals – Bengalis and so forth, people from other parts of India who may have been living in the north-east for decades. Nothing less than the elimination of non-tribals seems to be the goal of the young Khasi hotheads."

But wasn't there a problem with Bangladeshis pouring illegally over the border in their thousands? I had read of Indian government plans to fence off the entire border with Bangladesh in an effort to stem the tide. Surely it wasn't surprising that the Khasis, fewer than a million in number, were getting edgy about their economy and their culture?

"It has been blown out of all proportion. That fence is political. An idea. It will never be put up. Far too expensive and impossible to man. I'm sure the occasional Bangla finds his way over the border, but we have got to learn to live with the situation. The sad truth is that these tribals have only just emerged from the jungle, and I'm afraid some of them seem bent on going back there. Yes, things are looking pretty grim up in Shillong. I'm surprised the authorities gave you a permit."

8

It had surprised me too. One of the most frustrating jobs in India must be that of tourist director of Meghalaya, the state which the Khasis and their compatriot Jaintias share with the Garo tribe.

There is little point in five of the seven north-east Indian states having departments of tourism, because they are entirely closed to foreigners. The states of Assam and Meghalaya, however, are 'restricted areas' that, in theory at least, may, under certain circumstances, be entered by non-Indians. They have tourist offices, therefore, but next to no tourists, because prising an all-important 'restricted area permit' out of the Indian bureaucratic labyrinth is sufficiently protracted and exhausting a trauma to deter all but the most fanatical of terrorists and the most masochistic of researchers into the exotic by-ways of Welsh Presbyterianism.

Applicants who, after months of uncertainty, are refused a permit are invariably told, if told anything, that it is for their own safety. But the government in New Delhi does not, I think, give a burned chuppati for travellers' safety; more to the point is the 'oxygen of publicity', and how to prevent it fanning the fires of tribal unrest. While the Ayodhya Temple riots, and conflict in the western states have received extensive media coverage, the authorities have been remarkably successful in deflecting attention from shadowy troubles in the north-eastern states.

Thomas Jones and the early missionaries took up to six months, sailing by sea and river, to reach the Khasi Hills. It can take the modern traveller nearly twice that time to work a passage through the fogs and bilious confusions of Indian bureaucracy — especially if he's a writer and, worse, a writer interested in missionaries. For if there is one class of person held more responsible than most for fomenting tribal separatism it is, in the mind of Indian officialdom, the missionary.

I had been amply warned of the permit problem by the late Rev. Ednyfed Thomas, a missionary who left the hills in 1965 and settled with his wife Gwladys in Penrhosgarnedd near

Bangor. Ednyfed, who died in 1993, spent much of an active retirement writing the definitive history of the Welsh mission to the Khasis and Jaintias, published in 1988 as *Bryniau'r Glaw* (The Rain's Hills). Having had years of improvising circuitous paths around bureaucracy's obstructionism, Ednyfed and Gwladys offered invaluable advice and encouragement.

They seemed unperturbed that not only was I not a member of their Church, I was not even a Christian. The militant atheism of my early adulthood had given way in recent years to an agnosticism tinged with a kind of zen pantheist hankering, and I wondered if, in Ednyfed's eyes, this scrambled egg of a non-religion might be deemed a modest improvement. "Yes," he said, with an air of quizzical hopefulness. "And who knows? A visit to Khasia might have the effect of turning you into a Presbyterian. And then, after that, you might possibly become a Christian."

Although the Thomases had managed to gain entry in 1991-Ednyfed was preacher-of-honour at the Shillong golf course gala– they considered that my chances early in 1992 were slim. Owing to a prolonged postal strike, they had had little news from their friends in the Hills; the indications were, however, that renewed unrest had provoked central government into suspending Meghalaya's Legislative Assembly.

I had started applying for a visa and permit in October 1991, hoping to make the trip in March the following year. There had been no replies to the numerous applications I had sent to India House in London and to the authorities in New Delhi and Shillong, so in January I resolved to supplement the letter-writing campaign with a phone offensive.

"You want to go where?" snapped a busy, tired voice at India House.

"Shillong."

"Ceylon?"

"No, Shillong, in the Khasi Hills."

"Khasi Hills?"

"Yes, in the state of Meghalaya."

"You mean Meghalya?" He pronounced it as some people pronounce 'Himal(a)ya'.

21

"Yes, I think so."

"It is very wet up there. Why don't you go somewhere sunny like Goa?"

And so, for weeks, with a different hassled functionary almost every time I rang, these futile exchanges dragged on. If the line of 'the relevant authority' was engaged, they'd keep me sweet with a computer-tune rendition of "Bobby Shaftoe".

For a month or so, 'authority' seemed to reside, unpromisingly, in the postal department. The man there suggested that what was lacking was an official invitation from some respectable body in the hills, a writers' union perhaps? I had not been able to discover one. A university? I had written to the only one whose address I could find, but, owing no doubt to the postal strike, I had had no reply.

"In that case," said the man, "I suggest that you contact a newspaper there and get them to place a notice asking a suitable body to invite you."

Unable to imagine any 'suitable body' leaping at this unique opportunity to invite some unheard-of scribbler to the Khasi Hills, I phoned Alexander Frater at *The Observer*. March was less than a month away, and it was looking increasingly unlikely that I would secure the necessary documentation in time for my hoped-for flight. Perhaps the maker of *Monsoon*, who had blazed the daunting permit trail before me, would have some advice.

"Write to Mrs. Lakyntiew Richmond in Shillong," he said. "She helped on the film, and is the daughter of the influential MP, G.G. Swell. Lakyntiew should be able to help."

I wrote to Mrs. Richmond. "Write to Mark Tully of the BBC," suggested someone. I wrote to Mark Tully. "Send them swanky testimonials from the Welsh Academy and other august bodies," said someone else. I sent them swanky testimonials.

At the end of March, Amnesty International hit the headlines with a horrifying catalogue of police and army atrocities in India. The tribal people of the north-east were reportedly one of the five most victimised sectors of society. The charges were indignantly denounced by the High Commission in London; I felt sure that under these circumstances they would be less likely than ever to give a writer permission to enter the region.

I was by now in regular communication with 'First Secretary Visa' at India House. My anticipated time of departure having come and gone, I phoned to insist – after half a dozen "Bobby Shaftoes" – on a straight answer as to whether or not they were going to allow me into Meghalaya. "Give me your number and I will call you tomorrow morning," he said.

Towards the end of the following morning, he did indeed call. "I have been in touch with New Delhi," he said, "and they have told me that they would be very unlikely to grant a permit within the next few months."

"So they are refusing me permission to enter Meghalaya?"

"That would be a reasonable interpretation," he replied. "There may be some possibilities towards the end of the year."

Though this seemed a somewhat spectral straw, I gladly clutched it, and resolved to spend the coming months researching the historical context and attempting to make contacts in the Khasi Hills. Was I doomed to share the fate of the Rev. J. Hughes Morris who wrote his pioneering history of the Mission's first ninety years, and many articles about the Khasis, without ever setting foot in India? This diminutive dynamo of a man, so short that colleagues looked out for him with concern if he had to pass a large dog in the street, spent most of a long working life perched on a high stool at the Mission headquarters in Liverpool. "Yet," Ednyfed had told me, "he managed to convey a living and correct picture of life in the field."

One day in May, after a morning in the library, I returned home to find a message to phone India House. I dialled the number and asked to be put through to First Secretary Visa. The music while I waited had changed from "Bobby Shaftoe" to a lilting Indian *raga*. Could this be a sign?

"The Government of India," announced the familiar voice in London, "has considered your case and agreed to your request. A permit will be issued for a period of one month."

One whole month rather than the usual maximum of ten days: this was more than I had dared expect. But was it, I wondered, a cunning ploy to offer me entry in the monsoon period, when the leeches would be rampant and the rain-blinded hills would be a-slither with deadly blue kraits – an offer they might plausibly expect me to decline? I was being unwarrantedly cynical. The permit would be valid from the date of entry, be that sometime next week or in six months' time. I could go, if I wished, in October, after the monsoon.

Officialdom had effected at last, as they say in babu-speak, "the needful and obliged"; though quite who or what had brought about this change of heart remained to be discovered.

Since this book was first published it was announced, in June 1995, that the restrictions on travel in Maghalaya had been lifted.

9

Belgium, Germany, Austria, Romania . . . soon enough the hubristic constellations of urban Europe gave way to darker ground as our jet sailed east: Bulgaria, Turkey, Iran, the night below us as black now as the star-pricked night above, and the Commander and the Bangladeshis all slouched in sleep.

The missionaries, I suppose, were 'Universalists', solemnly convinced, with most architects of Empire, that their faith and their civilisation had identified the common core, the universal 'human nature' that underpins all the diversity of human custom. Those 'Others' in the world, ungraced as yet with consciousness of this irreducible 'human nature', practised certain manifest inhumanties, such as *suttee* or human sacrifice, which it was their civilising mission to terminate.

Wherever there's a missionary there'll be camped nearby his traditional rival the anthropologist, with an entirely opposed set of assumptions. The anthropologist, as 'Relativist', tends to hold that all forms of behaviour are merely local, and that there can be no such thing as 'human nature': what is 'natural' in Merthyr Tydfil will probably be abominable in Khartoum. If there are people who regard clitoridectomy or drinking twelve pints a night as 'natural', who is the anthropologist to attempt to hold them back?

The logic of 'Relativism' would seem to condemn us to complete moral inertia, while that of 'Universalism' may be deployed to define 'the perishing heathen' as less than human, justifying, if need be, the slave trade and British genocide in Tasmania and Empires of all sorts.

I cupped a hand to the porthole and peered out at the stars.

"It is a truth universally acknowledged . . ." we so grandly proclaim, without having consulted even the Andromedans. Could we not contrive, on this blue tormented planet of ours, some functioning convergence of the 'Universalist' and 'Relativist' creeds, a new humanism which understands and celebrates the huge differences that exist between peoples – an aspect, surely, of the sustaining variety of terrestrial life as a whole – at the same time as it nurtures belief in the existence of some shared humanity? One more tall new order for these dark days, and the stuff, no doubt, of dreams . . .

Twenty thousand feet below, in Iran maybe or Afghanistan, I could squint here and there the fuzzy glow of a settlement's lights, as faint as a distant galaxy.

10

Less than a mile from Thomas Jones's last home in Wales, Llifior Mill, Aberriw, stands Maen Beuno, a skewed, stubby monolith which is said to have been the first pulpit of the sixth- and seventh-century saint, Beuno. As he was meditating one day by the river, Beuno heard from the opposite bank a sound that hurt his ears – the voice of a Saxon calling to his hounds. "My sons," he told his monks, "put on your clothes and shoes, and let us leave this place, for the nation of this man I heard setting on his hounds has a strange language which is abominable. They have invaded this land and will keep it in ownership." So Beuno abandoned Aberriw to the English onslaught and decamped to Gwynedd where his mission was to prove comparable with that of Dewi Sant in the south.

Montgomeryshire has some thirty churches and twenty holy wells dedicated to the uncanonised but revered missionary saints of the dawn of Celtic Christianity. They evangelised not only the entire population of their homeland but travelled overseas – to Ireland, Brittany, Cornwall – to spread the gospel and found new churches. Welsh missionaries of the eighteenth and nineteenth centuries would undoubtedly have been aware of the remarkable achievements of their 'Dark Ages' precursors.

They were themselves scions of a new missionary age inaugurated by the great religious awakening that began in the 1730s. The preaching of Howel Harris, Trefeca and Daniel Rowland, Llangeitho, the hymns of William Williams, Pantycelyn – names intimately familiar to Khasi Presbyterians – were instinct with missionary zeal, anticipating uncannily sometimes the exotic fauna of far-flung mission fields:

> *Mae gelynion yma'n llechu,*
> *Wn i bryd daw llew i ma's,*
> *Ac y rhua fe arna i'n greulon,*
> *Bwgwth llarpio'th ofnus was;*
> *Eirth, llewpartiaid, seirph, gwiberod,*
> *Yn cytuno'm lladd i'n un,*
> *Nid oes dim a geidw f'enaid,*
> *Ond dy allu di dy hun.*

(Enemies here are hiding,/I know not when some lion may emerge,/roaring cruelly at me,/and threatening to tear thy faithful servant to bits;/bears, leopards, serpents, vipers/agree together to kill me,/nothing will preserve my soul,/save only thine own power.)

Williams, indeed, seems to have been under something of an Asiatic obsession. Believing that "getting to know the earth is part of a Christian's education", he frequently digressed in his evangelistic writings in order to furnish his readers with detailed inventories of the glories of India – exotic treasures like

Calico, Muslin, Silk . . . and precious stones of several kinds . . . ; a great deal of *Pepper* also is grown in *Malabar,*

26

and [from India comes] *Saltpetre, Indigo, Cardamum, Opium*, and a great variety of drugs.

Having succeeded by the end of the eighteenth century in snatching back the majority of their countryman from the benightedness into which their souls had fallen, the Methodists were ready to turn their attention to 'the perishing heathen' further afield.

The closing years of the century saw the formation of a number of overseas missionary societies, the first of which, in 1792, was William Carey's The Particular (Calvinistic) Baptist Society for Propagating the Gospel among the Heathen, later known simply as the Baptist Missionary Society. The second to form, in 1795, was the nondenominational London Missionary Society, whose leading Welsh supporter was the Methodist luminary Thomas Charles, Bala (1755-1814), founder of the Bible Society and champion of the Welsh Sunday Schools. The LMS, launched to the strains of Pantycelyn's "O'er those gloomy hills of darkness", was the society to which, initially, the Welsh Methodists contributed their funds. Thomas Charles organised collections, and levied congregations for regular donations to missionary activity which, he declared, was "the most important, the most necessary, and the most sacred and glorious work of which our world knows" (*Y Drysorfa Ysbrydol*, June 1799). People travelled many miles to attend his big public missionary meetings, though not all had gold or silver to give. One old man offered the produce of a cherry tree; another poor but not ungenerous supporter gave one of his small flock of sheep, calling it "the missionary sheep".

The very first Welsh missionary was probably the Rev. Dr. Thomas Coke (1747-1814), a Wesleyan Methodist who went to the West Indies in 1786. He also made numerous journeys to Ireland and America, and set sail for India in 1813, dying on the voyage. The Calvinistic Methodists' pioneers were channelled, like the funds from Welsh congregations, through the LMS. The first was the renowned John Davies, Tahiti (1772-1855), followed by Evan Evans and Isaac Hughes who went to South Africa in 1816 and 1823, respectively, and Josiah Hughes who left for

27

Malacca in 1830. An account of John Davies's voyage to the South Pacific in 1800, written by Thomas Charles from an interview with the ship's captain, caused a considerable stir. "Fervent prayers and praises have been offered by our people, who knew nothing at all of it before, or of the state of the heathen world," Thomas Charles wrote to the secretary of the LMS. "Their hearts being warmed towards the cause, their purses began to open. After announcing it in our chapel, and saying it was intended to make a collection, one good woman brought me FIVE GUINEAS, bedewed with tears of joy that she possessed so much money, and had lived to give it to so good a cause." He went on excitedly to outline his plans for a missionary magazine, *Y Drysorfa Ysbrydol*, but ended on a more sober note: "Whilst you supplicate the throne of grace for our brethren in distant lands, do not forget the poor Britons among their barren mountains".

The brethren in distant lands that initially most excited the solicitude of the Welsh were the long-lost descendants of Madoc in America and their even more benighted Celtic cousins in Brittany who had "departed from the true faith, and were lying under the iron yoke of the great Antichrist, the Pope." The Irish were perceived as being, for similar reasons, in dire need of Cymric enlightenment, and a short-lived Welsh Baptist Missionary Society was formed in 1820 to effect "the evangelisation of the Celtic races". The Madoc fever waned, but the Calvinistic Methodists did indeed send one or two missionaries to do battle in Brittany with the Pope and his adherents' "great and besetting sin of drunkenness"; they also sent a missionary to the Jews in London, but neither venture resulted in many converts.

It was the missionary endeavour in Africa, Asia and the South Seas that caught the public's imagination. News of the pioneers' often heroic exploits and daunting hardships took many months, if not in some cases the best part of a year, to reach home, and was eagerly awaited. Passed round by word of mouth or in the pages of journals such as the *Trysorfa*, these stories of courage, resourcefulness and dedicated spirituality must have intrigued and inspired many youthful "poor Britons among their barren mountains" and in the choleric valleys of the teeming industrial south.

The ambitions of one of those restless young Britons were to damage beyond repair the long-standing if increasingly sour relationship between the Welsh Methodists and the LMS.

When the Calvinistic Methodist College opened at Bala in 1837, Thomas Jones, aged 27 and convinced of his vocation as a missionary, was among its first batch of students. The training at Bala was designed for young men intending to serve in the home pastorate; it seems probable that there was little, if any, education offered in missionary practice.

He was ordained in a presbytery at Bala on New Year's Day, 1840 – the year in which the LMS would send Dr. David Livingstone (1813-73) to Africa. As the most famous missionary since Saint Patrick, Livingstone was destined to become a great British hero.

It was to the LMS that Thomas Jones offered himself at first. India, he was adamant, was where he wanted to serve, but the LMS's medical examiners reported to their board that "the functions of his liver were imperfectly performed and that a hot climate would aggravate this – a dry climate of moderate temperature would be best". They recommended a South African posting, but Thomas Jones, his heart set on India, produced assurances from three independent doctors, including the celebrated Dr. Addison of Guy's Hospital, London, that he was entirely fit for life in the subcontinent. Neither Thomas Jones nor the LMS could be budged from their positions, with the result that in January 1840 the society severed its connection with the headstrong young Welshman, precipitating a crisis which was to result in the Methodists breaking entirely with the London Missionary Society.

The consequences of this showdown must have been foreseen by Thomas Jones and his supporters. From 1835, if not earlier, an increasingly vociferous movement within the church had been arguing for the Calvinistic Methodists to establish their own missionary society. It was felt that the formation of an independent organisation would arouse in congregations a keener commitment to "the great work of evangelising the heathen world", and stimulate them to greater generosity. Above all, there was mounting impatience with the perceived hostility of the London Missionary Society towards the Welsh Methodists. Although the LMS had started out as a nondenominational organisation, its management during the 1830s had slipped almost entirely into the hands of the Independents. They had rejected, without apparent good cause, a number of Welsh missionary candidates, and the outcome of Thomas Jones's testcase application was awaited with intense interest.

Liverpool was at that time headquarters of the Welsh Calvinistic Methodists. When Thomas Jones returned there by train after the negative confrontation in London, the disappointment among his friends was profound. Three days later, on 31 January 1840, they convened in the vestry of Rose Place Chapel, Liverpool what was to be an historic meeting of ministers and leading laymen. It was proposed and, after heated debate, accepted "that we incorporate as a Foreign Mission Society, and that rules be drawn out to be presented to the Quarterly Association at Llanfair Caereinion".

A minority of those present opposed the plan, fearing that in the mood of resentment and indignation that had been aroused by the London Society's attitude, this was too serious a step to take hastily. How could so small a Society operating in an impoverished country like Wales afford to support such an ambitious project?

A leading opponent of secession was the Rev. John Elias (1774-1841), the mightiest preacher of his age who, as a fiercely dogmatic and authoritarian hyper-Calvinist, was known by his enemies as 'the Pope of Anglesey'. Radicalism in any shape or form was anathema to this hard-line conservative who resisted every movement towards freedom of thought and action, dubbing as 'rebels' the supporters of such measures as the 1832 Reform Bill. *The Dictionary of Welsh Biography* describes him as "a man of strong will, an inflexible mind, and imperious nature, [who] could not be easily opposed"; with his booming voice and physically animated mode of address, he often enough made oratorical mincemeat of 'rebels' and their impious causes.

As a law and order zealot, hot for sending in the police and the army at the earliest sign of unrest, he, like many others who were influential in the governance of this young church, would have been implacably hostile to Thomas Jones's stand against authority.

The anti-secessionists had three months to rally a coherent opposition, but in the event they failed to do so. The number of LMS supporters at Llanfair Caereinion on April 28 was small, and, fortunately for the separatists, the Rev. John Elias, with his flailing arms and stabbing forefinger, was absent through ill-health. Thomas Jones and his sympathisers had used the intervening months in energetic campaigning, raising on visits to various parts of north Wales "a great storm of indignation" against the London Society. When the contending parties met at Llanfair Caereinion, a town in Thomas Jones's home county which had long supported the idea of separation, the odds were stacked very much in his favour: the meeting voted by an overwhelming majority for the break-away movement. The Rev. John Elias and other leaders subsequently condemned the "unfair and exciting appeals made to men's prejudices", and "the immoderate haste" shown in deciding so grave a question at so "unrepresentative a gathering". Such criticisms were not without substance, for members in the south of the country, and others, had not been given a chance to state their views; it was not, in fact, until June 1843, after much debate throughout Wales, and long after Thomas Jones had arrived in India, that the Overseas Missionary Society was formally accepted by the whole church. Thomas Jones had, effectively, bounced the Calvinistic Methodists into sending him to India.

After the Llanfair Caereinion meeting, things moved fast. The first job of The Welsh Missionary Society, as it was called initially, was to decide where in India to send their man. The Rev. Jacob Tomlin had recommended not only the Khasi Hills but the Manipur Valley and the central province of Malour. When Tomlin met Thomas Jones in Liverpool he strongly recommended him to go to the Khasi Hills. An obvious advantage of a place like the Khasi Hills, where there was no *purdah* or caste system, was the probability that a self-contained people with their own 'minority' religion would prove much more malleable than adherents to one of the major faiths: it was axiomatic that Muslims were impossible to convert, and Hindus, with the possible exception of those from the lowest castes, were hardly less intractable. By 1840, when the semi-official committee of the fledgling society found itself faced with making a serious choice, their indecision was compounded by the additional suggestion from Dr. John Wilson, of the Scottish Church Mission in Bombay, that Gujurat might prove a fruitful area. The choice was at this stage somewhat academic, because they did not have the money to send anyone anywhere.

But Providence, once more, seemed to guide their hand. While the directors were hesitating as to where to send their missionary, a generous offer of a considerably reduced passage to Calcutta was interpreted as a sign from God that the Khasi Hills should be adopted as their chosen field. It would seem that Captain J. Johnson of the Jamaica, a cargo vessel with a few cabins for passengers normally let as a captain's perk, was prevailed upon by two prominent Liverpool Methodists, the ships' chandler Richard Roberts and his son the Rev. John 'Minimus' Roberts, secretary of the mission, to knock £50 off the fare to Calcutta, to enable the embryonic mission to make a start with its work.

Collections were taken, bags were packed, and opposition to the new Society melted away as church members and elders, even Rev. John Elias, rallied round to wish *bon voyage* to the Calvinistic Methodists' first missionary to India.

11

"And with your fruit juice, my friend, the Rajasthan desert." The Commander nudged me awake to take delivery of a breakfast tray, and nodded towards the window.

The rising sun had gouged the hilly desert below us with deep troughs of shade, which narrowed and darkened as the sun climbed higher. There seemed nothing but rusty wasteland, in all directions, for as far as the eye could see – not a hint of green, not a trace of habitation except for, rarely, a sketchy outline in the dust of some long-abandoned fields.

"Looks like Mars, doesn't it?" said the Commander. "There are hundreds and hundreds of miles of this, and it's spreading daily. Too many people, not enough productive land, that's India's problem. They say, you know, that in a few years' time we Indians will outnumber even the Chinese. We need a disaster, something to kill off a few million of us – but not me, of course, I don't want to be wiped out. And that's the problem, isn't it? We all want to live."

To our left, in a while, New Delhi was visible, and, soon after that, the dazzling, jagged expanse of the Himalayas, the mountain desert of 'eternal snow' that rebuffs the worst of the northern winds and keeps India's climate tropical.

From on high, the little settlements dotted around Bangladesh's maze of delta inlets looked homely enough among their bushy palms, but, as our 747 lowered to land, the ramshackle precariousness of these rotting tin sheds was all too plain. Pincered between the lethal surges of the Bay of Bengal and the annual deluge of monsoon water, much of it draining off the Khasi Hills, these coastal Bangladeshis are seasoned precisans of life's murderous whimsicality.

At Dhaka airport I lost the Commander, presumably to a more direct connection than mine turned out to be. It was mid-afternoon, hours later than scheduled, before my border-hopping flight turned up. I'd spent the day crossing and uncrossing my legs, nodding off and jerking awake in a lounge loud with the blare of three TVs, one belting out Bengali programmes, another booming forth the BBC's *Late Show*, and a third blasting us with 24-hour CNN. My restless semi-slumber was ambushed at one point by an American advert's slushy choric version of the lullaby "*Huna'n dawel, annwyl blentyn*" which, in that stuffy international no-man's land, induced an unexpectedly sharp sting of *hiraeth*.

It is possible, if your itinerary is organised tightly enough, to travel from Wales to the Khasi Hills in less than a day, discomfited only by a little high altitude turbulence and the onset of mild jet lag. With a return ticket in your pocket, you'll know when, to the nearest hour, you may expect to be at home again, unpacking your bags.

When Thomas Jones, aged 30, and his pregnant bride Anne set sail for India on 25 November, 1840 they were taking a gigantic leap of faith into an unknown from which, as they and their friends were all too aware, they might never return. Only one of the Welsh missionaries, Evan Evans, had ever come back to Wales, and he had died at Llanidloes less than six months after his arrival in 1827, his health broken, at the age of 35, by ten years in South Africa. On the very day of their departure, although the sad news would take another six months to reach Liverpool, Josiah Hughes died in Malacca of cholera, at the age of 36.

The people in Liverpool who had fought with such daring and urgency to found a missionary society were no strangers to the kind of poverty and disease they imagined Thomas Jones would meet in India. Founder members of the committee included a joiner and builder, a coal merchant, a chemist, a hymn-writing tobacconist, a blacksmith, a sawyer, a banker and JP, a tailor and workers in shipping, many of whom had lived hard, penurious lives. All were more than familiar with the destitution and sickness that surrounded them in the town. They had lived through cholera epidemics, one of which, in 1832, had carried away 1,500 people; they knew what tuberculosis and scarlet fever and diptheria could do. Typhus was ever present, and in 1847 they would see 15,000 people in Liverpool wiped out by typhus and famine, as a consequence of the Irish potato famine and the influx of starving refugees. The medical missionary Dr. Arthur Hughes, who died in 1996 and was among the last of the missionaries to leave the Khasi Hills, was a Liverpool Welshman who well understood the founders' motivation. "For them," he

34

once suggested, "amidst the degradation and destitution, the hope of the Gospel was the only sure light and joy in life. The Gospel of salvation was the motivating power in their lives, and they did what they could to propagate it, at home and abroad."

The Overland Route across the Isthmus of Suez had been pioneered in 1839, but it was not until 1842 that it offered a regular service between the Mediterranean and the Red Sea. The Suez Canal was not opened until 1869. The first telegraph line between India and Europe was not working until 1865, and the direct line to England not until 1870. News could travel only as fast as the first available ship: if you sent a letter from Calcutta to Liverpool, it would be perhaps a year before you could anticipate a reply.

When, therefore, travellers boarded a ship at a British port they might be entering a state of limbo in which they were lost to the world until, half a year or more later, they finally reached their destination. Was Thomas Jones aware that the ship which took the Baptist missionary William Carey to Calcutta in 1793 had taken five months less two days to reach the port, and that for three months of their voyage Carey and company saw neither land nor sail?

The barque *Jamaica*, built in Liverpool in 1834, normally sailed to and from the West Indies, but she seems to have been chartered on this occasion for a one-off voyage to Calcutta. Only one other ship sailed from Liverpool to India that month, most of the India traffic at that time sailing from London. On the understanding that the ship would sail on November 5, the mission's supporters held a farewell meeting at Rose Place Chapel on November 4. Seven hundred people managed to find a place inside, but many had to be turned away. It was crowded and stuffy in the chapel, but all were content to sit out the meeting which went on for no less than three and a half hours. Throughout the city in preceding weeks, and in chapels all over Wales, well-wishers had gathered to pray for the missionaries' safe conduct.

But bad weather kept the *Jamaica* in harbour for nearly three weeks more. She was berthed at the George Dock, a site now occupied by the Liver Buildings and the Customs House; the dock was often called the Welsh Basin on account of the Welsh ships that unloaded slates and masonry there for the building of Liverpool's docks and houses. Rain seems to have been responsible for some of the delay: they were loading the vessel from unprotected dock-sides, and may have had to wait for breaks in the cloud before putting on board the more perishable goods. Then there was the death and destruction caused by a ferocious storm on the night of November 17: a coaster, the *Lord Nelson*, was wrecked on a sandbank; the *Scotland* from Quebec was forced to anchor off the Formby bank with its masts gone; and another large ship was driven ashore near the Formby lighthouse with only its foremast left standing. It is more than likely that Thomas Jones, kicking his heels around the pierhead, watched with some disquiet as a steam-tug towed this stricken vessel into harbour the following morning.

When conditions improved, a new date was set for the *Jamaica*'s sailing, and on November 24, the eve of departure, a final prayer meeting was held in Rose Place Chapel. Small wonder, after so much shipwreck close to port and so many lives lost, that Thomas Jones was moved to remark at this farewell gathering, "I am told that it is a good ship, and the captain is a kind man, nevertheless I would put more trust in the prayers of my friends than in any of these things to get me safe to India".

And when they went aboard the *Jamaica* on November 25, he asked the ship rhetorically, "Tell me, is it to the Judgement or to India that you will take me?" Every one of the several hundred friends who gathered on the quayside to see them off must have wondered with intimations of dread, as the dockhands flung the hawsers from their bollards, if they'd ever see those two faces again.

Although Thomas and Anne Jones were travelling under sail, the recent introduction of steamships on certain lines was halving journey times and encouraging more wives and families to accompany their men to the distant outposts. The Empire was becoming less exclusively a man's world; but, as Anne Jones was to find, it remained a mercilessly tough and hazardous one.

We can imagine them after a week at sea, during which they had safely crossed the Bay of Biscay, catching sight of Madeira and then, some days later, the Cape Verde islands. They would be companioned through the latitudes by a constantly changing guard of birds: sea-swallows, boobies, gulls of many kinds. In tropical waters the flying fish would rise on all sides, scudding hastily along the surface before the dolphins, bonitos and albacores that would leap around the vessel for hours on end. Occasionally a lone shark might follow in the ship's wake, and hang there grimly for days.

Soon after crossing the Equator they'd have spotted, no doubt, their first few pintados, or Cape pigeons, which, over the next two thousand miles, would steadily grow in number, until at the Cape of Good Hope, after about ten weeks' sailing, they'd find themselves escorted by swirling flocks of them, scores of gulls and perhaps from time to time an albatross.

But Anne Jones, who was ill and in discomfort for the entire voyage, could hardly have taken much pleasure in these exotic sights. The Cape breezes must have come as a welcome respite after the punishing heat of the Equator. But, refreshed after putting in at the pretty little way-station of Simonstown for victualling and refurbishment, they would soon have to endure the even harsher temperatures of the Indian Ocean's equatorial regions.

Sailing north past Madagascar, they might perhaps have spared a prayer for David Jones (1797-1841) and his Welsh Congregational colleagues who, in 1818, were the first missionaries on the island. Their LMS-sponsored mission, beset with family tragedies from the start, had run into a storm of persecution in the mid-1830s: the missionaries and their converts had had to flee for their lives to Mauritius and the east coast of Africa. They had nevertheless succeeded in establishing twenty-five schools, and translating the Bible and other major works into Malagasy – an important contribution to Madagascar's culture that is remembered to this day.

Two months after rounding the Cape, the *Jamaica* was nosing through the Sundarbans, the low swampy islands, dense with dwarf-palm and mangroves, which surround the approach to Calcutta. At the mouth of the Hooghly a pilot and his assistant would have been taken on board, it being the latter's job to plumb the water's depth every few minutes to ensure safe passage through the estuary's treacherous sandbanks.

The celebrated botanist Sir Joseph Dalton Hooker, author of *Himalayan Journals*, will guide us the last few miles. "Higher up the River Hooghly is entered, and large trees, with villages and cultivation, replace the sandy spits and marshy jungles of the great Gangetic delta. A few miles below Calcutta the scenery becomes beautiful, beginning with the Botanic Garden. Opposite are the gardens of Sir Lawrence Peel, unrivalled in India for their beauty and cultivation, and fairly entitled to be called the Chatsworth of Bengal. A little higher up Calcutta opens out with the batteries of Fort William in the foreground, thundering forth a salute."

The *Jamaica* dropped anchor on 23 April, 1841, after a gruelling voyage which, like William Carey's nearly half a century earlier, had taken precisely two days short of five months. As Thomas Jones helped his now heavily pregnant and exhausted wife into the lighter that would ferry them to the landing *ghat* he might well have imagined that the worst of their troubles were over.

13

My flight from Dhaka to Calcutta, crossing both the border and the Tropic of Cancer, took about twenty minutes.

Approaching the airport at Dum Dum, birthplace of the expanding bullet of the same name, I could make out among the swaying palms of an endless jungly fen many ochre-brown mansions, long peeled of paint, a minaret in the distance and what looked like the steeple of an Anglican church. And even here, on the edge of the runway, sagged one or two sackcloth lean-tos.

A dusty Ambassador, the ubiquitous Indian saloon modelled on the 1957 Morris Oxford, sped across to our plane to collect a crumpled woman in a blanket. She had surgical tubes sticking out of her nostrils and looked close to death. The rest of us were ferried across the tarmac by bus, to be processed in a grey hall with dim fluorescent lighting.

As you emerge from 'the formalities', there, behind a barrier at the airport's outer doors, are the shouting and flailing taxi touts.

A number of tourists had 'disappeared' lately; the Commander had advised me to take an official taxi and not to go unregistered into that good night. But the taxi office was closed. There was, however, an official bus. A woman in an orange sari was selling tickets for it, and it was leaving immediately. Would it be going anywhere near Meghalaya House in Russell Street? "To the door, sir. Here is your ticket." She pointed out the vehicle's roof, just visible above the heads of the clamourous hustlers who lunged to grab my custom – "Change money, mister? Rickshaw? Taxi?" – as I slipped their net and made for the bus.

There was no one else aboard this battered old wreck, not even a driver, but I wasn't alone for long. Half a dozen child beggars were soon giggling around me, pushing hard for cash. A man who turned out to be the driver hopped aboard and chased them off, slamming the door behind him and removing the handle. The children scurried back in through the bus's missing windows, and resumed negotiations. The driver returned, chased them away again, and stretched out on one of the seats. I pointed quizzically to my watch.

"No petrol," he said. "We wait."

The sun's afterglow gave a pinkish tinge to the sultry grey evening as mournful women with naked babies on their shoulders came one by silent one to my open window, jabbed at their wide mouths with forefingers and thumb, and gestured imploringly towards their motionless children. I sweated. The driver dozed.

After half an hour the bus had attracted about a dozen fares, enough to buy petrol and, presumably, deliver the necessary profit. The ticket-seller climbed aboard, nudged the driver from his dreams, and we were on our way. The hour-long drive began briskly, as we rattled down the highway scattering pigs and swerving past cows asleep in pot-holes; but it ground ever slower as we approached the traffic-clogged chaos of the city proper.

I had read about Calcutta, seen films, talked to people who had been there, imagined in advance "the most wicked place in the Universe" as (the spectacularly well-travelled) Robert Clive once described it. But still, on that bus ride, still I gawped and sometimes flinched at the strangeness that assailed me on every side. The neon boast of a towering Hilton consigned to impeccable transience by the plague scene from the middle ages at its foot. Children scratting in rubbish for food and fuel. Water buffalo submerged in foetid green pools alongside huge modern tenement blocks with only candles to light them. A little girl about the age of my three-year-old Branwen weaving a path through roaring traffic with a naked baby in her arms. A man lifting his *longhi* to take a shit in the gutter. Women suckling babies outside rag bivouacs. Walls plastered with dung patties. The overpowering stench of exhaust fumes spiced with smells of burning as pavement dwellers everywhere cooked their evening meal. And shouting and laughter and bells and hooters. No matter that all traffic seems jammed in a gridlock, the horns in India go on getting pummelled, as if sheer hooter decibels were enough in themselves to shift any blockage.

"Typical European," I could imagine the Commander despairing. "Fixated like a rabbit by the glare of Calcutta's awesome drama. Squalor and filth, that's all you people have eyes for, squalor and filth and misery."

By the time we reached the broad avenues of what seemed the city centre it was dark. "Russell Street?" I shouted to the woman who had sold me the ticket.

"Russell Street?" she echoed blankly.

"You said the bus would drop me in Russell Street."

"Bus don't go to Russell Street."

One of my fellow passengers, who seemed to have heard of Russell Street, yelled something at the driver, the bus slammed to a halt, and I was waved vaguely up a lightless alley, struggling to swing my brute of a pack onto my back as a gaggle of streetkids pawed at me for money.

I was heading, I hoped, for Meghalaya House, a kind of hostel for people from the Khasi Hills, run by the state government. My 'postal friend' the Khasi poet Desmond Kharmawphlang, with whom I had managed to make contact during the months of waiting for a permit, had said he would see that I was reserved a room there.

I stumbled on, over rubbish and dozing pye-dogs, and turned into a broader street lit by little more than the glow from the little 'chula' braziers of the pavement people, and fluorescent spillage from the occasional small shop. Yes, said a paper-seller, this was Russell Street, and down there on the right was Meghalaya House.

The guard at the iron gate nodded me through towards a grand four-storey Regency town-house, the light from its open front door fanning out in welcome across the drive. Inside there was music and laughter and the tang of cooking, but alas – a misunderstanding – no room for me.

Back I trudged towards "the city of dreadful night", my pack now as heavy as a corpse. Beggars at my elbow, pye-dogs, shit and piss at my feet, streetkids fumbling for the zips on my pack, I lurched on. At the end of the street, lit up like a liner, was the impossibly expensive Park Hotel: $100 a night.

In a maze of crowded alleyways I came upon the Fairlawn Hotel which had a courtyard with fairylights and bronzed Australians drinking ice-cold beers. That too looked pricey, but my stand against rip-offs was weakening. A hustler reeking of booze sprang out from behind a shrub.

"Fairlawn full, my friend, but come with me, I fix you up good."

I followed my boozy leader down a confusion of passageways, up some steps into a concrete building, down some steps, along a rubbish-strewn corridor, into a lift, up some more steps, along another corridor and into a place called the Gujral Lodge, "cheap, no bugs, lock on door". The room I was offered was depressingly claustrophic – a brick wall had been built about eighteen inches from its window. But it was reasonably clean and affordable, and I was ready for bed.

"I wait for you in morning, sir," said my twinkling courier as I slipped him his *baksheesh*. "Take you Kali Temple."

I hoped not. Tomorrow I would go in search of the Scottish Cemetery – my guide looked puzzled – and the grave of Thomas Jones.

14

Loth even to attempt a retracing of last night's convoluted approach to the Gujral Lodge, I followed the stairs straight down to the street. It was obvious why my tout had chosen so circuitous a route: had he exposed his client to the caked vomit and diarrhoea jumbled up with broken glass and rubbish scattered down the stairway he might have found himself suddenly bereft of a customer.

On one of the landings was a generator the size of a tractor which juddered into raucous action, immediately beneath my room it seemed, whenever there was a power cut. It had been a noisy night. In addition to the roar of the generator the incessant skreek of a cricket lodged somewhere in a door jamb, the yelps of street dogs, the cries and shouts and throat-raking gobbings, there had been the regular explosions of firecrackers. For this was the time of the Durga Puja, the biggest festival of the Bengali year, when, over four days in October, the irrepressibly exuberant citizens of Calcutta defy their desperate circumstances to celebrate Durga, the matriarchal alter ego of Kali. It is after Kali, the savage Hindu goddess of destruction, that Calcutta is named. The Durga Puja falls as the punishing humidity of the monsoon season has begun to surrender to the cooler days of Calcutta's merely torrid 'winter'; the people of 'Kali-ghat' look to Durga for protection from evil and the promise of better things to come.

The firecrackers were still banging away, unsettlingly like bombs in this edgiest of knife-edge cities, as I headed up sumptuous, beggar-gliding Park Street in the direction, I hoped, of the Scottish Cemetery. I had a rough plan from the people at Meghalaya House, but no one on the street seemed to have heard of the place. They pointed instead to South Park Street Cemetery whose hump-backed vaults loomed like stone elephants above a wall as high as one of the city's cannibalised double-decker buses.

Like Government House where the Viceroys ruled as though monarchs themselves, and like Lord Curzon's Victoria Monument with its imperial icons and regal proclamations engraved in stone, South Park Street Cemetery reminds the visitor that Calcutta, built by the British in the middle of a noxious swamp, was, at least until April Fool's Day, 1912, both the capital of India and second city of the largest Empire the world has ever known. Here, among stately avenues of domed sepulchres, obelisks and classical columns, the ghosts of Empire most densely and ostentatiously clamour.

South Park Street Cemetery, the city's oldest, first opened its wrought iron portals in August, 1767 at the height of the annual sick season – the liveliest time of year for Calcutta graveyards. With its weed- and litter-free shady walkways, its discreet gardeners tending variegated shrubberies, and tomb-restorers dozing on manicured lawns, the cemetery still exudes an air of decorous and moneyed high Anglicanism.

The mightiest grave here, a skyscraping obelisk, is that of a famous Welshman (of sorts), the philologist Sir William Jones (1746-94) who, having learned Sanskrit, was the first person to argue a common source for the Indo-European group of languages. "Accomplish'd JONES", as he was apostrophized in a contemporary poem "On the Restoration of Learning in the East", was a judge and pioneer Orientalist who founded the Asiatic Society, an organisation which, disdaining notions of racial superiority, shared its discoveries eagerly with indigenous Bengali intellectuals. *The Indian Observer* described him at his death as "that celebrated and illustrious man who has opened the long-hidden mines of Oriental literature, and displayed them to the European world." His work inspired the founding in 1800 of Fort William College which was established to provide colonialist Brits with a grounding in Indian culture. Although he was the youngest son of the renowned mathematician William Jones (1675?-1749) of Llanfihangel, Ynys Môn, and a member in later life of the Cymmrodorion, Sir William spoke no Welsh. A British ambassador in Paris once presented him to the King of France as "a man who knows every language except his own."

A near neighbour of Sir William is another Welsh notable, the legendary beauty Rose Aylmer with whom the poet Walter Savage Landor fell in love when he met her in October, 1796 among the "low roses, yellow snapdragons, and thousands of other plants" of Swansea burrows. He was twenty one and she sweet seventeen. But, as a nineteenth-century biographer noted, Landor "was in no position to make honourable advances" because he was living at the time with his mistress Nancy Jones on whom he had fathered a daughter, recently deceased: "Without her brother's formal permission to pay his addresses he could not offer words of love, but he probably showed his attraction, waxing sentimental as was his instinctive habit with women, and since she welcomed his company, he had reason to suppose she was not indifferent to him."

Rose, the only daughter of the fourth Lord Aylmer, and subsequently step-daughter of Landor's friend Howel Price of Laugharne, affected the poet both emotionally and artistically. One of the books she lent him, borrowed from Swansea circulating library, was Clara Reeve's *Progress of Romance* which inspired the epic poem *Gebir* (1798) that made him famous. But their trysts on "the most beautiful coast in the universe", which seem to have haunted him to the end of his days, lasted only eighteen months: in the summer of 1798 Rose was taken out to India by her aunt whose husband, Sir John Henry Russell, was a Bengal judge (Calcutta's Russell Street is named after him). There, in 1800, at the age of twenty, she died. Landor's "Abertawy", a lyrical evocation of one of their meetings on Swansea's "lonely strand", concludes elegiacally:

> Where Ganges rolls his widest wave
> She dropt her blossom in the grave;
> Her noble name she never changed,
> Nor was her noble heart estranged.

Cholera, some say, was the cause of death; others claim it was dysentery, brought on "by indulging too much with that mischievous and dangerous fruit, the pineapple."

In comparison to Sir William's vaunting monument, Rose Aylmer's whorled and tapering column, nestling in foliage, strikes a more plangent, feminine chord. Inscribed at the base of her tomb are the best-known lines of Landor's entire *oeuvre* and the most famous of all imperial epitaphs:

> Ah, what avails the sceptred race!
> Ah, what the form divine!
> What every virtue, every grace!
> Rose Aylmer, all were thine.
>
> Rose Aylmer, whom these wakeful eyes
> May weep, but never see,
> A night of memories and sighs
> I consecrate to thee.

These verses, composed "when I was cleaning my teeth before going to bed", capture the sense of vulnerability and disenchantment that shadowed the British Empire even at its most thrustful. Most heyday imperialists genuinely believed that it was, in Queen Victoria's words, their Providential task in life "to protect the poor natives and advance civilisation". But in the mountains, deserts and jungles of Empire, self-doubt, like disease, often nipped at their heels.

Landor survived his Swansea love by 64 wayward years. After his death in 1864 a packet of hair found in his desk turned out to be not Nancy Jones's, as suggested by one of his poems, but Rose Aylmer's.

If South Park Street Cemetery is a necropolis for the captains of Empire, the humbler Scottish Cemetery in Karaya Street a few hundred yards away is the long home from home of its auxiliary ranks. It is a rambling and dilapidated jungle of a place with thousands of tombs, some, on the day I visited, exposed to sunlight by the annual slash-and-burn clean-up, many more of them submerged in dense tropical umbrage. How, I wondered, as

I pushed at the rickety gate, how would I find among these long-abandoned sea-captains, jute masters and men of the kirk my solitary Welsh Calvinistic Methodist?

As I closed the gate behind me, a *chowkidar*, removing reading glasses, emerged from the gatehouse. His air of puzzled surprise suggested that visitors here were few.

"There's probably not much point in my asking," I began, "but you wouldn't happen to know where I can find the grave of a Welsh missionary by the name of Thomas Jones?"

"Thomas Jones? Of course. Follow me, if you please."

He led me fifty yards or so up the grassy main aisle and there, in a clearing on the left, beneath the bay-green leaves of a *kath tagar* tree, was the dazzling white rectangle of our hero's grave. Incised in Italian marble, beneath an open stone bible bearing the legend "Safe in the arms of Jesus", were the words:

In loving Memory of
REV. THOMAS JONES 1.
THE FOUNDING FATHER OF THE KHASI ALPHABETS
AND LITERATURE AND THE PIONEER OF THE WELSH
PRESBYTERIAN MISSION IN KHASI HILLS.
DIED 16th SEPTEMBER 1849.
THE TABLET IS PLACED
BY

THE KHASI JAINTIA PRESBYTERIAN SYNOD

"Very sad," said the caretaker, "a very sad and lonely death."

"You know a bit about him, then?"

"The Khasis tell me. They come on pilgrimage. A few years ago, before I took this job, the grave was level with the ground, just another lost stone. Then the Khasis came to look for it, and built it up with this marble. Now many come."

"What about the other graves?" I gestured toward the acres of Machonochies, MacLeods, Duncans, Fergusons.

"Nobody comes now, nobody bothers. Their relatives and friends all dead or gone to Scotland."

Thomas Jones's grave, he said, was about the only one that people came to see. Indeed, it was a main reason why St. Andrew's Church kept the cemetery open.

The caretaker's name was Ian Mitchell. His father, he explained as we trailed among the tombs, had been an English surveyor, his mother a member of the Garo tribe, who live immediately to the west of the Khasis. Born in 1933, he had never been back to the Garo Hills, and didn't expect that with a monthly salary of 500 rupees (£10) he ever would. This wage, he said, was 300 rupees down on his previous job with an engineering concern, but it represented, in the most literal of senses, a living.

I wondered how long it would be, with tenement blocks pressing in on all sides, before the developers converged on these prime downtown acres. Lesser sharks had already removed much of the best marble from the tumbled, gaping graves, and every scrap of lead lettering on every single headstone had been studiously prised away, leaving only rivet holes to read the inscriptions by.

Occasionally, said Ian, the beggars would invade the cemetery looking for somewhere to live; then, being himself not a strong man, he would have to hire a couple of local heavies to return the squatters to the street.

He invited me into the gatehouse, which was also the one-room home that he shared with his solemn wife and a skeletal chicken. It was neat but sparse, with a makeshift single bed, a set of shelves with a few paperbacks and personal oddments, and a plank settle. As Ian's scrawny arm reached under the bed for the old leather-bound records of the cemetery, it struck me that all that separated these two survivors from the lethal poverty of Calcutta's homeless thousands was this ramshackle boneyard and a Welshman's grave.

15

All day, every day a sweating leper juddering with fever lies where he's been dropped in Jahrwahal Nehru Street, his teeth pressed hard against the pavement, his jumbled limbs incapable of movement, apart from an arm-stump incessantly wagging. His minders have spread alongside him a large rectangle of blue plastic, pinioned by stones, for the merciful to toss their *paise* to.

Twenty yards further on, there's the alarming sight of what appears to be a headless corpse, stretched out on its back. Getting closer, I see that the 'corpse' has either found or made for himself a small hole in the pavement into which he has lowered his head, which he has then covered entirely with gravel. With a stone in his right hand he taps the pavement spasmodically; with his left he bangs a tin mug on the ground, beside the levelled off gravel beneath which he has buried his face.

Midway between these two desperados: an image of transcendent tenderness: around a foot-high broad-leaved plant pushing up through a crack at the edge of the pavement, someone has balanced eight or nine stones, to make a rickety little fence. It is still in place two days later.

16

Thomas Jones, overshadowed by palms, and circled by vultures and huge black kites, seems a long way from the shallow, secluded valleys and the soft, wooded hills of *'Paradwys Cymru'*. But he would probably have been less dismayed by Calcutta's endemic wretchedness than is the modern visitor, because he would have been only too familiar with comparable scenes of misery at home. His was a profoundly troubled 'paradise'.

He was born on January 24, 1810 at a small farm called Tan-y-ffridd in the parish of Llangyniew, between Llanfair Caereinion and the village of Meifod. His birthplace, like Llifior

Mill, Aberriw with which his name is more commonly associated, is typical of the border style of half-timbered house that came to be built in the later, peaceful years of the fifteenth century. Tan-y-ffridd, as its name implies, is situated below a half-mile ridge of what was once mountain pasture but is today a forest of pine trees; sheep still graze the lower slope, and in many ways this quiet, hidden valley seems little changed in nearly two hundred years. Outwardly, the house too seems little altered, but the sharper geometry of the rear portion is evidence of a recent extension which has doubled the building's size. Inside, everything has been modernised and the irregularities of the old structure forced into compliance with the clipped, clean lines of the new.

Thomas was the second son of Edward and Mary Jones, who were to have ten children altogether. His father was a wheelwright and carpenter from Meifod, his mother, born Mary Owen in the parish of nearby Llanfihangel-yng-Ngwynfa, 'St. Michael's in Paradise', was from the same locality as the celebrated hymn writer Ann Griffiths (1776-1805). Mary's people would have been close associates of Ann Griffiths's family, for both were among the pioneers of Methodism in their district. It was in Mary's home, a farm called Penllys about half way between Llanfihangel and Pontrobert, that the Methodist cause, serving the neighbourhood of Pontrobert, first established itself. Ann Griffiths, coming rather later to Methodism than the rest of her family, accompanied her brothers to the Methodist meetings at Mary's family home from about 1797. It was then that Ann started composing the hymns that were to shake the chapels of Wales to the rafters, and are sung nowhere today with greater fervour than in the Khasi Hills. In spite of the scornful denunciations heaped on the new sect by the majority of Anglican priests, the Penllys Methodists soon grew too numerous for their farmhouse meeting place; sometime around 1800 they transferred to a purpose-built chapel at Pontrobert.

Thomas Jones's family no doubt transmitted to him their pride in being so actively involved in what amounted to a revolutionary upheaval in the religious life of Wales, instilling in him a confident, venturesome spirit which was later to find expression in his determination to follow through to a successful conclusion whatever task he set out to accomplish.

His wife Anne, whom he married shortly before departing for India, was also steeped in the Methodist traditions of mid-Wales. She was the grand-daughter of one of Daniel Rowland's followers, Thomas Rowlands, who farmed at Llwyncoppa, Adfa. His farmhouse was the main meeting place of the Adfa Dissenters until they built their own chapel in 1742. Anne was related distantly, through the Swancotts of Llanllugan, to William Lewis, who would become Thomas Jones's first co-worker in the Hills.

Another native of Llanfihangel and a regular worshipper at Penllys was John Davies (1772-1855), the weaver's son who sailed as a missionary to the South Sea Islands in 1800 and died there fifty-four years later without once revisiting the land of his birth. As 'John Davies, Tahiti' he is probably the most famous of Welsh missionaries; Thomas Jones would have been brought up on family recollections of John Davies and stories of his adventures in that almost incomprehensibly far-flung place. Davies wrote regularly to John Hughes (1775-1854), the minister at Pontrobert, who would have passed on to the community at large the latest eagerly awaited news of his friend's exploits: his encounters with all manner of strange creatures and stranger people, his eventual mastery of their language, his translation into Tahitian – single-handed – of *Pilgrim's Progress* and thirteen books of the Bible.

Montgomeryshire in the early nineteenth century was, like much of rural Wales, an area of considerable poverty and distress. A short-lived boom in small industries such as slate-quarrying, lead-mining, tanning and, above all, flannel-weaving did little to relieve the hardship of those who lived on the land. Life in the burgeoning townships to the south, where the world's first industrial revolution was well underway, was squalid and severe enough: the average life expectancy there was a mere 20 years, and three-quarters of those who died were children under the age of five. But country people, reduced to landless destitution by unofficial enclosures, often saw a better life for themselves among the smoke and noise of the coalmines and iron foundries, and flocked there, in a memorable phrase, "to seek their freedom" from the shackles of near – and, in 1817, actual – famine in their sheep-bitten hills. From 1815 until 1850 the depression in Montgomeryshire was acute and unrelieved.

Liverpool, 'the capital of north Wales' and gateway to the Empire, seemed to many to offer an escape from rural hardship. Edward Jones removed his family there when Thomas was about three, plying his trade as a wheelwright. But in 1819, as a consequence of failing health, he brought his growing brood back to the sweeter air of Montgomeryshire. After a short stay at Brithdir, he became a tenant of Llifior Mill, Aberriw, known at that time as Tŷ Brith or Pied House Mill - 'Pied' describing the black-and-white appearance of both the mill and the nearby farmhouse to which it belonged. He continued to work as wheelwright and carpenter, and introduced each of his sons to woodworking skills. Thomas worked initially for his father, but subsequently became a miller, itself a well-regarded and highly skilled craft.

Aberriw, or Berriew as it has been Englished, would have been an important focus of economic, social and religious life in the early nineteenth century, and the mill, situated a stone's throw from the main road that linked nearby Welshpool and Newtown, the county's two main towns, would have been a hive of activity. Carts laden with grain from outlying farms, some of them more than a day's travel away, would come creaking down a track that cut across the grassy slope opposite, over a narrow ford and onto the muddy yard in front of the mill. Often, the visitors would have to stay overnight, the men sleeping in a loft above the stables where their horses were bedded down. This constant flow of all kinds of country people would have led to an exchange of a wide variety of skills and ideas. Young Thomas, with an enquiring and agile mind, and gifted with his hands, soon added other crafts to those of carpenter and miller: he became a proficient cooper, learnt how to burn lime, and took a special interest in farming. He was to turn this extensive knowledge of rural crafts to good account when he reached the Khasi Hills.

The mill is occupied today by Jan and Mike Harris Edge, a retired English couple who, with considerable energy and sensitivity, have worked hard to restore the house, which had suffered much neglect. I was taken there by Bill Price who is head of religious education at Newtown Comprehensive, and who works enthusiastically to keep the memory of Thomas Jones alive in both his pupils and the wider community. Jan and Mike knew nothing of Thomas Jones when they bought the mill. But one day, Jan told me, a man came and asked permission to fish in the stream, which he had done from time to time in the past.

"He said in passing that someone had lived here who translated the Bible – into Welsh, I thought. No one locally knew anything about this, but we got piles of books, and gradually picked up a bit here, a bit there, slowly getting quite hooked on the subject as the person got more and more real. Then we actually found his name: Thomas Jones!"

Eventually, Bill Price made contact with Jan and Mike, and they learned more. They are proud of the mill's associations with Thomas Jones, and were delighted when, just before Christmas 1991, some visitors from the Khasi Hills called at Aberriw to see the mill for themselves, and, Bible in hand, stepped over the threshold and into the very house that Thomas Jones stepped out of all those years ago, Bible in hand, with such momentous consequences for the Khasis.

Tucked in between the rear of the mill and a field that sweeps upwards to Pied House Farm is the now empty leet, the basin into which water would have been diverted from the stream, to drive the great iron mill-wheel. The wheel now lies slumped and motionless in its trough at the side of the milling shed, entangled in a glorious blaze of virginia creeper. The mill workings themselves, and most of the milling shed, are not those of Thomas Jones, for a fire destroyed the old mill shortly after he left for India. Mike and Jan had hoped to restore it to working order but, at about £100,000, the costs were prohibitive.

In 1819, the year Edward Jones brought his family back from Liverpool, there were riots in Newtown and Abermiwl which the Montgomeryshire Yeomanry were summoned to put down. Thus began two decades of violent unrest.

The governance of Britain was in crisis throughout this turbulent period, and the ruling classes lived in fear of revolution. Wales, with its distinct religious, political and linguistic identity, gave the Establishment particular cause for concern. There were dozens of strikes and riots in the south; in Merthyr Tydfil an armed rebellion of industrial workers faced the guns of the Argyll and Sutherland Highlanders, and twenty men died; thousands more workers marched on Newport in support of basic democratic rights as enshrined in their leaders' famous Charter, and again met the guns of the British state; exploitation led to unionisation, and a self-aware Welsh working class sprang into articulate life.

The very first outbreak of Chartist violence occurred not in the south but in Thomas Jones's mid-Wales in 1839. At Llanidloes, about 23 miles to the south west of Aberriw, the presence of a squad of London policemen, who had been sent there because of fears of an uprising, so enraged the local textile workers that they stormed the Trewythen Arms where the police were staying. For a week the Chartists held Llanidloes, and order was not restored until infantry from Brecon and the Montgomeryshire Yeomanry arrived on the scene. By this date, Thomas Jones was committed to spiritual radicalism, but the intense Chartism of his region, which caused such alarm in London, could not have escaped his notice.

There were other discontents. A scheme to extract more taxes from tenant farmers by establishing toll-gates on main thoroughfares was meeting with growing resistance; this was to erupt throughout Wales in the legendary Rebecca Riots. There was widespread anger against the workhouses of the new Poor Law, one of which – at Forden – was situated barely two miles from Llifior Mill. Thomas Jones, whose later championing of exploited Khasis showed him to be an instinctive supporter of the underdog, must have shared in the community's general revulsion at conditions in the Forden House of Industry: here hundreds of destitute adults, and scores of children under the age of four, were confined in foul discomfort as the only alternative to starvation. Parents were kept separated from their children, and the able-bodied were flogged for slacking at their labour.

There were riots aplenty in this supposed 'backwater' of mid Wales, and the Montomeryshire Yeomanry were called out on numerous occasions to 'pacify' a desperately angry peasantry struggling to survive on little more than potatoes and oatmeal.

Living at Aberriw, Thomas Jones was balanced geographically between representatives of two major contending forces.

Down the road in a southerly direction lay Newtown, birthplace of Robert Owen (1771-1858) the saddler's son who, developing practical and civilised solutions to the economic and social chaos of the early nineteenth century, won world-wide fame as the founder of Utopian socialism. Faced with an industrial crisis at the end of the Napoleonic Wars, the government had called him in to advise them on what should be done. Although Thomas Jones could not have reconciled himself to Owen's hostility to religion, much of the Montgomeryshire thinker's social polemic, encountered possibly in such works as the influential *A New View of Society* (1813), may have presented itself to the fair-minded young Christian as a compassionate politics for the future.

A short distance away in the opposite direction lay Powys Castle, dynastic home of political beliefs and practices rooted in pre-feudal times – and still a major force in the land. This, one of the grandest stately homes in Wales, had been the residence for centuries of the Earls of Powys. In 1784, a Powys heiress, Lady Henrietta Antonia Herbert, had married the son of Sir Robert Clive "the mighty conqueror of India", as they referred to him at the time. This Powys Clive was himself governor of Madras (1798-1803), and on his return to Wales was appointed 'Lord Lieutenant – Governor, in effect – of Montgomeryshire (1804-1830), backed up with a string of honorific titles – Baron Powis of Powis Castle, Baron Herbert of Chirbury, Viscount Clive of Ludlow, and Earl of Powis. A Tory, he voted by instinct against the measures of social amelioration proposed by the Reform Bill. In 1830 he was succeeded as Lord Lieutenant by his son, who maintained a similar political line and took a leading part in suppressing the Chartist uprisings. Here, virtually on Thomas Jones's doorstep, was an ancient dynasty of high panjandrums whose influence and wealth, much of it lately carried home from India, were inescapable.

It is tempting to imagine that as he passed the Powyses' impregnable 'Red Castle' on his way to and from Welshpool, Thomas Jones the social improver might have looked forward with a forgiveable degree of relish to evening the score in favour of the oppressed as soon as he could get to India.

The Powys family were but one of an entire class of frequently absentee, rack-renting landlords against whom the tenant farmers and peasantry of Wales had set their teeth in moral and sometimes physical opposition. As antagonism grew between the landed gentry and the labouring people, so a chasm yawned between the Established Church – identified increasingly as the church of capital, social injustice and an alienating Englishness – and the Nonconformists, with their roots embedded in the traditions and language of the people.

In spite of poor or non-existent schools, and unremitting deprivation, the farming populace was not without culture. There would have been wide-ranging discussions at the Mill not only around the practicalities of existence but on intellectual, political and, of course, spiritual matters.

In 1810, the year of Thomas Jones's birth, there were 74 Nonconformist chapels in Montgomeryshire. By 1830 that number had more than doubled to 154, three times more than the number of churches. Despite the activity of Baptists and Congregationalists since the 1650s, Montgomeryshire was by the middle of the nineteenth century overwhelmingly a Calvinistic Methodist preserve, testifying to a tremendous energy among the Methodists in this region.

Thomas Jones, brought up a Methodist, was a faithful attendant of the church meetings that were held at Fferm Tŷ Brith (Pied House Farm, as it is today) on the hilltop just behind the Mill. But it was not until 1835, at one of the grand Association meetings held at Bethel, Llanidloes that he found himself brought under those deep religious impressions that were to change the course of his life, not to mention the course of Khasi history. He began to preach, his first sermon, on the exhortation "Turn ye to the stronghold!", touching on a theme distinctly prophetic of evangelisings to come.

17

Upstream from Calcutta lies Serampore where in 1799, under the King of Denmark's protection, the Northamptonshire Baptist and social radical William Carey (1761-1834) established what became famous worldwide as "The Cradle of Modern Missions".

In the 1830s the Baptists at Serampore sustained a short-lived and largely fruitless mission to the Khasi Hills, but they later developed strong ties with the Welsh from the earliest days of the Methodists' considerably more successful mission. This historical association, and the continuing importance of Serampore College as a focus for Indian Christianity, called for a visit.

A train to Serampore, then a rickshaw to the college: Ednyfed Thomas, on the phone before I left, had made the trip sound like a jaunt from Swansea to Llanelli. So spurning Meghalaya House's offer of a "friendly taxi with no-cheat driver", I opted for the cheaper rough-and-tumble of public transport.

I had thought that by about 9.15 a.m., as I crossed the Hooghly towards Calcutta's twin city of Howrah, the worst of the rush-hour would be over. I was wrong. The Indian working day, a couple of hours shorter than ours, seems not to get underway until between 10.00 and 10.30 p.m., so the astounding tidal bore of humanity that boils twice daily through Howrah Station was starting to surge through the neo-Gothic concourses and subterranean broadways just as I began dithering around in search of the booking hall. Buying a train ticket, I had been warned, was an agonisingly slow business – "In India, my friend, we have eternity" – involving interminable queues and hours of waiting. So I was surprised at how quick and easy it was, and how few travellers were doing business at the booking hatches. It soon became apparent that with trains and buses as hypercrowded as Calcutta's, there is no practical point in bothering to buy a ticket: not all the ticket inspectors in India could possibly keep tabs on the resistless legions that sardine aboard the city's sagging public vehicles.

"Platform three, at nine fifty," said the clerk at the hatch. What could be simpler? But as I headed out against the inflowing commuters, such was the density and force of the human current that I could make little progress against it. They were coming now in their hundreds of thousands, wave on surging wave down a set of steps ahead of me which were as broad as a six-lane highway, but nowhere near broad enough for the ever tighter, ever mightier swell that built against my reed-like insignificance. Soon I could neither move forward nor stand still, but was swept along with the crowd, faster and faster, in precisely the opposite direction to that intended. The only thing for it was to try to tack obliquely downstream towards a cast-iron stanchion and anchor myself in its current-breaking lee. I managed to reach the pillar and nestled there, buffeted by the white-shirted torrent, for ten or fifteen minutes, until it seemed that the flow had subsided sufficiently for me to attempt, once more, to move against it.

English is officially India's *lingua franca* but only about three per cent of the people speak it. I could find no one on platform three who understood a word of the language, but I did what I could with gestures and repetitions of the word 'Serampore?'. The general view seemed to be that it was the next train. So when the next train nudged the buffers and its crushed thousands had poured down platform three, I stepped aboard. "Serampore?" I asked a traveller who had a couple of bony chickens dangling from each hand. He shook his head authoritatively, so I returned to the platform. This kind of thing happened with two or three more trains, and I wondered if those who nodded happily when I pointed to a train and said "Serampore?" did so not because they knew anything about the Serampore service but because they thought that that was what I wanted to hear. I suppose I could have spent the entire morning getting on and off trains that may or may not have been going to

Serampore, but I had only that day left before flying out of Calcutta, and couldn't afford to waste any more time.

Reluctantly, I admitted defeat, caught an autorickshaw to Meghalaya House and asked for their friendly no-cheat taxi. It was costlier, perhaps, than an ordinary taxi but the Bengali driver was nifty, prudent and determined, and therefore eminently worth his hire in a city where driving is a manic game of push-and-shove. "Slow drive, long life" is the widely ignored jingle seen on the rear of many an Indian lorry; truer to the spirit of Indian road sense is another common tailboard motto, "Blow Horn – Good Luck".

Serampore is some sixteen miles north-west of Calcutta. After crossing the Hooghly on the great Vivekananda road-and-rail bridge, the broad and congested highways of the city area give way to narrower roads snaking alongside the western bank of the river which, glimpsed between factories and houses, is the only major open space in the seemingly endless urban clutter of Calcutta's hinterland.

The College is a defiantly out-of-place neo-classical edifice; it is separated from the murky expanse of the Hooghly only by a broad sweep of lawn, an ornate wrought iron fence and a pair of huge baroque gates. Freshly decorated for its 175th anniversary in golden yellow paint with slate-blue trimmings, Serampore College looked as palatial as any structure that this city of (now crumbling) palaces might have boasted in the vainglorious days of the Raj.

The early British rulers of India were hostile to missionaries; indeed, missionary activity in British India was illegal until 1813, and sea captains were banned from accepting missionaries among their passengers. It was the East India Company's view that they were in India to make money, not to interfere with the indigenous culture and religions, which might irritate the timorous natives and tip them into commercially damaging rebellion. It was therefore in little oases of non-British India that the Protestant missions sought to establish a toehold. The first, set up in 1706 by King Frederick IV of Denmark, was in the tiny Danish settlement of Tranquebar on the Coromandel coast in the south-east. This Royal Danish Mission established five operational principles that became ground rules for most subsequent missions, including the Welsh: the church should set up schools to ensure literacy among Christians and thereby direct access to the Word of God; the Bible should be available to Christians in their own language; evangelists should have an accurate knowledge of the mind of the people; personal rather than mass conversion should be the aim; and as soon as possible a native church, with its own native ministry, should come into being.

Arriving in India in 1793, William Carey had to evangelise surreptitiously while working up country as an indigo planter. In 1799 he joined four other missionaries who, refused a licence by the Company, established their mission base at Serampore which, like Tranquebar, was a Danish settlement, until it was sold to the British in 1845.

From here the Northamptonshire shoemaker would witness daily the smoke curling from the riverside funeral *ghats*. Britain, Carey believed, was rotten with guilt for ruling Bengal yet turning a blind eye to the evils of *suttee* (widow-burning) and the bloodier excesses of indigenous custom. It was Europe's mission to carry civilisation abroad, and he wanted to see his country doing much more for India's good.

Two of Carey's associates soon died, as did his deranged wife, but with the remaining two, the self-educated former weaver Joshua Marshman (1768-1837) and the printer and journalist William Ward (1769-1823), he embarked on an unflagging regime of preaching, teaching, translating and building. The 'Serampore Trio', as they became known, enjoyed the support of various organisations and individual benefactors in Britain and America, as well as King Frederick VI of Denmark. But they also sank into the mission the considerable sums they earned as independent professionals: Carey, for instance, continuing the linguistic tradition of Sir William Jones, worked as Professor of Sanskrit and Bengali at Fort William College. It must have amused him that his paymasters there, the sternly anti-missionary East India Company, were contributing so handsomely, through his salary, to the missionary cause.

My Serampore contact was 'out of station' on the day of my visit, so I arrived at the Principal's chambers unexpected and unannounced. The Principal's wife, a stout woman in a sari, welcomed me, a little distractedly, into the capacious and exceptionally high-ceilinged apartment that had been built and lived in by William Carey and his extended family of missionaries. She apologised, in the half-shuttered gloom of the lounge, for her husband's absence. He had suffered a heart attack while visiting the United States, and had undergone major surgery. Such were the pressures and difficulties of the present time that she could not, she regretted, take me round in person, but she would ask a student to show me the college.

My guide, Lal, was an undergraduate from Madras whose Hindu parents had disowned him for turning Christian. He showed me first the student hostel built like an Oxbridge college around a grassy quad, and he talked hesitantly about some deep trouble in his life that had caused him to question his Hindu upbringing. "I found peace at last in Jesus Christ. My mother and father will have nothing to do with me, but my brother and sister are still good to me, they understand."

On then to the palatial main building. Its echoing hallway was dominated by twin cast iron and brass stairways which had come, said Lal, from a burned out palace in Denmark – another gift from the Danish King. Tucked beneath the stairs was the door to the little Carey Museum where portraits of the King and Queen of Denmark flanked the missionary's desk and his alabaster bust. Here too were his bow-bellied pulpit, his grandfather clock, his letter-writing case with a phial of quill nibs, and samples of the many Asiatic languages and scripts into which the mission translated the bible. In a glass cabinet stood a miniature steam engine which Carey brought with him from England: this, the first steam engine ever seen in India, was precursor to the battalions of steam engines that were to transform the country's communications and economic life.

These crowded mementoes were to be transferred to a major new Carey Museum that was under construction in a corner of the front garden. It was to have been ready in time for this year's jubilee celebrations but, still at the wet concrete and scaffolding stage, it looked about a year behind schedule. It was nevertheless an ambitious undertaking, with big money behind it, possibly from the American Baptists, many of whom had left their signatures in the visitors' book.

We moved on, through the King of Denmark's towering gates, to the river's edge. Carey's first convert, Krishna Chandra Pal, was baptised in these waters on 28 December, 1800. Over the next ten years 300 more Hindus were converted. "Thus," said Ward, "the door of faith is open to the Hindus, and who shall shut it? Thus is the chain of caste broken, and who shall mend it?"

In 1813 Krishna Chandra Pal was sent by Carey to attempt to evangelise the Khasis from a base at Pandua, a trading centre at the foot of the Khasi Hills below Cherrapunji. Although situated in the plains, and these days part of Bangladesh, Pandua belonged at that time to the Khasi kingdom of Sohra (Cherrapunji). During his eight-months stay, Pal succeeded in baptising seven individuals, two of whom were Khasis; some 600 Khasis and eight native chiefs turned out to witness the immersion in the Dlebolisshore river.

Carey was encouraged on Pal's return to begin a translation of the bible into Khasi. "This week," he wrote home, "we have obtained a person to assist us in the translation of the scriptures into the Khasi language and I believe the only one who can read and write." Khasis tend to think that this first translator was himself a Khasi, although there is no record of his name, and the *New Testament* translation in the Bengali script which resulted from his labours was so imperfect as to be quite unintelligible to its intended readers.

Pal, who is considered to be the first missionary of North-East India as a whole, never returned to the Khasis. There was no further contact between Serampore and the Hills until 1832 when Alexander B. Lish, an Anglo-Indian who was only eighteen years old, was sent as a missionary to Cherrapunji, where a British military station had been established.

Lish's mission was supported by William Carey in person, who every month set aside fifty rupees of his pension to send to the Khasi Hills. Towards the end of his life Carey worried what would happen to the mission in Cherrapunji after his day, but a woman in England sent him £500 to enable Lish's work to continue. Baptist missionary records for this period having been destroyed in London during World War II, the identity of this benefactress remains dark. But the late Dr. Arthur Hughes of Liverpool once raised the intriguing possibility of a 'Welsh connection'.

Carey had significant links with Liverpool: as an eminent botanist, he was a Fellow of the Botanical Gardens of Liverpool; furthermore, the treasurer of the Serampore group, Samuel Hope, was a Liverpool man. He lived in Hope Street, a stone's throw from the Mount Street home of the Rev. John 'Minimus' Roberts, who was secretary of the Welsh Mission for the first twenty-five years. Nearly all of the Liverpool members of the mission's committee lived within half a mile of Samuel Hope's house, and it is more than likely that as members of the same intellectual circle, Hope and his Serampore supporters would have shared excitedly with their Methodist friends news of Lish's pioneering mission to the Khasis. "I have often thought," Dr. Hughes told me, "that it would indeed be a delightful thing to have it established that the lady who in 1833 sent William Carey that money for work on the Khasi Hills, was a Liverpool Welsh lady."

Lish stayed at Cherrapunji for six years, learning the language, opening a number of schools and retranslating the *New Testament*. This, again, was in the Bengali script and proved inaccessible to the Khasis, accounting in part for Lish's relative lack of success in spreading the gospel. He seems to have failed to win a single convert, but he did manage to persuade a small party of Khasis to accompany him to Calcutta in 1833 for his ordination at the Lal Bazaar Chapel. This metropolitan visit, possibly the first by Khasis, fired them with enthusiasm for the wonders of urban civilisation, but they, like the rest of their compatriots, remained stubbornly resistant to the religion on which that civilisation claimed to be founded. Serampore called Lish back to base in 1838, and abandoned the Khasis to their intractably heathenish ways.

The Christians at Serampore have long since given up baptisms in the Hooghly. "Far too filthy," said Lal, pointing to the slime green mudflats at our feet. "The Hindus still bathe in the river, but we would not consider it. To them it is a sacred river, a branch of the holy Ganga that springs from the head of Shiva the destroyer. But we think of the pollution, the rotting corpses."

"Do you see many bodies?"

"They wash up here on this muddy bank, maybe two or three together. The college has made complaints to the municipal authorities, but it makes no difference. The Hooghly is a holy river, they say. Whatever has been put in it must remain where it is, not pushed back in or taken out and interfered with. So we have to put up with the smell, for many days sometimes, until a high tide carries them away again."

Carey, Marshman and Ward, giving everything they earned to the mission, died poor men. They are buried in a tumbledown English cemetery, strewn with cowpats and convolvulus, about half a mile from the college. Most of the brick monuments here are crumbling to dust, and every tomb has been picked clean of its lead letters; discernible occasionally is the faintest shadow of the Grecian filigree that once proudly festooned the fancier piles. Admirers of the 'Trio' have honoured each of them with a grand memorial, retouched lately with rich yellow paint for the jubilee celebrations. Such vanity would not have been to the founder's taste: he left instructions that his funeral was to be "as plain as possible"; he also chose the inscription for his grave: "A wretched, poor and helpless worm,/On thy kind arms I fall."

18

The Baptists of Calcutta, well established by the 1840s as a dynamic and influential presence in the city, gave Thomas and Anne Jones a hearty welcome.

The Rev. Jacob Tomlin, who 'discovered' the Khasi Hills for the Welsh, noted during a visit to Calcutta some years earlier "the delightful and cordial union which subsisted amongst the

Lord's servants of all denominations"; though I don't suppose he included in his rosy ecumenical picture the followers of the Pope, that "great foe to Christ and his gospel".

Among the non-Baptists waiting to receive the new arrivals was the renowned Church of Scotland missionary Dr. Alexander Duff (1806-78) who thanked God that "gallant little Wales" had awakened to her missionary responsibilities. The Serampore 'Trio' were by now all dead, but their close associate Dr. John Mack, who with Marshman's son had taken over the running of the College, was also on hand to greet the couple from Wales.

The Joneses lodged, as had Tomlin before them, in the home of a Mr. Grey, a prominent Baptist layman, and his wife. They expected to stay at the Greys' only a short time before continuing their journey, but no sooner had they arrived than Anne, weak and sickly from the voyage, gave birth to the child she had been carrying those anxious sea-borne months. The baby died the same day.

Anne was now seriously ill – Thomas was later to write home that it was a miracle she recovered – and it was clear that they would have to postpone the last leg of their journey until she was fit enough to face up to its demands.

Her recovery, in Calcutta's searing heat, was painfully slow. For weeks that turned into months, Thomas wandered the broad streets and stately gardens of this strange new city. Younger even than New York, it had grown from nothing but a village to become, by 1773, the headquarters of the East India Company and the chief centre of government in India.

Central Calcutta today, with its architectural cribs from the imperial capital, looks in certain lights like a long unpainted, disastrously stressed London. But in Thomas Jones's time it was a dazzling if somewhat weather-battered city of white plastered walls and neo-classical columns, where the Europeans lived in grand homes around the abundant green acres of the Maidan, and retired at 1 p.m. to take a siesta. Those who lived in the 'white city' kept as far away as possible from what they referred to as the 'Black Town'.

I can imagine Thomas Jones strolling through the bazaar, lingering at a spice stall over the rich sweaty bloom of *jeera* or brushing a hand against some silk newly boated down from the Khasi Hills; and then, perhaps, cutting across the Maidan, still today a sweet green oasis, to see if there were an American ice ship anchored in the Hooghly. Ice, which sold for a penny a pound, was greatly prized in this foul climate as a life-saving remedy for inflammation and fever.

Worried about his wife he certainly was, but it would have been against the drift of his questing intelligence for him to be bored. There were things to be done, equipment to be gathered and people to see, the better to gird himself for the challenge that lay ahead.

Visiting Alexander Duff, he would have found himself caught up in one of the great debates of the day: should the medium of instruction in government schools be English or the classical languages of India? Duff was a leading advocate of higher education as a means of producing an educated Christian population and of bringing the gospel to the intellectual élite. He had a vision of the mud-and-thatch village school developing in time to become a university.

Thomas Jones would have heard from Duff how his first conversions of young men from leading Bengali families had caused a furore: there had been riots, court cases and the boycotting of his school; one or two converts had even been kidnapped and disappeared for ever. The parents of many converts had reacted as had those of Lal, my Serampore guide, and rejected them entirely, a situation which often led to missionaries adopting the outcasts as their sons and raising them in their own homes. Out of such defensive measures grew the 'mission compound' which not only protected converts from intimidation but also ripped them clean away from everything that defined them as Indian, and threatened to turn them into honorary white men.

The argument over language had been settled, officially, in 1835 when the very English and hugely influential T.B. Macaulay (1800-1859), who was a member of the Supreme Council in Calcutta, tabled his infamous proposal that English should be the medium of instruction in an education system geared to the creation of a westernised intellectual élite. The standard 'mission compound' model adopted by the Welsh would indeed lead to something of a westernised élite, but it is as well for Khasi culture that Thomas Jones, and most of the missionaries who followed him, proved resistant to Macaulay's anglicising fervour.

Thomas Jones was not disconcerted by the failure of both Pal and Lish to introduce literacy to Khasi culture. Serampore's John Mack handed over to him all the documents containing the translations of Khasi already attempted in the Bengali script, which he surely found as baffling as did the Khasis. He had a radically different approach in mind, and, preparing for the time when he would have his own translations of the scriptures ready for printing, he no doubt called at the Baptist Mission Press, at 44 Lower Circular Road, to discuss publication timetables and procedures.

By the beginning of June Anne was sufficiently recovered to undertake the long river journey to the Khasi Hills, but sickness, for the rest of her brief life, was never far from her door.

19

I had toyed with travelling to the Hills by train, to be more intimate with the people and the land's unfolding. But I'd decided, even before my bungled efforts at Howrah, that the 1,000 miles journey up and around the border of Bangladesh would eat away the best part of two days, which was time I was disinclined to squander on the curiosities of an Indian train ride. Rather than snail my way along two sides of a triangle, I'd fly straight there, a distance in a north-easterly direction of about 300 miles.

The Indian authorities did me a favour, as it turned out, in refusing me entry earlier in the year. Had I pitched up in the Khasi Hills in March, as originally intended, I'd have been under-researched and bereft of contacts. During the extra half year of preparation, I managed to read a lot more about the Mission, and opened up a fruitful correspondence with a wide range of cultural, political and religious figures, some of whom had been influential in persuading the authorities to grant me the all-important 'RAP' (Restricted Area Permit).

Alexander Frater's *Monsoon* documentary had suggested that thanks to the Welsh presence the Hills were alive with the sound not only of hymns but of poets. It seemed tantalisingly possible from the drift of his commentary that the Khasi Hills represented a far eastern outpost of the venerable tradition of the *bardd gwlad* (folk poet). But having scoured the libraries of Britain on the inter-library loan system, I found little in the way of translations or critical writing that lent much weight to this attractive notion; furthermore, if the following snatch of supposedly twentieth-century 'Anglo-Khasi' verse was representative, the Khasis seemed to be mired in a Victorian time-warp of altogether somebody else's making:

> Lo, down the vale, how merrily
> The streamlets danced along their beds
> Of flowery fields and grassy meads,
> E'er swarmed by the laborious bee.
>
> Thus throughout nature, vast and great,
> A kind of renovation flowed:
> The earth with radiant beauty glowed,
> In all its verdant bloom arrayed.

I was open to the possibility that, as with some early English versions of Welsh poetry, a certain something might have gone adrift in translation. But it was difficult to derive much encouragement for this wishful thought from most of the critical writing that was attempting to persuade me of the splendours of Khasi literature:

> The present Bible form has helped much evaluating the standard of Khasi literature, equipping high vocabularies and use of idiomatic phrases which come at all instances to the mark that the original meaning of such biblical thought has not been dimmed in the concurrent phases varying to

theological dogma, dramatic episodes, proverbs, sermons, doctrines, parables, allegories, historic incidents, outlook of divinity and other associated ideas.

What did it all amount to, I wondered, having slogged through several studies written in this pantomime Oxbridge vein? A couple of positive impressions emerged strongly, however: there was music out there, and there was an extraordinarily rich oral tradition of story telling. Surely such a culture had its poets too; but who and where were they?

By chance, the spring '92 edition of *Poetry Wales* carried an article on contemporary Indian poetry. The author, Bibhu Padhi, praising the "tribal lyricism" of a certain Robin Ngangom, singled him out as one of the most promising talents on the Indian literary scene, and regretted that because the poet lived "in a town called Shillong on the southwest fringes of Orissa" he had not enjoyed the attention accorded big city poets. Had I stumbled at last, in spite of the puzzling association of Shillong with Orissa, on a Khasi poet? Or was there more than one Shillong in India? I wrote to Bibhu Padhi for further information, and he wrote back with Robin Ngangom's address, switching Shillong this time from Orissa to Arunanchal (sic) Pradesh, which is rather like exiling Swansea to mid-Devon.

I followed a hunch rather than Bibhu Padhi's zany geography and wrote a letter to Robin Ngangom in Shillong, Meghalaya. Within a couple of weeks he wrote back, with poems, newspaper cuttings and a clutch of what turned out to be indispensable names and addresses, mostly of poets and writers. To my relief there was not a streamlet or grassy mead to be seen in the selection of poetry he had taken the considerable trouble to type out for me: these boys, as he said, had cut their teeth on Lorca, Seferis, Arghezi, Neruda and the hard-edged modernists of the Third World; they were keen too on Dylan Thomas and Alun Lewis (who died not so very far from the Khasi Hills), but they were palpably of their own time and place. I was suddenly among friends. He also advised me that although 'Khasia' was a term often used by the Welsh and other outsiders, it had pejorative connotations for the Khasis themselves, and was rarely used.

As for Robin, he was not, he said, a Khasi but a Meitei from nearby Manipur, who had been living in Shillong for many years as a university teacher. One of the writers he urged me to contact was his friend Desmond L. Kharmawphlang, a poet and lecturer who was working towards a Ph.D. on Khasi folk tales: "I personally feel he would be the best interpreter of his culture and people."

And so it turned out to be. Soon Desmond and I were in regular communication. One of his letters included an appealing description of him as a folklorist, tramping through the jungle "with only tape recorder, a supply of batteries, notebooks, anti-malaria pills and a trusting heart." Desmond was full of encouragement. The 'RAP' and my trouble with the bureucrats? Desmond had detailed and useful advice. Accommodation? He'd fix it up. Transport? No problem: the family car and a driver would be at my disposal; Desmond himself would be my guide.

The last letter I had before leaving for India was from Robin. There had been, he said, a bit of trouble in Shillong. "Student unrest (they call it here in India) and other ethnic organisations demanding very legitimate rights (that's what I feel). But then politicians and twisted minds make the best of such situations and unfortunately only the poor and the simple get hurt. One day we may have replicas of mini-banana republics in the North-East. At the moment we are firmly united with mainland India by absolute corruption and consumerist mania. But don't let all this worry you. Things will be all right, I know."

Direct flights from Calcutta to Shillong are few, and involve what can sometimes be a hair-raising landing at the little mountain strip of Umroi, just outside the city. Most travellers to the Khasi Hills fly to Guwahati which is 63 miles north of Shillong, and just over the state border in Assam.

I phoned Desmond the night before I left Calcutta to ask about buses from Guwahati to Shillong. "The bus will not be necessary," he said. "The poets will be there to meet you."

20

The north-eastern states of India – Assam, Arunachal Pradesh, Manipur, Meghalaya, Mizoram, Nagaland, Tripura – are joined to the rest of the country by the thinnest of umbilical cords, the 12-miles wide Siliguri pass which links North Bengal with lower Assam. The states swell out from the pass like an amorphous speech bubble, bounded by Bhutan and sad Tibet to the north, China and Burma to the east and Bangladesh to the south.

Home to some 35 million people, roughly 4% of the total Indian population, the region comprises 7.7% of the total Indian landmass. These tribal territories are so marginal to 'mainland' thinking that they are sometimes missed off maps of India altogether. Indeed, the British toyed with the idea of making the hill tracts of Assam a Crown Colony or Protectorate independent of India. The Governor of Assam, Sir Robert Reid, argued that the hill tribes "are not Indians in any sense of the word, neither in religion nor in language, nor in appearance, nor in habits, nor in outlook, and it is by an historical accident that they have been tacked on to an Indian province." His plan was abandoned in 1946, but for a year or so the hill tracts enjoyed a brief spell of independence, as tribal leaders debated whether or not to join the new India.

The Khasi Jaintia Hills, to use their full modern name, are a diminished, but nonetheless formidable, eastern flourish of the great Himalayan upheaval that resulted from a spectacular clash of continents 40 million years ago. What is now India detached itself from what is now Antarctica and crept northwards along the ocean floor at speeds of between one and eight inches a year. It was about 90 million years before 'India' bumped gently into Asia, but with that amount of mass behind it, the momentum transformed the topography of a continent. The impact threw up the Himalayas, and northwards, the enormous Tibetan plateau, which at 15,000 feet has an average height greater than America's or Europe's highest peaks.

The Khasi Jaintia Hills, occupying an oblong east-west plateau, are between four and six thousand feet above sea level.

They reminded the missionaries of home: there was something of Gwynedd's rugged *hauteur* about the Khasi Hills, and in the *moelydd* of Jaintia they found echoes of the gentler slopes of Montgomeryshire. At 6,022 square miles, this was a country only a little smaller than their own, some thirteen thousand sea miles away.

This plateau is surrounded on all but its eastern flank by watery flatlands: the mighty Brahmaputra flows through the Plains of Assam to the north; to the south lie the Surma Valley and the Plains of Sylhet and Cachar. These alluvial lowlands of clay and sand are only a few feet above the level of the Bay of Bengal. Spread invitingly for miles at the plateau's feet, they once enticed the warrior hillmen to rich and easy pickings of women, loot and land. Now, with the onset of global warming, the people who live on the plains have a bigger, more capricious enemy to gnaw at their imaginings.

21

The dramatic topography of the region, and the Khasis' provenance as a celestial people, are explained by the story of *Ka dieng iei*, or "the forbidden tree".

It grew on a mountain top about eight miles to the west of Shillong, and was the biggest tree in the world. Indeed, so far-flung and tall were its branches that they covered the entire face of the earth and tickled the very toes of heaven, where there lived, with God their creator, the sixteen clans of humankind.

The tree was a bridge between heaven and earth. Every morning, people shimmied down its branches to work in their fields, and every evening they climbed back up to take their rest in the House of God.

Now God had created nine suns, and though they shone all day, the tree's branches were so many, its foliage so thick that the earth languished in shadow, and people grew impatient with the gloom that hung over their fields. What could be done to get more light? It was resolved to hold a durbar of all the creatures on earth, for in those days man and beast talked to each other, and there was only one language known in the world.

"We must cut the tree down!" the durbar decided. So they took up their axes and hacked all day at the tree, until nightfall drove them away to their beds.

The next morning, returning to their labours, they were astonished to find not a trace of the gaping wounds their axes had made in the trunk of the tree. Some ran away, fearing the influence of evil spirits. The remainder renewed their assault on the tree.

But the next day and the next, the tree, when they returned to it, stood whole and unblemished. How would they ever complete their task?

They held a second durbar at which a small bird offered an explanation of the problem, and a solution. "It is the tiger who spoils your work," she said. "He comes at night and heals the tree's wounds by licking them. If you want to stop him, wedge your axes in the trunk with their blades facing outward. When the tiger comes to lick the tree, he'll cut his tongue and be frightened away."

The axemen did as the bird advised. Sure enough, when they returned the following morning they found their previous day's handiwork, slicked here and there with blood, just as they had left it. They set to without delay, and soon they succeeded in felling the tree.

Light and heat from the nine suns, hotter and brighter than they had ever imagined, now engulfed the world. Every green thing shrivelled, lakes and rivers ran dry, all creatures on earth, man and beast, were tormented with heat and the folly of what they had done. In chopping down the tree, they had sundered their connection with God, and introduced suffering and death to the world. And they had cut themselves adrift from many of their compatriots: on the day they felled the tree, only seven of the clans had descended to earth: nine of the sixteen were now stranded in heaven.

After many failed attempts to win God's forgiveness, the seven clans on earth eventually persuaded a bird, a lowly scruff of a fowl, to fly up to heaven and intercede with God for foolish, suffering humanity. God was moved by the bird's plea, and agreed to remove eight of the nine suns, leaving just one. So pleased was God with the bird's intercession that he equipped him with a scarlet comb, a dashing new coat and an arching plume of tail feathers, and appointed him governor of the day and night.

The seven earth-bound clans were known from then on as *Ki Hynniewtrep*, "They of the Seven Huts", and their country became *Ri Hynniewtrep*, "The Land of the Seven Huts". Although relieved of the ferocious heat of all those suns, they were never reunited with the heaven-bound clans, who remain in the sky to this day. The stars, it is said, are the lamps they carry when they come together in their markets.

The Khasi's land of *Hynniewtrep*, and the plains that surround it, still bear the stigmata of the great tree's fall. The branches fell on Bengali country, laying the land flat and spreading on its surface a fertile mulch of foliage. The trunk and colossal boughs of the tree crashed down on Khasi terrain, making such indentations in the earth that the country to this day is all mountains and gorges.

22

Another way of looking at the Khasis, the anthropologist's, is to deduce from their language, their stories, and their Mongoloid physiognomy that time out of mind ago they migrated to the hills that now bear their name from somewhere in south-east Asia. But where, precisely, and when?

That such questions fuel endless debate among the ethnographers and socio-linguists is hardly surprising, for there are precious few clues to build a theory on: no written Khasi record until the Welsh arrived, no clear folk memory of a terrestrial place of origin, and a cosmology based exclusively on the hills around Shillong.

Ethnically, it is agreed, all natives of the Khasi Jaintia Hills are Khasis, although the darker-skinned Jaintias (also known as

Pnars or Syntengs) have their own traditions and dialects of Khasi, and like to be distinguished from, rather than subsumed by, their Khasi kin when reference is made to the tribe as a whole.

It has been suggested that Khasi history began, as perhaps did Welsh, in about the fifth century AD. The little that has been done with Carbon-14 dating argues that the Khasis' megalithic culture was flourishing by the late thirteenth century. But nothing concrete is known of the Khasis before the sixteenth century, and their name, if the philologists are right – 'Kha' ('born of') + 'Si' ('the primal mother') – tells us more about the centrality of their matrilineal practices than their place of origin.

Soso Tham (1873-1940), their greatest poet, makes much in his work of the Khasis' belief in a 'Sottijuk' or Golden Age when they were at one with each other and the natural world. People and animals spoke the same language; they led righteous and religious lives, uncorrupted by materialism and the cash nexus; they worked hard in their fields by day, and rewarded themselves at night by visiting girls and singing songs; and anyone who flouted their Eden's taboos would be destroyed by thunder and a tiger.

In the Jaintia Hills where, it is believèd, the Khasis first settled before spreading westward, old sages refer to the site of their lost Golden Age home as 'Sohphoh Lynrum', a land abundant in Khasi pears. But it's not to be found on any map.

Could the Khasis be the aboriginal inhabitants of India, it is sometimes asked – pushed to the mountainous periphery when the Aryans moved in four thousand years ago? Does their popular notion of heaven as the place where the mountains and the sky become one suggest the Himalayas as their source? Were they driven by war or natural disaster from a homeland far to the east – somewhere on the Mekong River, maybe? And what of a possible Burmese connection – the annual tribute in the form of an axe that the Khasis used to pay to the King of Burma?

In the absence of definitive answers to these stabs in the ethnic fog, it is generally accepted that the Khasis are descended from the Austro-Asiatic Mon-Khmer peoples, a derivation that would connect them to the Burmese, the Kampucheans and perhaps the Malays.

A certain confusion about identity, compounded by centuries of historical amnesia: no wonder the Welsh felt at home in these Hills.

23

The Brahmaputra, which rises in southwest Tibet as the Tsangpo, is a sprawling giant, as wide as a Swiss lake, by the time it washes past Guwahati. It still has a couple of hundred miles to roll before it merges with the Ganga and is splayed out through innumerable delta channels to the Bay of Bengal. As our plane tilted to land, I caught a glimpse of the river, its greenish grey expanse streaked with sand spits and cultivated islands the size of Lundy. Until the later nineteenth century, there being virtually no roads in this part of the world, a boat up the Brahmaputra was about the only means of approach to the northern Khasi Hills.

Guwahati, sometime capital of Assam, was the base between 1829 and 1836 of a Scottish Baptist missionary by the name of James Roe. In addition to venturing into the Hills on fruitless preaching expeditions, Roe ran a Company-supported school in the town, mainly for young men from the neighbouring hilltribes. David Scott (1787-1831), resented 'pacifier' of the Khasis and administrator of a large part of East Bengal (as it was before it became Assam), sent a number of hillmen to Roe's school, including three Khasis. One or two of these pupils may have subsequently assisted young Alexander Lish in his inadequate attempt to retranslate the Bible. When Serampore pulled out of missionary work in Guwahati and Cherrapunji in about 1838, they offered the two fields to the American Baptists, who already had work in Upper Assam. The Americans accepted the Guwahati station, but declined Cherrapunji, leaving the Khasi field unadopted until the arrival of the Welsh a few years later.

The Khasi Hills, jungly green waves of them, now filled my porthole. After more than a year of busy preparation and dispiriting uncertainty, my goal was in sight, I had arrived. Or had I? As the only white man on the plane, I was the centre of official attention as soon as I entered the arrivals hall. I was taken aside by two cheerless functionaries who riffled repeatedly through my passport, giving me long, quizzical gazes, and muttering to each other while shaking their heads. They seemed to have overlooked the all-important 'RAP', stamped unequivocally at the front of my passport. I pointed it out to them.

"No guarantee of admittance," said one of the men, "I am in charge here, not London or Delhi."

More riffling and muttering and questions.

"The purpose of your visit is tourism?"

"Yes," I lied.

"Very well," said the arbiter of my mission's fate, reaching for a rubber stamp. "You may proceed to Shillong."

I swung my leaden pack onto my shoulders as if it had been a satchel of feathers, and, beginning to realise how close I'd come to expulsion, headed across the hall towards a crowd of expectant faces at the entrance.

And there in the throng were three young men waving and calling my name: Robin and Desmond and their friend Ananya Guha. The poets.

"Welcome to the Khasi Hills," said Desmond. "We can't believe they let you through."

"You had us worried there," said Robin. "There must be some mistake – thank goodness! Let's get out of here before they change their minds."

They lead me across the carpark to a dark blue Ambassador in the shade of a tree where their driver Mohammed, a slim young Muslim with Clark Gable moustache, is buffing the car's paintwork.

They explain to me, as we cruise towards the Hills some ten miles distant, that the "bit of trouble" to which Robin had referred in his letter had escalated into the bloodiest explosion of communal violence ever known in Shillong. Twenty-eight people, according to some reports, fifty according to the BBC, had been killed and scores injured; the city was now under a 5 p.m. curfew, in an attempt to forestall further outbreaks of violence.

"It's being presented to the world," says Robin, "as Khasis, or tribals, against non-tribals – "

"Which means people like me," says Ananya, who is of Bengali stock, although he was born in Shillong, at the Welsh Mission Hospital. "I feel insecure now for the first time in my life."

"But," continues Robin, "it's more complicated than that, with religion playing a part and politicians winding things up for all they're worth."

This trip down to Guwahati is the first time since the upheaval that these three friends have dared get together.

"Ananya," says Desmond, "is like a brother to me, but up until now it has been too risky for us, a tribal and a non-tribal, to be seen together, especially in a car. We could run into a roadblock, perhaps set up by tribals, perhaps by non-tribals. Whoever the aggressors, I or Ananya would be powerless to prevent the other from being hacked to death."

Suburban Guwahati, with the odd working elephant padding along the tree-lined main road, seems almost to have 'arrived', subtly and unobtrusively, among the paddies and wooded wetlands of its fecund plain. Guwahati proper, however, is as cluttered and noisy as downtown Calcutta, although its hilltop temples to Kali and the nine planets, and the Lugano-like splendour of its waterfront still strongly evoke the days when, as the beautiful city of Pragjyotishpur, it was known as the Eastern Metropolis of Astronomy and Astrology.

Although Shillong is only 63 miles from Guwahati, it can often take three or more hours to cover the distance. It is too late in the day for us to reach Shillong before the five o'clock curfew, so Desmond has made arrangements for us to stay the night at Nongpoh, half way between the two cities. His friend Richard, a government official in Nongpoh who spends most weekends with his girlfriend in Shillong, has left his home and his cook at our disposal.

As we wind into the Hills, the road gets narrower, and the traffic – mostly lorries – slower and denser. Mohammed is the most avid hornblower I have yet encountered, maintaining a continuous barrage of beeps even when there are no other vehicles in sight. The rule that drivers should stick to their own side of the highway seems in India to enjoy the status merely of a loose suggestion, particularly on blind hairpin bends which are the preferred stretches of road for overtaking. He who blares wins . . .

We are now in Meghalaya, says Desmond, but fifty or sixty yards away, on the other side of the tight little valley whose western side we are climbing, is Assam. "This is a good part of Assam to live if you're a boozer. It's a dry state, apart from on Thursdays, so if an Assamese over there gets thirsty, all he has to do is hop across the valley into Meghalaya."

Thick jungle rises steeply on all sides, its lush lime greens burnished gold by the late afternoon sunlight. These deep valleys act like an echo chamber on the blatter, blares and screeches of the trucks, but in spite of the noise and exhaust fumes billowing from hundreds of vehicles an hour, the roadside seems a popular place to live or set up shop. Simple thatch and matting huts line the way, some built out from the road bank and balanced precariously at the rear on bamboo stilts.

There's a living to be made from truck drivers, breakdowns, accidents and traffic jams on this feverish north-south artery, nowhere more so than in the straggling truck-stop settlement of Beltola. Here thousands of lorries, for mile after mile, are parked in the oily dust at the side of the road, as their drivers take a rest or a meal, a woman or a drink, and get that tyre fixed, those spongy brakes sharpened up in one of Beltola's many repair shops. As in parts of Africa, it is the truck-driver, with his casual sexual encounters all over the land, who is perceived as the biggest disseminator of the HIV virus. The first AIDS case in India was reported in 1986. If current trends continue, about five million people will be HIV positive by the year 2000, and the number of AIDS cases will exceed one million. Suggested solutions to a potentially catastrophic AIDS explosion range from free condoms with petrol, to building more railways; but there are those, like my old travelling companion the Commander, who wonder, *sotto voce*, if AIDS might not be the great pruner which they believe their overpopulated country needs.

Indian trucks, with their Taj Mahal windows and garish paintwork, their garlands and tinsel, are loud witnesses to their drivers', and a region's, religious predilections. Here in the heavily Christianised north-east the lurid Shivas and Kalis that bedeck the cabs and headboards of many Indian lorries run into stiff competition from the equally lurid icons of Christianity. The coal-laden Tata bearing down on you with neon Virgin, fairy lights and rosaries is sure to be in the providential control of a Khasi Catholic, of whom there are some 200,000.

By six o'clock it's getting dark, and we are now well into bandit country. This stretch of road is notorious for highway robberies: men leaping out of the jungle with guns, forcing vehicles to a halt and stripping their occupants of all valuables. Robin jokes that if the bandits were unlucky enough to pick on our car, all they'd get out of us would be a few poems.

Having passed safely through bandit country, we pull up at a little wineshop to buy beer and whisky, then drive on to Nongpoh. Mohammed, like other drivers, is in the habit of switching off the engine and coasting at every downhill opportunity. He also likes to switch off the headlights.

Desmond's absent friend lives in a spacious government-owned bungalow with eight or nine rooms, set back a little from the main road. Waiting to receive us are the cook and an assistant who take orders for the meal, and settle us in a tall blue room with a couple of hareskins and a clock on the otherwise bare walls. They even open and pour our beers for us, but there is none of the self-effacing deference about them that is normally associated with 'servants'. They too join in the conversation when their duties in the kitchen permit. So does an almost speechlessly drunk youngster in a red baseball cap who drifts in from a neighbouring house and solemnly parrots everything that Desmond says, while understanding barely a word of it. He makes up his mind that my beard and longish hair qualify me as a guitarist. "Eri' Chlapton, Shimmy 'Endrix," he slurs, waving a battered six-string at me. "You play, you play, Eri' Chlapton . . . " I bash out a few clumsy chords of twelve-bar which seem to throw him into a floor-staring trance, whether of pain or ill-judged ecstasy I can't tell, then I hand the guitar over to Desmond who, like every other young Khasi, really can play the thing – Van Morrison, Bob Dylan, lyrics and all. When the conversation turns to poetry our visitor quickly tires of trying to repeat words like Akhmatova and Tsvetayeva and staggers away into the night, muttering "Eri' Chlapton, Shimmy 'Endrix, where you goin' with no gun in your hands . . ."

It all seems suddenly difficult to believe: that here I am, drinking Indian beer and talking about poetry in the middle of the Khasi Hills, with the jungle's orchestra of crickets and cicadas, swell on swell of that narcotic music, pulsing in my ears. Is it a dream or is it a dream?

"A nip of Scotch?" asks Robin, handing me an amber tumblerful. No dream can recreate that fiery bloom: no doubt about it, I am awake and kicking in the Khasi Hills.

As Robin pours for the others, Desmond begins to tell us about Nongpoh and his work in this area. This part of the Hills is home to the Bhois, one of the five sub-tribes of the Khasi people. In spite of the busy highway that cuts their territory in two, there are villages only a few miles into the 'interior' with little experience of the outside, 'civilised' world.

Of course, the Khasis were weaving stories and minting songs long before the Welsh with their Bible and tonic sol-fa arrived on the scene. Still very much alive is their age-old oral tradition of long, extemporised narratives with musical accompaniment, and it is to the remote 'interior' villages that Desmond treks to make recordings of this rich material.

With their sacred groves and ancestral reverence for nature, these 'backwoods' folk have developed a knack for taking what they need from civilisation while abandoning the rest. One figment of modernity they have decided they can certainly do without is a uranium mining industry. Government scientists have detected significant deposits of uranium in the West Khasi Hills, possibly the largest hoard of uranium ever discovered in India, if not, indeed, the world. But the farmers there, and many

80

other Khasis only too familiar with the damage already done to their country by the large-scale exploitation of natural resources, particularly timber, want the mineral to stay where it is.

"When government officials, backed up by the police, went in there to make further investigations," says Desmond, "they came out like greased lightning, with arrows sticking out of their arses."

We bed down at about midnight in a little dormitory of mosquito-netted four-posters. My friends advise me to tuck the net securely under the mattress, Bhoi country being notoriously malarial. Trucks continue to rattle along the main road most of the night, but the only thing that intrudes on my dreams is a curious metal banging once in a while, never more than half a dozen blows, as if someone were beating a steel ploughshare with a shovel.

24

In Thomas Jones's time, the Khasi Hills were part of the huge province of Bengal, as was Bangladesh (or East Pakistan as it was between 1947 and 1971). Therefore the most direct route to the Hills was not, as today, through their northern 'back door', but from the south.

The flavour of that journey, which since partition it has been virtually impossible for an outsider to attempt to retrace, is vividly recreated in Merfyn Jones's novel *Ar Fryniau'r Glaw* [On the Rain's Hills]. Merfyn, twelve years a missionary in various north-eastern fields, was only a visitor to the Khasi Hills, but he has a firm grasp of the language and culture. I called to see him and his wife Dilys in their retirement bungalow in Tywyn shortly before I left for India. He told me that he reconstructed the journey mainly from missionaries' letters published in *Y Drysorfa Ysbrydol*, fused with his own considerable experience of '*y popty poeth*', the 'hot bakehouse' of the plains as they used to call the Sylhet region. The novel, which won first prize in the 1978 Pontrhydfendigaid Eisteddfod, is in the form of letters sent home by Mary Lewis, wife of Thomas Jones's co-worker the Rev.

81

William Lewis. A gripping yet faithful account of the early years of the Mission, it had little need of 'novelist's licence' in its making, so inherently dramatic are the true-life events it recounts.

It was possible, from the 1830s onwards, to make the trip, or part of it at least, by river steamer, but the early missionaries still undertook most of the journey in the traditional manner – by budgerow, a shallow-draught country boat with a plaited bamboo roof set amidships; two men with long boat-staves, one fore, one aft, would pole the craft slowly along, assisted by wind and the currents. The missionaries' luggage and one or two items of furniture – a writing desk, perhaps, Nain's chest of drawers – would travel in an accompanying vessel.

The journey, by air and road, that took me just a few hours to make, took mid-nineteenth-century travellers a good three weeks. After several days drifting down the Hooghly, they'd find themselves mazed in the Sundarbans, the low swampy grounds where the Ganga discharges into the sea through its 150 miles wide delta, which they would have to cross on their way to the town of Barisal and the chief ingress to 'the river of rivers'. From foggy dawn to dusk there'd be little to see among the Sundarbans except densely forrested islands of dwarf date-palm. Occasionally an enormous crocodile might glide down the foot-high mudbanks, leaving a deep furrow ploughed in the ooze by his tail.

From the northernmost inlet of the Bay of Bengal, their budgerow, having cleared the Sundarbans, turns into the main stream of the Ganga and sails north-west inland until it takes a rightward turn into the delta of the Surma. They are soon in the marshy freshwater Jheels whose vegetation differs radically from the maritime Sundarbans. Devoid entirely of trees and shrubs, the Jheels are covered in ten-feet high tropical grasses.

Sir Joseph Dalton Hooker travelled this way in 1850. "We often passed through very narrow channels, where the grasses towered over the boats," he wrote in his *Himalayan Journals*. "The boatmen steered in and out of them as they pleased, and we were utterly at a loss to know how they guided themselves, as they had neither compass nor map, and there were few villages or landmarks; and on climbing the mast we saw multitudes of other masts and sails peering over the grassy marches, doing just the same as we did . . . Often we had to retreat from channels that promised to prove short cuts, but which turned out to be blind alleys. Sometimes we sailed up broader streams of chestnut-brown water, accompanied by fleets of boats repairing to the populous districts at the foot of the Khasia, for rice, timber, lime, coal, bamboos, and long reeds for thatching, all of which employ an inland navy throughout the year in their transport to Calcutta."

After a couple of mosquito- and leech-ridden days in the delta, the travellers would enter the Surma itself, which is as defining of the plains to the south of the Khasi Hills as the Brahmaputra, flowing roughly parallel to it, is of those to the north. Rising in the region of Manipur, the Surma receives the waters of the Cachar, Jaintia, Khasi and Garo mountains, draining an immense area of some 10,000 square miles. Hooker describes it as "a full and muddy stream flowing west, a quarter of a mile broad, with banks of mud and clay twelve or fifteen feet high, separating it from marshes, and covered with betel-nut and cocoa-nut palms, figs and banyans."

We don't read much of the Sundarbans in Merfyn Jones's novel, but the river passage through the Jheels and along the Surma is beautifully evoked. His narrator, Mary Lewis, describes their party being poled upstream during the day, and sleeping on the floor of the budgerow at night, having eaten a meal cooked by one of the Bengali boatman on a big stone at the stern of the vessel: boiled rice, fish, goat or chicken curry, and "a kind of pancake made of coarse flour". A fire would be kept burning on that stone all day, so that boiling water would be constantly available for brewing tea. She finds the boatmen very clean, washing every morning, and rubbing their teeth with a sliver of wood called 'neem', "but not so clean in their habits – washing out their mouths with filthy water from the river, and dipping the kettle in the same water – sometimes a putrid pool – to make tea . . . It's not surprising that so many come down with cholera and dysentery . . ."

She is apprehensive too about some of the natives in the riverside bazaars. "Very dark-skinned people, hundreds of them. I feared they might turn on me like a pack of dogs. Ali the boatman warned us not to go into such places. 'Police far away,' he said. They know, these people, that the law isn't particularly strong outside the main Indian towns."

After about a week pushing against the gentle current of the Surma the travellers' budgerow arrives at Chattuck. Spread before them at last are the Khasi Hills. "From this place," writes Hooker, "the Khasia mountains are seen as a long table-topped range running east and west, about 4000 to 5000 feet high, with steep faces towards the Jheels, out of which they appear to rise abruptly. Though twelve miles distant, large waterfalls are very clearly seen precipitating themselves over the cliffs into a bright green mass of foliage, that seems to creep half way up their flanks . . . [The cliffs] seem to rise out of the Jheels so abruptly as to remind one of some precipitous island in the ocean."

Chattuck was developed from the late eighteenth-century onwards as an important trading centre for goods from the Khasi Hills – oranges, potatoes, coal, iron, timber, lime – most of which found their way to markets in Calcutta. The entrepreneur behind the growth of the town was an Englishman by the name of George Inglis (1774-1850). Arriving in the area at the age of twenty, he built up an intimidatingly powerful company which cornered the market in every lucrative commodity the Khasi Hills could produce.

Remember the name Inglis. It was this man's son, as we shall see, who drove Thomas Jones to his death.

At Chattuck the budgerows, too cumbersome to negotiate the rivers leading towards the mountains, normally decanted their passengers and freight into a flotilla of narrow-gutted two-man canoes. Each canoe carried just one passenger, who had to lie on his back, protected from sun or rain by a plaited bamboo roof.

Travellers bound for Cherrapunji would be paddled as far as Pandua in the shadow of the Khasi Hills. Here they'd meet with crowds of lighter-skinned people, looking more like Malays or Chinese than the plainsmen of Bengal: Khasis.

Nineteenth-century travellers seem unanimous about the sublimity of Pandua and the approach to the Hills, but some of them, such as Robert Lindsay, found the natives anything but sublime. Pandua, he wrote in his *Anecdotes of an Indian Life,* forms "one of the most stupendous amphiteatres in the world. The mountain appears to rise abruptly from the watery plain, and is covered with the most beautiful foliage and fruit-trees . . . which seem to grow spontaneously from the crevices of the lime-rock. A more romantic or more beautiful situation could not be found than the one then before me. The magnificent mountain, full in view, appeared to be divided with large perpendicular stripes of white, which, upon a nearer inspection, proved to be cataracts of no small magnitude; and the river, in which the boats anchored, was so pure that the trout and other fishes were seen playing about in every direction; above all, the air was delightful when contrasted with the close and pestilential atmosphere of the putrid plain below, so that I felt as if transplanted into one of the regions of Paradise. But the appearance of the inhabitants of this garden of Eden did not enable me to follow out the theory I could have wished to establish; it certainly deserved a different style of inhabitants from those wild-looking demons then dancing on the banks before me."

Thomas and Anne Jones, travelling at the height of the monsoon, would have had a very different kind of journey from that of Hooker or Lindsay. From May to October, when the Surma can rise by as much as fifty feet, most of the plains are under water. With just a few islets of higher ground showing above the surface, it must have seemed to Thomas and Anne Jones that they were lost on a bewildering inland sea.

Any sense of deliverance from the muddy deep, as they disembarked at Pandua, must have been short-lived. How to scale those towering limestone cliffs, thousands of feet higher than any mountain they had ever seen in Wales? Today there's an engine-punishing zigzag road to wind you to the top along chasms and around hairpin bends, but in those days man- and woman-power was the only way. Chests, trunks, wardrobes, pianos: it was by human muscle power alone that you would haul them to the top. Even before reaching the cliff-face, there was an eight-mile track, twisting through pineapple and orange groves, that was far too rough for ponies; so everyone had to walk, the Khasi porters carrying burdens of ninety pounds or more in conical baskets on their backs, with a broad strap around their foreheads taking most of the weight. The wheel, at this time, was a relative novelty to the Khasis, not that there were many places in their rugged land where this newfangled device would have been of much use. The basket, or *khoh*, varying in size but usually tapering to a point, was the main means of transporting goods – as it still is today for most short-distance loads.

At the cliff-face itself the walker, if bold enough, turned into a climber, ascending some of the trickiest verticals on a series of bamboo ladders. The Khasis, with their spectacularly muscular legs and a sure-footedness that seems to survive the attrition of both rain and rice beer, take to such work as if born to it. Not so, often enough, the vertiginous European with no head for heights: he or she would be strapped into a *thaba*, a special man-carrying basket and ferried up the face on a native's back, with thunderous waterfalls on all sides.

Thus wet, fearful and wide with wonder, the stranger approached Cherrapunji.

25

There was some concern, over a hurried breakfast on the verandah, that we should set off from Nongpoh in good time. "We need to be on the road to Shillong before the trouble-makers are up," said Robin.

The mysterious metallic banging that had punctuated an otherwise morphean slumber came again as we downed our boiled eggs and sweet milky tea. "It's the time-keeper," explained Desmond. "In some of the villages they employ a man to beat out the time, on the hour, throughout the night."

It could not have been anything other than a Sunday morning. As Mohammed, who had spent the night on the back seat of the car, bowled us blaringly on our way, we passed many family groups walking to church in their Sunday best, with pink-edged bibles tucked beneath their arms.

Those of a less sabbatarian inclination were hard at work in their paddy fields in the narrow valleys below us. These yellowy green patches of cultivation seem vulnerably provisional: rampant jungle, its wispy bamboo latticing the sky, its ropes of bindweed strangling telegraph poles and fences, rears from the edge of almost every field and seems poised to reassume the land the moment a farmer turns his back.

The valleys' quick little rivers and feeder streams were clay-grey with pollution. This didn't seem to bother the truck drivers. Wherever the road dipped down to the riverside, there'd be a Tata or two parked on the verge, and their occupants, perched on a boulder mid-stream, splashing their bodies and towelling themselves down.

Towards the end of our journey the country opened out, with bare mountain ridges, like those of north Wales or Scotland, stretching into the distance on all sides. The Khasis too have their drowned valleys: at Barapani they dammed the river Umiam to form a huge lake. It powers a hydro-electric station that makes Meghalaya, alone of all Indian states, self-sufficient in energy. Lake Umiam is popular with fishermen, and would be with tourists too, were it not for the central government restrictions that keep north-east India a relatively tourist-free region. With its fir trees and mountains, its anglers thigh-deep in world-inverting waters, Umiam seems interchangeable with a slice of Gwynedd – until a worker elephant comes plodding round the corner with a tree trunk in tow.

The last ten miles are steep and twisty, for the road from Barapani has to rise another two thousand feet to take us into Shillong, which sits at five thousand feet above sea level.

The Shillong skyline is dominated, Rio fashion, by what at first appears to be a huge stylised crucifix, with a curiously truncated cross-bar. The even curiouser plumes of smoke issuing from the top of this 'crucifix' suggest, of course, that it is no such thing. It is, in fact, the perenially belching smokestack of

87

the Welsh Mission Hospital which is rarely out of sight for long, wherever in this city of hills you happen to be.

We enter Shillong through what is one of the most intensely Khasi districts, passing along a street where several people were murdered in the recent troubles.

All, this morning, seems a picture of sabbatarian rectitude. The shutters are down on most of the makeshift little shops that line the road, and the traffic, by Shillong's standards, is light. Beneath the Douglas firs and Scots pines and dreamy pink clouds of blossoming cherry, there are scores of well-dressed people, bibles and hymn-books in hand, making their way to and from the numerous churches – Presbyterian, Catholic, Anglican, Unitarian, Pentecostal – that throng the city, some as grand as cathedrals, others no larger than wayside chapels.

Most church-going women wear an ankle-length overgarment of brocaded and fringed silk, known as the *jainsem*, and a shawl called the *tapmoh* covering head and shoulders. This is widely held to be the Khasi woman's traditional outfit, but it's a 'tradition', some say, only as old as the Welsh Mission. The missionaries' wives, scandalised by the flimsiness of Khasi dress, hastened to cover their converts' near-nakedness with yards of silk and woollen cloth, leaving only the face and ankles for a sinner's eyes to light upon.

Their menfolk, particularly church elders, dress much as a deacon in Wales might dress: neatly pressed dark suit, a triangle of pristine handkerchief peeping from the breast pocket, and shiny black shoes.

Many, many hundreds of Sundays ago the streets of Wales must have looked like this.

26

Surely, by now, they'd have washed the blood from the streets? There seemed to be splatterings of it everywhere, as if the victims of a mass stabbing had gone reeling through the city spraying white-washed walls and concrete pavements with fatal effluxions of gore. Then I remembered *kwai*.

The chewing of betel nut (strictly speaking the 'areca' nut; the 'betel' is the vine leaf it is eaten with) is to many Indians as the chewing of gum to Americans. They've been doing it for perhaps 8,000 years. But in the Khasi Jaintia Hills, betel-munching capital of the world, the consumption of *kwai*, as they call it, is a ritualistic necessity of life, as fundamental to the human condition as air or water. When a man dies the Khasis say that he has gone to eat *kwai* in the House of God.

Our first port of call, having arrived in Shillong, was Desmond's parents' place in the Laitumkhrah district. His father is the leading Khasi novelist Leslie Hardinge Pde, who manages to be both a popular and critical success. In spite of a punishing workload as Meghalaya's Commissioner of Labour, Mr. Pde has written five novels, a play and many articles, and translated into Khasi some of the classics of Indian literature. As we ate a sumptuous lunch in the family's cool, dark kitchen he talked of his latest project, a translation of Dante's *Divine Comedy*: he had just begun work on part one, *Hell*. How, with his professional and family commitments, did he find time to write at all? "I ask myself the same question," he replied.

Khasis view with incredulous dismay the Western nuclear family and its tendency to abandon its 'redundant' elders to solitude or unhomely 'homes'. The Kharmawphlang family compound, three small bungalows housing five generations, typifies the Khasis' traditional extended family. The children grow up nearly as close to uncles, aunts and cousins as to their parents; grandparents and great-grandparents have an honoured and active role to play in family life. If anyone is sick, or simply weary with the weight of years, there is always someone to look after them.

The compound is tucked onto a ledge of land overlooking the bungalowed hills and corrugated roofs of southern Shillong. It is overshadowed at the rear by a gleaming stand of banana trees, their leaves flashing like blades. Down the sharp slope in front are a few square yards of vegetable plot which Mr. Pde tends devotedly each morning, along with his chickens and his flower beds, before leaving for the office.

Having eaten, we moved from the kitchen to the compact reception room, with its brass-topped tables and Catholic icons. It was time to *bam* (eat) *kwai*.

The partaking of *kwai*, which varies in significance from the utilitarian to the sacramental, may be as formal or as casual as you desire. Everyone chews it, and everyone as a consequence has a reddened tongue and mouth, and teeth stained a dark orange. Some people chomp the stuff all day, gobbing out the bitter, rust-red juices with vomitously loud rakings of the throat. Others, as on this occasion, take *kwai* after a meal for its refreshingly astringent aftertaste.

But it is, above all, when two or more are gathered together that *kwai* comes into its own as a token of acceptance, friendship and equality. The story is told that a poor man once invited a rich man to his house, but, being penniless, he and his wife had nothing to offer their guest by way of hospitality. The couple were so ashamed that they jointly committed suicide. The rich man, horrified at this outcome and stricken with guilt, also killed himself. Khasis everywhere were shocked by these deaths: it was decided that in future it would be as well for everyone, whatever their economic standing, to offer visitors *kwai* as a welcoming gift: being common and inexpensive, anyone could afford it. And so it was, that *kwai* became the basic symbol of Khasi hospitality – which is as bountiful, I imagine, as any in the world.

Desmond's sister Loreta, who is also a writer, hands round the little *kwai* basket, and everyone helps themselves to a segment of betel nut and a leaf of what the Khasis call the *tympew* vine, which is the colour and consistency of a bayleaf; into each has been folded a dab of limestone paste. You adjust the quantity of lime to suit your palate – chalky smears of excess lime are conspicuous throughout the Hills as a kind of pointillist frenzy on walls, signposts, trees, table-legs. Too much lime, Loreta warns me, will set my head spinning. I brace myself for an 'experience', wrap the leaf around the nut, and chomp.

Betel, which has been compared somewhat extravagantly to the peyote of Mexican Indians, is supposed to be a 'mild stimulant'. It is not so much hot as dry. In fact, it is like a desert exploding in the mouth. The only thing, alas, that *kwai* stimulated in me was a raging thirst for an ice-cold beer. It left, to be sure, a pleasantly 'clean' aftertaste, but I felt I could get the same effect from a toothbrush without first having to gobble my way through the Sahara.

Kwai, I concluded, must be an acquired taste, like whisky or laver bread. In spite of this disappointing first encounter, I would persevere and trust that habituation would eventually attune my unsophisticated constitution to *kwai's* tonic delights.

The strictly abstemious missionaries, whose experience of drugs began and ended with tea, looked askance at the Khasis' addiction to *kwai*, but they must have realised that attempting to outlaw the betel nut would have been as futile as trying to ban rugby balls in Wales.

"When the British came to the Hills," chuckled Mr. Pde, "they were confronted by all these 'terrible people who spat blood' and were fond of painting their teeth an ugly red. 'These are bad habits,' the missionaries told them, 'You should change your ways.' And the answer the missionaries got back was 'Why should we? Only dogs and the British have white teeth.'"

27

The poets fix me up with a room – "bedbug-free", they are assured – at the Hotel Prakash, whose glossy plastic sign advertises "Fooding and Lodging". At less than £2 a night, it's cheap and unpretentious, and even has a 'bathroom' attached, a bit like a fragment of cowshed, with a bucket and occasional running water (cold). It's also, after the lino has been swept and the surfaces swabbed, reasonably clean.

Ananya, who lives with his mother just opposite the Prakash, remembers the place when it was a notorious drinking den. "I was in Southall last year, and I would say that bars here are not like pubs in Britain. People go to bars not to chat and play darts but to get drunk, full stop. There was boozing and fighting here all the time. The locals couldn't put up with all the noise, so they complained to the district durbar, and the durbar instructed the bar to close down."

The Prakash then reincarnated itself as 'Hotel and Restaurant'. I doubt that on the 'fooding' front it will ever loom large in the 'eatery' guides, but it proved an unusually characterful and convenient place to stay. For the first few days I seemed to be the Prakash's only customer; then the curfew began to ease and trade picked up. Most guests were Indians, on business rather than pleasure; none of them were Europeans or Americans. Indeed, I saw not a single white face, apart from the cracked specimen in the mirror, during the whole of my time in the Hills.

The Prakash, which is Bengali for 'light', is an echo of 'mainland' India. The little reception lobby, where joss-sticks smoulder before a garlanded portrait of a revered guru, declares the Hindu faith both of the family who run the hotel and of most of their workers.

As I sit, on my first evening, writing a letter home, there's a knock on the door: "Phone, Saheb." I take the call in the owners' quarters. It's Bari, Loreta's husband, phoning from the Kharmawphlang compound, which is only just down the road, to check that all is well with me on my first night under under curfew. After the call, the owners, a shy and smiling couple in their mid-twenties, ask me to stay and drink tea and eat a little curry with them.

He, Pinky, is a Bengali and his wife, Nupur, a Punjabi, so the language of their home is a fluent English, because neither speaks the other's native tongue. Where this arrangement leaves Pinky's mother, a solid but welcoming Hindu mama who speaks not a word of English, I am not quite sure. Although both Pinky and Nupur were born in Shillong and can understand Khasi, both deny that Khasi is anything other than a dialect – though of what, they can't say.

Pinky and Nupur have a big colour t.v., and watch a lot of BBC on it. They want to know what I think of BBC news. And what do I think of India? Is it backward? Why and how are the British more 'advanced'? What does it mean to be 'advanced', and is it, anyway, a good thing?

The curfew, says Pinky, is particularly unpopular with local Hindus. "It has completely put a damper on the Hindu community's Durga Puja and Diwali festivals. Normally everyone is out in the streets and letting off fire-crackers, Christians included. But this year nobody can get together. All you hear are a few isolated bangs behind closed walls."

They show me proudly round their cosy little apartment. In their bedroom one of their fifteen male staff, a boy in his late teens, is rocking their new baby boy to sleep. Nupur asks to see photographs of my two small daughters, Angharad and Branwen, and is so taken with the girls that she says we must come to an arrangement for her son to marry one of them.

My room at the Prakash is on a concrete balcony that runs round three sides of a courtyard. In the yard itself is Pinky's brother's motor-repair business, drilling and banging away from dawn till curfew, to the ghetto-blaster accompaniment of heavy metal and Hindi pop. Beyond the hotel's gates is Police Point, Laitumkhrah's busiest junction, where taxis mass and buses hover to drum up custom for the run to Iewduh market on the other side of town: "Iew! Iew! Iew! Iew! Iew!" crescendo the touts all day. Whenever a truck rumbles past the whole building shudders to its foundations, and I wonder how the Prakash would perform in an earthquake.

The curfew had its advantages. At 5 p.m. all this bustle and noise, except for the Hindi booms and trills from the t.v. down in the lobby, would come to an abrupt halt. Confined to base like everyone else, I'd make use of the evenings' enforced tranquillity to keep up with the invaluable theses, books and articles that were being fed to me by university and church historians. By nine or ten o'clock the avid film-fans below would normally have taken to their beds, restoring to the night a silence, broken only by the yelping of pye-dogs, that seemed to echo in clarity and crispness the effervescent lights of the Milky Way.

28

Before the Apollo astronauts in 1969, before the satellite probes of the 1950s, even, no doubt, before Galileo and his sea-supposing telescope, the Khasis had come to certain well-pitched conclusions about the nature of the surface of the moon.

U Bynai (Moon) and Ka Sngi (Sun) were brother and sister. The Sun, who was some years older than her brother, had helped rear the boy, cradling him in her arms and carrying him on her back as a mother would. She grew in beauty with each year that passed, and he grew also, into a wayward and lusty youth.

The Sun's beauty obsessed the Moon, so that he yearned to love her not as a brother loves a sister but as a man loves a woman, flesh to flesh. One day in spring, he could contain himself no longer and advanced on his sister, blurting out his body's desire for her.

"Get away from me!" cried the Sun, enraged at the wickedness of her brother's passion. She ran to the hearthstone, snatched up a handful of ashes, and hurled them in his face.

The Moon until this moment had shone as brightly as the Sun, but now, ashamed and covered with ashes, his light shrivelled to a cold white glow.

The Sun, from then on, would live nowhere near the Moon. She still spends her life running away from him, and he still spends his in haggard pursuit. Often, after sunset, the Moon is to be seen with his ash-soiled face mounting up in the heavens to gaze longingly after his beautiful sister, and trying in vain to catch up with her.

29

One of the many people to whom, in increasing desperation, I had written for help in my long campaign to secure a visa and permit was Mrs. Lakyntiew Richmond, who had been a production assistant for Alexander Frater when he brought his film crew to the Khasi Hills in 1990.

I wrote to her, at Frater's suggestion, in January, 1992 but months of silence ensued. Then, in September, shortly before leaving for India, I received an encouraging note from her and a copy of the souvenir programme of the Thomas Jones Sesquicentennial Jubilee held the previous year.

As her office was in the same part of town as the Prakash, I phoned to suggest we meet. Within the hour we were drinking coffee together in my room. Khasi women, confident scions of their tribe's ancient matrilineal system, exhibit no trace of the self-effacing timidity found in societies that deem it improper for a woman to enter a stranger's hotel room.

Far from suffering loss or neglect, my appeal to Lakyntiew had been receiving, in those months of silence, her most diligent attention. It soon became clear that it was thanks to her, and the influential offices of her father, the MP Professor G.G. Swell, that the authorities had decided after all to grant me a 'Restricted Area Permit'. She showed me a copy of a letter that her father had written to Professor Barrister Pakem, Vice Chancellor of Shillong's North-Eastern Hill University. Professor Swell asked the Vice Chancellor to invite me officially to Meghalaya, in view of the "great and fundamental contribution the early Welsh missionaries made to the religious and cultural life of our community." This having been done, Professor Swell was in a position to take up my case with the Government in New Delhi and the Indian High Commission in London. "The needful and obliged" was soon afterwards on its way to a grateful yet puzzled petitioner in Swansea.

The MP, who divides his time between the Hills and New Delhi, was in town for a brief spell, so later that day Lakyntiew drove me up to the family home in Nongthymmai so that I could thank him in person for his decisive efforts on my behalf.

G.G. (pronounced 'eg eg', Welsh-style, as are most of the letters in the Khasi alphabet) Swell is generally considered the most able politician yet produced by the Khasis, and one of the most eloquent parliamentarians in New Delhi. His political stature is such that in 1992 he was one of the three principal candidates for the Presidency of all India. Had he been successful he would have swopped his comfortable, but modest, two-storey home for the British-built Presidential Palace in New Delhi which is so colossal that Buckingham Palace in comparison might almost pass for its gatehouse.

Swell is famous above all as the strategist whose political and diplomatic skills led the Khasi, Jaintia and Garo peoples to the achievement – bloodlessly – of their own fully-fledged state of Meghalaya in 1972. Previously, thanks largely to the cartographic whims of outsiders, their territory had been considered part of Bengal and then, after a redrawing of the map in 1874, part of the province of Assam.

There are few who see Meghalaya as the perfect solution to the tribes' political and social problems. The state is "misbegotten and misnamed", say those who feel that the Khasi Jaintias have nothing in common with the Garos except a matrilineal social system, and who resent the non-tribal name of Meghalaya ('abode of cloud') that was conjured up for them by central government's geographer general. But Meghalaya has given these hill people a platform for the expression of their tribal (and largely non-separatist) aspirations that had been much agitated for. They have considerably more democratic control over their internal affairs than our somewhat larger 'nation' of Wales enjoys. I met several members of Meghalaya's Legislative Assembly who were astonished to learn that the country whose Presbyterians had trained them so well in political leadership was itself without a parliament and run from London by viceregal remote control.

As in most Presbyterian homes, as soon as we arrived out came the tea service and a generous spread of tea-cakes and pastries. Eg Eg Swell proved somewhat less rotund than the image evoked by his Humpty Dumptyish and, by all accounts, self-chosen name. The sobriety and gravitas of the Presidential candidate and elder statesman found sartorial expression in an immaculately tailored brown pinstripe suit with matching waistcoat – a gravitas, however, that hit the rocks at shin level where, in a pair of gleaming plasticated platform-heel boots, the spirit of Gary Glitter suddenly took command.

A member of the characteristically prideful War sub-tribe from the south of the Hills, he'd started out as a teacher of

English in Shillong. After teaching in Ethiopia, he had joined the diplomatic service while still in his early twenties: Norway, Burma and Canada had been among several foreign postings.

"Then, in 1984, after Mrs. Gandhi was assassinated, I quit the foreign service," he said. "I was asked to join the Congress Party, but I left them and am now a member of the Hill State People's Democratic Party. I have been in office now for five terms of five years apiece. And for three of those terms I represented this area with the intention of winning a separate state for the Khasis. I was a lone voice at the time, but we got there in the end."

He had also, added Lakyntiew, been Deputy Speaker of the Lower House of Parliament.

I expressed some surprise that a non-Hindu, indeed a Presbyterian, had scaled such heights in Indian politics.

"I am not a churchgoing Christian," he said, "although I believe in God and believe in Christianity, while at the same time I have respect for all religions. But the Khasis, you know, imbibed more than religion from the Welsh. The habits of piety, frugality, hard work, love for your language, a care for your identity – all these things that are very much part of the Welsh way of being were somehow transmitted by the missionaries. The two peoples took to each other, there's a remarkable empathy between them."

Having made a career in national and international politics he was now, he said, increasingly concerned to re-root himself in his native culture. "Soso Tham, our great Khasi poet, remarked that we looked for wisdom everywhere in the world and were blind to the light of our own country's wisdom. This strikes a chord with my own experience. I was a little deracinated, I have to admit, but now I am trying to get closer to my own people.

"But I am also very happy and proud to be an Indian. The world is being churned up, horrible things are happening, but here, I hope, such things will not happen. We have a big safety valve: the Parliament and the people. The people of India are very wise people. For five thousand years we have suffered invasions, but people here have remained very wise."

Why, I wondered, had his bid for the Indian Presidency failed?

97

"I had the votes of the BJP and Janata Dal, but not of Congress. Even the representatives of Meghalaya did not vote for me, because it's Congress that rules in Meghalaya. So, it was a combination of party loyalty, political envy and enmity at work. If the Communists had voted for me, as at one stage seemed likely, I would have got in, but they switched sides, for their own reasons, at the last minute, and went with Congress. I got 33% of the vote, but it wasn't quite enough."

But he was looking to the future with the optimism of a true politician.

"Central government – Congress controlled, of course – don't want the regional parties to come to government again. So they're using jobs and money to induce people from the regional parties to come over to them, so that they can go on securing a majority. But there is deep resentment, and the coming election will show how people feel about it. We are confident that Congress will be defeated."

And another stab at the Presidency?

"'I strove with none, for none was worth my strife,'" he said, quoting Landor's "Dying Speech of an Old Philosopher". "'Nature I loved; and next to Nature, Art. /I warm'd both hands before the fire of life;/It sinks, and I am ready to depart' – but not perhaps quite yet. We shall see."

Our teacups drained, it was time for me to be heading back to the Prakash before curfew fell. I thanked Professor Swell again for his masterly string-pulling on my behalf without which, I was sure, I would never have made it to the Khasi Hills.

"I am delighted to have been in a position to render assistance," he said. "It was simply a matter of banging a few heads together."

Lakyntiew, dropping me back at the Prakash, was full of plans for the weeks ahead: an open-air presbytery, a picnic, a visit to her clan's sacred grove – and a meeting with Bah Bling, an authority on Thomas Jones and UFOs.

30

There are fewer beggars in Shillong than there are in Swansea. I saw only two, and neither was a Khasi.

For Khasis, as a rule, do not beg. Life, to be sure, is hard and plain for most of them, although not as drastically simplified by abject poverty as it is in many other parts of India. No matter how desperate a person's wants, the sense of collective responsibility is so deeply ingrained in Khasi society that begging is held to be a socially unacceptable solution, and a source of great shame to the begging person's entire clan.

It is the clan's responsibility to preserve its members from destitution, and to provide what material support a needy individual requires, until he is able once more to fend for himself.

This support is debited from a family's 'ancestral property', which is traditionally held in trust by the youngest daughter – a cardinal principle of the matrilineal system. If the person who has fallen on hard times is a drunk, he is given only his food.

"Have you no kith or kin?" exclaim Khasis, giving nothing, when a compatriot is found begging. And if he owns up to having no kith or kin he still gets nothing, because a Khasi bereft of relatives is likely to be a Khasi who has offended against the clan or family code, and has therefore disqualified himself as a worthy recipient of charity.

31

To Western interlopers the Khasis were mere 'slaves of nature', mired in darkness and superstition; the Empire, harbinger of light and progress, would teach them instead to be 'masters of nature'.

After two centuries or more of smog-fouled 'light' and earth-wrecking 'progress', the 'masters of nature' would do well to revisit the jungles and sacred groves of these 'slaves of nature'. They might learn something.

Nearly a hundred years ago the government official and ethnographer Lt. Col. P.R.T. Gurdon observed that "The [Khasis], like the Japanese, are fond of nature. A Khasi loves a day out in the woods, where he thoroughly enjoys himself. If he does not go out shooting or fishing, he is content to sit still and contemplate nature. He has a separate name for each of the commoner birds and flowers. He also has names for many butterflies and moths. These are traits which are not found usually in the people of India."

Heading out towards the Mawphlang sacred grove, with Lakyntiew at the wheel and a picnic in the boot, we passed many a reminder of Shillong's status as the biggest military cantonment on the north-east frontier: the Garrison Ground, where a band was marching to the bagpipes; an army recruitment centre; the ornate portals of some brass-hat's residence guarded by two stiff sentries in white puttees and crimson cockades. On flat stones in the porridge-grey River Shyrpi a dozen *dhobis* were flailing the army's dirty washing; others, on a grassy bank nearby, were laying out rank on rank of 'clean' shirts and trousers to dry in the sun. The army, of late, had been erupting in nasty red skin-rashes, and the finger of official suspicion had pointed to the putrid Shyrpi.

"Let's hope this leads to some kind of clean-up," said Lakyntiew, who is a founder member of the Meghalaya Women's Alliance, which was formed recently to give women a stronger voice in social and environmental issues. "When the forces see that something on their doorstep needs doing they usually get it done – take this road, for instance."

We had wound steeply away from the city, and were now gliding, smooth as ghee, on a long straight road flanked by regimented pines: no pot-holed switchbacks for the military. To our left, the Pentagon-style grandeur of Eastern Air Command's h.q. – the only air-conditioned building in Meghalaya – with a jet-fighter rampant on a plinth out front, and every paintable surface whitewashed, including the occasional monolith, marooned on the wrong side of the war machine's fence.

Mawphlang, which became an important regional base for the Mission, lies 14 miles south-west of Shillong. *Maw*, meaning

100

'stone', as common a prefix as *'llan'* in Wales, usually refers to a stone that has been designated as a 'remembrancer' of some historic event. *Phlang* means grass, so the village's name translates as 'the grassy stone'. Rock and rich vegetation are certainly the genii of this particular place. Slate was mined here until the 1880s, and cromlechs and monoliths abound, the most striking ones being two sharp black sentinels, about fifteen feet high, near the centre of the village.

The Mawphlang sacred grove, or *law lyngdoh*, is the biggest in the Khasi Hills. Indeed, it is not so much a grove, more an extensive forest, situated, as are most such groves, just below the brow of the hill on which the village stands. Roughly oval in shape, it is separated from the village by an extensive sweep of greensward which, with its scattering of cromlechs and standing stones, looks from a distance like a crazy-golf course for giants. On its further side it drops sharply away into the top end of a gorge.

We coasted down the grassy slope and parked at the edge of the forest, beside a cromlech whose upper surface was about two feet above ground level – Khasi cromlechs are rarely much higher.

"This will be our table," said Lakyntiew, spreading out our picnic on the mini Pentre Ifan.

"Mightn't we be offending the cremated dead?" I wondered. But Lakyntiew, pointing to a cowherd enjoying a cromlech-top smoke nearby, assured me that these stones have always had their uses for the living too.

The grove is shared between the half dozen or so ruling clans of the Mawphlang *Hima*, or state. Centuries ago a battle was fought for this forest between the clans of Mawphlang and those of Nongspung. Villagers still point to the large black honing stone where the Mawphlang warriors sharpened their swords before vanquishing the Nongspung upstarts. The victors cut off the head of the chief of Nongspung, and carried it through the forest to the clan mother's cromlech where their priests performed rites of thanksgiving.

Lakyntiew belongs to the Lyngdoh clan, two or three thousand of whom meet on this green about once a year, Christians and non-Christians alike.

"It wasn't until recently that I attended my first clan gathering," she says, "and it affected me profoundly. It made me want to learn more about my people, to get closer to my roots. The clan is a wonderful support network, giving money to its poor members, helping those in difficulties and honouring the achievements of those who have distinguished themselves in some way.

"One very important thing about these gatherings is that you get to know other members of the clan, because it's an absolute taboo, even among Christians, to marry within the clan. It's quite possible for a boy and a girl to court each other and get close to marriage, and then find out they're related in some way. So it's good for us to get to know our own clan. Our custom of marrying outside the clan means that congenital defects are virtually unknown among the Khasis."

After washing our dishes in a stream, Lakyntiew led me into her clan's grove.

The sacred groves of Khasia, all of them virgin forests, stand as potent witnesses to this people's desire to live in harmony with nature. The Khasis have been ecologically sensitive 'environmentalists' throughout their history, long before 'green thinking' began to impinge on the profligate consumerists of the West; in spite of the benefits of 'progress' they still manage to nurture a vision of the ecologically balanced good life that is of the greatest significance to a species grown lethally careless of its dependence on the planet's well-being.

The richness of the flora and fauna of these Hills astonished botanists such as Hooker who recognised, as early as 1850, that "the Khasia flora . . . is, in extent and number of fine plants, the richest in India and probably in all Asia." His botanical survey of the Hills lists a remarkable 250 varieties of orchid, and dozens more have been found since. "I doubt whether in any other part of the globe the species of orchids outnumber those of any other natural order, or form so large a proportion of the flora."

However, the fauna of the Hills, ever since the Rev. William Morgan Jenkins's tiger extermination campaign of the 1890s, and probably earlier, is not what it was. As the hunter-gatherers turned into farmers, the tigers, leopards, elephants, deer, bears and wolves slunk gradually away from the populous areas; they are found today only in the gorges and the jungles of the interior. With India's population increasing by 17 million every year, which is equivalent to the population of Australia, it is difficult to see that species such as the Bengal tiger will survive much longer.

There were hardly any birds in the Mawphlang grove that afternoon, the only sound being the whine and skreek of cicadas, and the chatter of pebbly streams. But the air smelled sweet and earthy, and the flora, in dramatic contrast to the sparse clumps of pine outside the forest, seemed in abundantly good heart.

Although the grove is associated with particular clans, anyone is at liberty to enter and take their ease here, for the Khasis do not believe in the ownership of land. There are, however, certain unwritten rules. You may drink the water, and eat what fruits, fish and fowl you desire, but not a sweet paper or fag-end may be left behind, and not so much as a leaf may be taken away. Even deadwood must be left where it lies, to rot down as mulch for moss and orchids, and habitat for insects. In former times, it was only when oak was needed to provide a sacred column for the *iing sad* (palace) of the chieftain's family that timber could be removed from the grove.

Oaks, as sacred to the Khasis as they used to be to the Celts, and tree-rhododendrons, their branches dripping with blue-vanda orchids, are probably the most dominant of the grove's hundreds of species of trees, flowers, ferns and grasses. The lichens and mosses flourish in such profusion that it's difficult to tell the matted stones of cromlechs from fuzzy lumps of rotting wood.

If you abide by the code of the forest, no harm will befall you. Indeed, the grove is famous as a place of refuge from any terrors, physical or psychological. Its calming, restorative powers were palpable within minutes of my entering its sun-shot green shade. But if you abuse the forest its guardian spirit, the Basa, will find you out.

103

The Basa in its benign manifestation takes the form of a tiger. The animal is never seen, though its hot breathing – "khor, khor, khor" – can be heard at your back as it pads behind you keeping danger at bay. But if angered by some defilement of the forest, the Basa appears as a snake and demands restitution.

Desmond's father told me several tales of 'Basa justice'. Fifteen years ago, for instance, a wood-seller stole some timber from the grove and traded it at a booze shop for a bottle of liquor, believing that having passed on the wood he might escape the Basa's attentions. But the next day the Basa, in the form of a snake, came looking for the wood. When the Basa appeared at the shop, the shopkeeper realised the snake's purpose – and where the wood had come from. "Please don't harm me," she begged the snake, "I have not myself done anything against the forest, but I promise to find out who stole the wood, and admonish the offender." Satisfied with this undertaking, the Basa slid away. The shopkeeper then tackled the woodseller who immediately confessed his crime, and carried the timber back to the forest.

Then there was the time a snake suddenly appeared in the home of a village elder, Myntri Bonik Blah. Members of his household rushed to kill it, but Myntri Bonik stayed their hand, remembering suddenly a wrong he had done the forest. Had he not fenced his garden with some timber that had been discarded after being used in the annual thanksgiving dance – timber that had come from the sacred grove. This was no ordinary snake, it was the Basa come to demand the wood's return. "Please forgive me," said Myntri Bonik to the Basa, "I will take the wood back at once." But he had many things to do and he forgot his promise. That night, tired after his labours, he pulled back the blanket on his bed and there, coiled on the mattress, was a snake twice the size of the one he had seen before. Myntri Bonik ran terrified from the house, tore up his fence and carted it straight to the forest. When he returned, the snake had gone from his bed and he was able to sleep.

On a grassy hillock perched on the edge of the forest's southern precipice there's the sacred omphalos of the Mawphlang grove, the box cromlech of *Ka Iawbei*, the clan

104

mother. Who, precisely, this primal ancestress was, and when her ashes were deposited here, nobody knows. But there's no escaping the reverence accorded her – the very siting of her tomb on this panoramic mound insists on her significance: to the north, over 200 miles away, the snowy glimmer of the Bhutan Himalayas; to the south, the gaping green wound of a canyon that stretches all the way to Bangladesh.

As if echoing the configurations of a traditional Khasi dance, *Ka Iawbei's* cromlech is encircled by half a dozen menhirs representing the males of her line. This cosmic 'dance in stone' is perfected by the fleeting presence of a visitor – a wispy pine, its scrawny trunk uniting heaven and earth.

The veneration of *Ka Iawbei*, a tribal mother as dynamic to the Khasis as was Ffraid (or Brigit) to the Celts of old, reflects the centrality of woman in a society that has maintained its unique matrilineal system in spite of all the Pauline misogyny that Christianity has been capable of throwing at it.

About half an hour's rugged walk downhill from the sacred grove there's the poignant and enigmatic grave of a child. It lies in a cluster of pines on the long-abandoned bridle-path that the British conquistador David Scott drove across the Hills in the late 1820s. The inscription on the tombstone reads:

To
A Child Fondly
Call'd Camilla
"Soft Silken Primrose
Fading Timelessly"
1843

And that is all. No family name, no age, no exact date, no hint of a religious affiliation.Why the secrecy? Who were the parents of this love-child, if love-child she was? A Khasi mother . . . a British father? And not your ordinary army wallah or commodities merchant of a British father, but someone sufficiently literate to be able to quote from the lesser works of John Milton:

O fairest flower, no sooner blown but blasted,
Soft silken primrose fading timelessly . . .

These are the opening lines of "On the Death of a Fair Infant Dying of a Cough", the earliest extant poem of Milton's in the English language. He wrote it at the age of nineteen, following the death of his two-year-old niece. There couldn't have been, in the Khasi Hills in the 1840s, many Englishmen conversant with the obscurer reaches of seventeenth-century literature; there couldn't have been many Welshmen either . . .

Yes, rumour has had it for years that Camilla was the 'illegitimate' child of Thomas Jones (not that the Khasis themselves – the non-Christians at any rate – recognise the odious concept of 'illegitimacy'). And the late Professor R.S. Lyngdoh, of the university in Shillong, lent authority to the rumour when, shortly before he died, he told a historian colleague that he had seen a document in the papers of the Deputy Commissioner of the East Khasi Hills District that mentioned Camilla's death and referred to her as the daughter of the Rev. Thomas Jones.

But that document has never resurfaced, and detractors have been busy undermining 'the Thomas Jones theory' by pointing to certain implausibilities. Take the date, for instance: 1843. This was long before his second, questionable 'marriage' as a widower. In any case, his first wife, Anne, was very much alive in 1843. So it would have been impossible, you see, for Thomas Jones to have been the father of Camilla. Wouldn't it?

32

"Violence is better than cowardice." "This is supposed to be a Hill State, not a Police State." "The Germans and the English are anti-alien – why not us?" "Non-tribal dogs get lost."

Graffiti howl through the frightened city.

When Thomas Jones arrived in the Hills in 1841 the Khasis numbered no more than 120,000. Although today there are nearly a million of them, they are only a drop in the swelling Indian ocean of 900 million. The influx of outsiders is imposing stresses on the culture that many Khasis feel are no longer tolerable. They remember smartingly the plains territory south of the Hills that was once theirs, until 'deleted' and sprawled over by Bangladesh. They witness with alarm neighbouring tribes and tribal states – Tripura, for instance – being inundated to the point of cultural extinction by tidal waves of outsiders. They are themselves a minority in their own capital; out of Shillong's total population of 300,000, little more than a third are Khasis.

The first of Shillong's ethnic clashes occurred in 1979, as a result of which non-tribals began moving away from some of the predominantly Khasi areas of the city. It's often towards the end of the monsoon season that trouble breaks out. In one of his curfew poems Desmond describes the September streets

> dotted with men in green,
> policemen,
> arsonists and
> miscreants,
> growing like unwanted sores,
> sighing under the burden
> of violence . . .
>
> . . . and voices are loudest
> of those who speak
> of stones, bullets, knives, fire.

This latest curfew had been imposed since August 12, in response to the blocking of main roads by the Federation of Khasi, Jaintia and Garo People (FKJGP): the Federation had thrown up its blockades in order to protest about the 'excessive' number of trade permits given by the government to non-tribals. In the heightened tension resulting from the curfew, related grievances were expressed with mounting anger. The FKJGP joined forces with the powerful Khasi Students' Union (KSU) to demand the reservation of 90 per cent of jobs for tribals, the scrapping of trade licences for non-tribals, an end to uranium extraction in the West Khasi Hills, and the renaming of Meghalaya to reflect its tribal identity. Young people, educated

107

for white-collar jobs that simply do not exist, were among the most militant protesters.

There were no doubt other key players with altogether shiftier motives. Indian politicians of whatever party seem to like nothing more than an outbreak of communal violence to boost flagging pre-election fortunes. It is widely believed that the spark which ignited October's conflagration, a petrol bomb lobbed into a taxi, was the work of some shady *agent provocateur*. The bomb, tossed perhaps arbitrarily into that taxi, happened to kill a non-tribal: the scene was now set for an orgy of violence.

"Riots are not new to Shillong but never before had the city seen as many gory scenes as it did between October 5 and 10," reported *The Times of India*. It went on to describe some of the atrocities. An entire family of eleven, including a 70-year-old grandmother and a nine-month-old baby, killed, their bodies wrapped in plastic sheets and dumped in a thicket. A 34-year-old Rotarian businessman dragged from his shining Maruti jeep, beaten unconscious and then burnt alive in his vehicle. According to *The Times*, 23 people were killed, and 137 were seriously injured; many of them were to die of their wounds in the days that followed. The killing of women and children was previously unheard of in this matrilineal society. "Who or what is responsible for the mindless violence that has torn the peaceful fabric of the city of pine trees and placid lakes?" agonised *The Times*.

Robin Ngangom, although a tribal 'outsider', has made Shillong his home and, grafting himself sensitively onto the culture, is perhaps the first such outsider to make use in his poetry of 'the matter of Khasia'. I asked him, as an observer of similarly stressed cultures elsewhere in the north-east, especially in his native Manipur, what he felt about the situation in the Hills.

"I am quite worried about the fate of the Meghalayans, because I don't want this land raped," he said. "You see, giving asylum to refugees on humanitarian grounds is fine, but the influx must stop now. This is India's dilemma which the western nations have ignored. India, the north-eastern states especially, probably has the biggest problem of migrant infiltration in the world. They don't come in ones or twos but in droves – from Bangladesh, from Nepal, from Sri Lanka, from Myanmar.

"Tripura is one sad example. The indigenous people there are being completely swamped by migrants from Bangladesh. These new settlers, highly procreative groups and therefore legion, have also become assertive and belligerent. Can you expect them to have any love for the language and culture of their hosts?

"In Shillong too, most of the Bengalis and Nepalis born and brought up here do not even speak Khasi, let alone know its myths or learn about its culture and art. On the contrary, the larger cultural groups – some very subtly – have tried to impose their language and culture on their hosts. For example, the Hindiwallahs from the cow-belt – Uttar Pradesh, Madhya Pradesh, Bihar – will call you a barbarian if you cannot speak Hindi. The Bengalis are not so crass, but they do suffer from a constipated cultural superiority. Such attempts at imposing culture and language, whether underhand or overt, must be resisted firmly.

"I would rather have just one culture, one nation, spread out harmoniously over this little globe of ours" – a mischievous smile crossed his lips – "where I can make love to women from all races and climes, without fear or shame. But this is wishful thinking. I've realised that tradition and identity must be preserved at all costs. Take, for instance, my own state of Manipur. It's a veritable melting pot. We have twenty-two major ethnic tribes there – probably the largest conglomeration of tribes in the country. Imagine the surfeit of dances, tales, crafts, myths, music, each tribe having a distinct role in the cultural make-up of Manipur. But I must point out that Christianity, in its worst Protestant form, has done a lot of harm there. The tribals have grown ashamed of their roots: whatever is not Christian is heathen and bad, and best forgotten.

"A friend of mine there asked an old Kuki woman, 'Mother, don't you miss your god Doibom whom you used to worship in the old days?' And the old woman replied: 'Eh! Doibom is Satan, we worshipped him because there was no other.' So the festivals, the rituals, the oral traditions, the songs which were the pulse of the people, the treasured ornaments, the pipes, the drums and fiddles are fast disappearing."

The anthropologist Verrier Elwin, whose widow still lives in Shillong, is much read and often referred to by Robin and other Shillong intellectuals. He quoted me a short passage from Elwin's work which, he felt, succinctly articulated the Khasis' present predicament:

> The inferiority complex is the knife that severs the link that binds the people to their past. If it continues to develop in the tribal areas it will destroy their art, culture and religion, for the people will not hold to something of which they have become ashamed; and it will lead to a collapse of moral sanctions and of the social organisation which at present hold the tribes together.

Returning to the Prakash after an afternoon with Robin, I nearly tripped over a set of wooden stays shoring up some new cement work in the stairwell. Pinky and Nupur had installed an impenetrable gate of iron bars between the stairs leading to their quarters and the rest of the hotel. There was no need to ask why.

33

"Mr. Jenkins! Oh, Mr. Jenkins!" I was being hailed from below by a voice straining to be heard through the Hindi pop and panel-beating of the Prakash forecourt.

There, among the limbs of a dismantled Ambassador, stood a stocky eighty-year-old in a crumpled grey suit, with a blanket hanging loosely from his shoulders. The weather to me was like a good summer at home, but the Khasis, especially the elderly, were already beginning to feel the dry season's cold.

"I am Mr. A. Blingstodar Diengdoh of Mawmluh village, Cherrapunji," he said. "Mrs. Richmond told me you are here."

"Come on up."

I recognised the name, and the bronzed mongolian head with its cap of silver bristles. This was surely Bah Bling. He had featured briefly in Alexander Frater's film, talking about Khasi history and UFOs.

"I am unable this morning to stay for discussions," he said, rolling energetically along the balcony. "There are elections soon, and I have much work to do on my campaign. But you will come, please, to my village of Mawmluh, and there we will talk of Thomas Jones."

"And UFOs?"

"Of UFOs and many other important things. You have come all the way from Wales to hear the Khasis sing your Welsh hymns. So you will come, please, to our church's presbytery at Laitkor, and there you will hear them. And then, please, in the afternoon of the same day you will return to Shillong for the Laitumkhrah Catholic parade. Then, please – "

"Well, I'll have to let you know about the Catholic parade," I broke in.

"That may be difficult," he said. "I have a number of houses and I am busy with my election campaign – I am everywhere. But our friend Mrs. Richmond will be able to find me. Now, please, before I go," – he pulled a camera from his pocket – "we will have some photographs. You too have a camera?"

Bling snapped me, I snapped Bling. Then, flinging his cape-like blanket around himself, he was gone, like an octogenarian Zorro.

34

The Khasi Jaintia Presbyterian Synod sent a ministerial jeep for me.

A sturdy Mahindra four-wheel drive is *de rigeur* for the modern wayfaring Rev. The driver ushered me to the front passenger seat; in the back were two portly gentlemen in grey suits: the re-translators. They had been sent to escort me to h.q.

The Welshman's bible, begun by Thomas Jones, completed by his successors and published in 1891, had, with certain

111

amendments over the years, served the Khasis well for a century. But the time had come, as it comes to most bibles, for the Khasi version to be modernised. It was necessary to weed out certain instances of 'missionary Khasi' and infuse the text with more indigenous idioms. The *New Testament* was already finished, and work was well in hand on the *Old*. I had assumed that the Catholics, the 'second force' in the Hills, would be collaborators in this major undertaking, but no: the two old rivals had been unable to agree on objectives and procedures, therefore the Catholics were working on their own version. Khasi Christians would soon have two new bibles to choose from.

Church House, the Synod's headquarters, was only about three miles away, but it is common for even short journeys such as this to take half an hour or more. Shillong, 'Queen of the hill stations of India', is being choked to death by cars and lorries. With the highest rate of car ownership in India, the city is surely only a year or two away from being immobilised by a permanent traffic gridlock. It is often quickest to walk from A to B, but even so it is difficult to take any pleasure in Shillong's pines and cherry trees, butterflies and mountains, so total is the assault on one's eyes and lungs by gales of exhaust-fart.

Older residents have a raking *hiraeth* for the Shillong of twenty or thirty years ago. "You can't imagine how lovely the city was when we were young," a Presbyterian in her seventies told me. She showed me an anonymous European's depiction of Shillong in the days of her youth:

> The rolling downs on all sides, picturesque waterfalls, rows of fragrant pine trees, red roads intersecting one another and pleasant grass-rides have made it an Earthly Paradise, where one may enjoy eternal peace, face to face with the naked, beautiful and all-perfect creation of the MASTER ARTIST, drinking deep of the sweet and healing fountains of Nature and forgetting the woes and worries of this torturing night-mare which men call life.

"But now," she sighed, "it's such a dirty, smelly, untidy place. So very sad."

Shillong manages, nevertheless, to smile through her tears. Remove the sewage and vehicle pollution (not to mention the desperate communal violence) from the picture, and you still have a proud and beautiful city.

It was little more than a straggle of villages until the British transferred their regional administrative headquarters here from Cherrapunji in 1864. Although no more than 35 miles away, Shillong's average rainfall was only five feet a year, compared with Cherrapunji's staggering forty or even fifty feet – a main reason for the move. Also, Cherrapunji had declined not only in military and political importance, but in its economic activity: production and trade were not what they had been in the 1830s. A more centrally situated civil station, with a cantonment for troops and sanatoria for Europeans, would make an ideal base from which to control the whole of Assam.

Shillong matured as a hill station whose setting, facilities and salubrity rivalled those of Simla and Darjeeling, and were famed throughout the eastern Empire. There was everything in Shillong that might be desired by the indigo planter from the interior or the government official from stifling Cal, up in the Hills for a month or two's respite from the sweat and tedium of life in the plains. A few chukkas at the Polo Ground or a round of golf; gin and male chinwag at the Club; a dance at Government House, followed perhaps, the next afternoon, by a stroll round Ward's Lake with the lovely Miss Fanshawe, up for the season from Cox's Bazar, and quite the niftiest little waltzer you ever did see; then, on a Sunday, communion of a rather different kind, at the sweetest little Anglican church, the only one in town – most of the others, believe it or not, being Calvinistic Methodist, set up for the natives by the Welsh, of all people.

The natives, like the Welsh at home, were expected to know their place. A strict apartheid operated in 'European Ward', Shillong's arboreal, bungaloid high ground, where a brown face was tolerated only if it was attached to a cook or a cleaner or a gardener. The natives belonged to the lower levels of town

113

which, according to the Rev. J. Hughes Morris (who had never actually been there), were infested with anti-social elements making the place "a seething cauldron of iniquity, sin and blasphemy."

An earlier commentator who *had* been there was the Rev. Jerman Jones (1833-1890) who described, in 1871, scenes of untramelled misrule, with "old and young, men and women, Khasis and Bengalis, darting to and fro, a rowdy, noisy crowd, swearing and cursing, drinking and fighting, gambling all day long and all night long." Shillong, declared the former Bethesda quarryman, was "the place most like my idea of hell as any I have yet seen on earth."

In 1872, therefore, the Mission opened a Shillong front. The Rev. Griffith Hughes, who was placed in command of the Shillong campaign, also complained in his letters home about the debauchery of the place. "I dare say that this is the most immoral place on the Hills," he wrote. "There's carousing, drunkenness, dancing, lewd singing, and gambling every night in Mawkhar, the village where the school house is, close to where the mission house is being built – it would fill any man of sensibility with dread and horror."

Those revellers of the 1870s would hardly recognise Mawkhar today. At its very heart is the Mission Compound, with key institutions of the Presbyterian establishment. There is Church House itself, at the end of Ceredig Road which is named after the one-time sailor from Ceinewydd (New Quay), the Rev. J. Ceredig Evans who became not only a distinguished headmaster but a member of the Assam government. There are two pioneering secondary schools; the Dinam Hall, whose name recalls the largesse of the Davies family of Llandinam; the cemetery, where many missionaries and their families are buried; and Mawkhar church, which has a capacity congregation, every Sunday, of 3,000 worshippers.

Just before we turned into Ceredig Road we drove through what looked like a huge jumble sale, with coats, shirts, dresses and jumpers arranged on hangers along the railings and spread all over the pavement. This, apparently, was charity clothing that Europe had given to Bangladesh; it had been hijacked by canny traders and sent up here in bales to be sold on the open market.

As we climbed from the jeep the translators pointed out a chunky, four-sided column in front of the church. It was the recently unveiled monument to the Welsh missionaries, whose names were already slightly fogged by the action of rain on limestone. There, among the 'Ambassadors for Christ', was listed Ednyfed Thomas's name. "A considerable honour," I remembered him saying back in Penrhosgarnedd, "and a little unsettling too, to see oneself on a monument and be still alive."

In the half-timbered Church House with its red tin roof, I was led down a dark, lino-clad corridor to an airy meeting room with lace curtains (another legacy of the Welsh, seen in homes all over the Hills). There, standing round a table beneath a touched-up portrait of their church's founder, a reception committee of half a dozen leading Presbyterians was waiting to greet me.

They were surprised but delighted, they said, inviting me to take the seat of honour beneath Thomas Jones, that I had, managed to gain entry to Meghalaya at this difficult time. The Mission Board secretary from Cardiff had also been expected, for a conference on how to defend the faith against materialism and consumerism, but his visit and the conference had been called off until peace and normality had been restored.

They resumed their places at the table, which was spread with a floral oilcloth; then tea and tea-cakes were served. What sort of contact, I asked, did they still have with 'the mother church'?

"We are in frequent touch with Cardiff," said the Rev. Dr. H.M. Rapthap, a small, beady-eyed man with a big job as the Synod's Senior Executive Secretary. "And we send two students a year to the theological college at Aberystwyth. There are personal contacts too with the retired missionaries – most of them came back last year for the Thomas Jones Sesquicentennial Jubilee. But as a church we are entirely independent of the Presbyterian Church of Wales – we have been independent, organisationally, since 1940, seven years before India as a nation gained her independence."

"From the very beginning, the Welsh attitude was different from that of the English and others," added Dr. Ivan M. Simon, a

115

linguist and lay churchman who has the moustache of a colonel but the gracious gentility of an Oxford don. "Right from the outset, they started raising up leaders from among the Khasis, and thought all along of a time when they themselves would have to leave."

"They tried their best to produce local leaders," said Dr. Rapthap. "It was very different with the Roman Catholic church, where there are very few local leaders. Many, about 75%, come from south India and other places."

There was no mistaking the warmth of affection for former missionaries such as E.W. (Ednyfed) Thomas, Miss Gwen Evans and the almost legendary Dr. Arthur Hughes, who was at that time Moderator of the Presbyterian Church of Wales. The general (and questionable) explanation for the missionaries' departure is that the Indian Government, fearing their supposed political influence, ordered them out of the country in the 1960s.

"At midnight, on December 31, 1969 – the Government's deadline – the last of the missionaries left the Hills for good," said the Rev. J. Fortis Jyrwa. "I remember vividly the farewell meetings here and at the airport. They were full of tears."

The Welsh presence in the Hills, the little gathering agreed, had changed the lives of the Khasis, whether Christian or not, immeasurably for the better. But their church was now mature enough for them to begin to question the missionaries' virtual demonisation of the indigenous culture and their imposition on the Khasis of substantially Welsh patterns of worship, to the exclusion of Khasi thought-forms and musical traditions.

"Among all the tribes in the north-east we were the first to become Christians," said the Rev. Jyrwa. "But only 54% of us are Christian – 300,000 Presbyterians and 200,000 Catholics. How is it that the Mizos are 100% Christian, the Nagas 90%, the Garos about 70%? If our missionaries and also our church had taken seriously the need to use and enrich Khasi traditional culture, things might perhaps have been different. Perhaps by now all Khasis might have become Christian. Genuine evangelisation means indigenisation, and this is the challenge that faces us today."

The Khasi Presbyterians are still expanding, nevertheless, at a rate of between three and five thousand new recruits annually. The same cannot be said of Welsh Presbyterians whose numbers have slumped from 80,000 ten years ago to 55,000 today.

I mention, as the meeting breaks up, my interest in attending a service or two, to hear a Khasi sermon and some Khasi renditions of Welsh hymns. "Come, please, to the English-language Sunday school service at Police Bazar," says Dr. Rapthap. "They have invited me to preach to them this Sunday, but I would like you, please, to speak in my place. A few words from somebody from Wales, it would be something special for our young people . . . "

I panicked for a moment among the clatter of teacups. Then, ah! I thought: the famous Khasi sense of humour. Me, of all unworthies, preach a sermon to the Khasis! The Rev. Dr. Rapthap could surely not be serious?

35

Mr. Pde sits me down in a wicker chair on his little cobbled yard, plonks an old sun-blanched straw hat on my head, and, as I munch through a breakfast of boiled eggs and toast, regales me with stories of SdUK, *Seng Biria U Khasi*, the Khasi Humour Society, of which he is dishonourable squanderer.

The oldest of SdUK's 13 all-female members is a venerable patriarch of 40 years of age. The youngest is 71-year-old Mr. Webster Davies Jyrwa, President of the Khasi Authors' Society and Station Director (Retired) of All India Radio. In their extra-SdUK existences they are all highly respectable top brass gentlemen, or, in SdUK terms, disreputable bottom tin viragos.

Every year the Society, formed in 1989 by Mr. Wan Kharkrang, Secretary of the District Council, stages a small private event boycotted by people from all over the Hills. "One year we held a fly killing competition – who could kill the most flies? Next year we are planning an Elvis Presley imitation competition male and female. And then there are the annual awards. The State, in its awards, concentrates on the top

117

achievers, but we concentrate on the bottom, the people who have managed to pass through lower primary school."

Easily the smallest and most forgettable SƏUK event ever was their chilli eating competition. "We had about fifty entrants from all parts of the Hills, and there were two doctors present to certify that the competitors were fit and taking part of their own free will. We sat them on stage in a semi-circle, with one judge per person, to make sure of no cheating.

"Each competitor was given a bag of 25 two-inch chillies, and some water and salt. At the sound of the whistle, they opened their packets and started chewing. Even the judges were sweating with the heat of those chillies! Contestants who managed to finish the first packet would be given another packet of 25, and so on."

The record that day was 113 chillies in five minutes, for which feat the champion chilli chomper was awarded Rs 1500 (about £30). "There were three or four women competing, and they did pretty well too. One woman ate 62 chillies, which is the current ladies' record."

The bilingual nature of these occasions adds to the gravity of the proceedings. For instance, Thailand to members of SƏUK is not Thailand but *'Rilbong'*, which is a straight translation into Khasi of 'thigh land'.

The moon, by now, was high underfoot. It was time for Mr. Pde to feed his chickens and return to the *Inferno*. I thanked him, SƏUC style, for the low solemnity of our midnight feast, handed back his moon-blackened shoe, and wished him a fond hello.

36

But the Rev. Dr. Rapthap had been serious.

It was World Sunday School Day, the biggest Sunday of the year at Police Bazar Presbyterian Church, which holds English-medium services for the city's Bengali, Naga and Garo youngsters, as well as for English-inclined Khasis.

I had hoped to sample today the famed Khasi treatments of Welsh hymns, but there was a strong flavour of happy-clappy evangelistic schmaltz about this all-English service – bouncy, fresh-faced songs to guitar accompaniment, rather than the *sturm und drang* of the great Welsh roof lifters.

Although I had sidled in fairly unobtrusively, it was obvious, from the 'discreet' turnings of young heads in front of me, that everyone was aware of my presence.

When the Rev. Dr. Rapthap was introduced at sermon time as "our very special guest", I thought I'd escaped official attention.

"I am going to surprise you all this Sunday," began Rev. Dr. Rapthap, adjusting the pulpit microphone. "I am not going to preach to you after all. You can hear me any time. Instead, I am going to ask Mr. Jenkins, our guest from Wales, to preach to us." He stepped down from the pulpit and beckoned me forward.

Like St. Govan, I could have called on the very geology of the place to open up and hide me from this terror, but St. Govan had contacts I don't have.

There was nothing for it but to go forward, plead total inadequacy, and persuade Rev. Dr. Rapthap to get back in that pulpit pronto.

"I really am in no position to deliver any kind of sermon," I stammered on the pulpit's threshold.

"Don't worry about a sermon," he said, placing a reassuring hand on my arm. "Why not talk to them about Thomas Jones – just for twenty minutes or so?"

The 'reassuring' hand was now urging me gently up the steps to the pulpit. And there I suddenly was, on a crumbling cliff-top about 500 feet above an alarming ocean of expectant faces, bright-eyed believers all, generously indulgent of someone they surely construed as one of God's quirkier messengers.

Twenty minutes on Thomas Jones. Recover from mental limbo article written six months ago. Rephrase to suit audience aged between four and sixteen. Open mouth. See if any words come out . . .

37

It was on June 22, 1841, at the height of an early monsoon, that Thomas and Anne Jones arrived at Cherrapunji.

The British, having recently 'pacified' the Khasis, had established a sprawling military station at Saitsohpen on the moorland at the foot of the rise on which the little town of Cherra stands. They had done a deal with the Rajah of Cherra Poonjee, as they called the place then: a thousand acres of his plateau in exchange for a similar spread of land in the plains of Sylhet. The British rifle having spoken so persuasively to the Khasi bow and arrow, it was an offer the 'friendly' Rajah was in no position to decline.

Although Cherra's inhabitants were found by most early European visitors to be, in Hooker's words, "sulky intractable fellows, averse to rising early and intolerably filthy in their persons", the place itself, and its temperate climate, seemed to be just what the doctor ordered. The Rev. Jacob Tomlin, for instance, whose family had been so poorly in Calcutta, was pleased to report that "After a short residence on the mountains, our health and spirits were much improved; and the children soon became rosy-cheeked, and delighted to enjoy their freedom, and to run about in the open air."

It used to be the custom, in the early days of the Company, for Europeans taken ill in the sultry sloughs of Calcutta to attempt to cure themselves by taking a sea voyage. They had nowhere relatively near at hand to compare with the Simla Hills to which their fellow colonialists in the Upper Provinces frequently resorted when their health broke down or the heat on the plains became too much for them.

It was David Scott, 'pacifier' of the Khasis and the Governor General's Agent on the North East Frontier, who most actively championed Cherra's suitability as both a military base and a 'sanatory' station, and by 1829 the barracks and bungalows for troops and convalescents were under construction.

It was envisaged that as many as 10,000 European soldiers might be posted here, but the plan died with its progenitor. Convalescent troops and civilians from Calcutta continued to avail themselves of Cherra's balmy altitudes, but it lost out as a resort to the superior charms and facilities of Darjeeling, and peace in the Hills led to a scaling down of soldiery as Cherra developed as an administrative centre. Its biggest drawback as a health resort was its extraordinary rainfall: the place was quite unsuitable as a sanatorium between the months of June and October.

When the Joneses arrived, the station had been, since 1835, headquarters of the Sylhet Light Infantry, a force of mainly sepoy troops under British command, who, having vanquished the Khasis, were charged with consolidating a Pax Britannica in Sylhet and the southern Khasi Hills.

Today not a brick remains of the military station – all has reverted to tussocky grass where once were arrayed the bustling lines of the native troops, the regimental hospital, and the huts of the grain hawkers, oil sellers and sutlers who supplied the wants of the infantrymen. But even in the mid-nineteenth century, when there would have been hundreds of soldiers and officials in residence here, there was, by most accounts, an air of desolation about the place. Hooker, who was here in 1850, found Cherra's "flat portion, where the English reside . . . as bleak and inhospitable as can be imagined; and there is not a tree, and scarcely a shrub to be seen, except occasional clumps of screw pine. The low white bungalows are few in number, and very scattered, some of them being a mile asunder, enclosed with stone walls and shrubs; and a small white church, disused on account of the damp, stands lonely in the centre of all."

It was in one of those low white bungalows, with the rain pummelling its leaky thatch, that the Joneses found a first, temporary shelter. The bungalow was the home of the invalided soldier Lieutenant William C.J. Lewin (1806-1846), his wife Jane and their growing family of, eventually, six children. Lewin, who saw action with the East India Company's Artillery when King Bagyidaw of Burma invaded Bengal, had been posted to 'salubrious' Cherra in 1836 after his health began to deteriorate. A devout Christian, Lewin had been a staunch supporter of the unsuccessful Baptist mission of Alexander Lish in the 1830s, and he had given a roof to the Rev. Jacob Tomlin on his visit to the Hills in 1837. No doubt Thomas and Anne came to Lewin's door equipped with a warm commendation from the English Baptist who had 'discovered' the Khasi Hills for the embryonic Welsh Mission.

John Whitehead, who has written a biography of the Lieutenant's nephew, T.H. Lewin, the great soldier-administrator of the nearby Lushai Hill Tract (now Mizoram), describes William Lewin as a new kind of servant of Empire. "In his high-mindedness he was representative of the new liberal spirit that, with the social reforms introduced in India during the first half of the nineteenth century, was beginning to inform the raj. Western ideas were being taught in the schools, Christian missions were proliferating. Efforts were being made to exterminate the thugs, the sect dedicated to ritual murder in the name of the goddess Kali; the practice of *suttee*, or widow-burning, was made a capital offence; and the first steps were taken towards the abolition of slavery throughout the country." (*Thangliena: A Life of T.H. Lewin*, Kiscadale, 1993). Close in both years and progressive outlook, Lewin and Thomas Jones had much in common; the Englishman was to prove a generous patron of the Methodists' Mission, and a willing participant in many of its ventures, one of which would speed him to an early grave.

The couple stayed with the Lewins for three astoundingly wet months – in August alone no less than twenty-two feet of rain fell on Cherrapunji. They burned coal fires constantly, but nothing could keep the mould from rotting their clothes and the damp from spoiling their papers.

"Mr. Lewin has shown us every kindness," Thomas Jones wrote home, "indeed, the very greatest kindness, because this

was the only house, or part of a house, to be found in the place . . .
We have only one room, at ground level, and at this time of year
it takes all Mrs. Jones's time and much of my own to keep our
few belongings, which have already been much spoiled, from
being utterly ruined . . . It might appear strange, but it's
certainly true that after one trunk has been opened and dried out
before the fire, the contents of the others have grown mouldy,
and if these things aren't taken out and dried before the fire,
they will quickly rot."

Cherra's long monsoon made it difficult for them to attend to
anything more than the chores of survival, although the
missionary was eager to get on with his work. "It is a lot easier,
perhaps, for you to imagine than for me to describe, the feelings
on our arrival of my dear companion and I: to traverse the great
oceans, to journey over lakes and up rivers, to expose ourselves
to a thousand dangers, and then to arrive safely at journey's end,
the field of my mission, and the village where I shall be working
and where I hope to unfurl the banner of the cross, and to
publish before long the good news of the gospel to thousands
who have never before heard its words of comfort."

But, as he wrote in his first letter from the Hills, he was
under few illusions as to the enormity of the task that faced
him. "A more pitiful, lamentable, and at the same time a more
inviting field for the Christian cannot be found. Here are
multitudes upon multitudes of untutored heathen, naturally
lazy and sluggish, living in filth and rags, afraid to wash a rag
lest it should wear out the sooner; depriving themselves of
proper clothing; niggardly hoarding up every *pice* they can get;
and if asked the reason why, they answer, 'that they may have
something to sacrifice when they or their friends are ill'."

From the military and government officials Thomas Jones
received little more than cool civility and undisguised
scepticism.

"Go home, Jones," advised a British official. "You may as
well try to instruct the monkeys in that tree as attempt to teach
these people."

38

"My abiding curse on the ugly, under-sized glass, and worse than that is the hand that didn't half fill it." So declared the itinerant harper Turlough Carolan, a fastidious connoisseur of hospitality in eighteenth-century Ireland. He would have approved of the Khasi Hills where the glass is invariably cornucopian, the hand that fills it blessed with a generous and frequent downward tilt.

There may not be anything in the bible warning Christians off the booze, but forswearing alcohol was as much a condition of church membership in Khasia as it was in Wales. Illicit tipplers caught in *flagrante delicto* with a bottle could expect denunciation and expulsion from the church, followed by months of social pariahdom. The ministers and elders are still strict teetotallers, and one of the church's formidable women's committees is dedicated to spreading temperance throughout the Hills. But the ordinary members tend to be considerably more relaxed about alcohol these days, and many enjoy the conviviality of a social drink or three.

"What would the deacons say if they knew you were knocking this stuff back?" I asked a group of Presbyterian friends, following my preaching debut, as we sat sipping Scotch in a comfortable home in the middle of Shillong's Mission Compound. Across the rooftops, half hidden by blossoming cherries, gleamed the whitewashed walls of the Welsh Mission Girls' High School, where most of the women present had once been educated in the paths of industrious sobriety. "Do they still expel people for drinking?"

"If the church threw out all the drinkers," said Esther Pugh, a retired teacher who was not herself a drinker, "they'd have nobody left, except me and one or two other old timers." She giggled impishly.

Our hostess was her sister Millionora, who runs the oldest bookstore in town. As bouncy a matron as Esther is wren-like, Millionora bustled about in the dining room next door, singing as she prepared our lunch. I could hardly believe my ears when I caught a snatch of song I had last heard from my daughters' lips a few weeks earlier:

'Mae gen' i dipyn o dŷ bach twt,
O dŷ bach twt, o dŷ bach twt . . .'

"Who taught you that?" I exclaimed.

"Our teacher at the High School, Miss Lloyd," said Millionora through a mouthful of masticated *kwai.* "Do you remember it, Esther?"

Esther was chuckling again.

"She never told us what it meant," continued Millionora, "but there's a word in this song – *'Mae gen' i dipyn o dŷ bach twt'* – everyone broke into naughty chortles – "which is a certain very bad word in Khasi, though we never told Miss Loyd about it and why everyone always laughed when she got us to sing it."

"*Twt,*" whispered her chubby, besuited son Kenneth, stooping to refill my tumbler, "female, er, anatomy."

"And do you remember this one?" said Esther, clearing her throat. "Let me see, now . . . *'Iesu tirion . . .'* Come on, Mil, help me out . . . "

The two sisters stood side by side, as timid and hopeful as a pair of ten-year-olds, their voices quavering thinly at first, then growing in confidence as the rather fuzzy words came back to them:

'Iesu tirion, gwêl yn awr
Blentyn bach yn plygu lawr . . . '

I felt for these two elderly Khasis as I had felt for Angharad and Branwen the first time they had struggled to sing their way successfully through a verse of this simple, child-like song, their infant hands pressed prayerfully together. It was indeed a scene of curiously transplanted Welshness, for the cheerful room in which we were assembled was as fussy with nicknacks and furniture as a Victorian *parlwr*: the souvenir jug with 'Beaumaris' inscribed on it, the 'Birds of Wales' tea-towel become a wall-hanging, and the brightly polished upright piano that is to be seen in many a Khasi home, invariably with a lace coverlet surmounted by family portraits, bible and hymn book, and, centre stage, a Thomas Jones Sesquicentennial memorial plate.

Some of the Welsh mementoes, explained Esther and Millionora, had been brought back from the land of 'the mother church' in the nineteen forties and fifties by their brothers, Orlando and Hollando. Both, at different times, had studied at American universities and had contrived to break the homeward journey with a tour of Wales and a visit to Liverpool, the perceived mecca of Welsh Presbyterianism.

But what of the surname Pugh? Esther's name and address had been given me by Bill Price, the Newtown school teacher who, researching into the Mission's support network in mid Wales, had unearthed the names of several Khasis, including that of Esther, whose education had been sponsored by local schoolchildren. In my brief correspondence with her, I had assumed from her surname that she had married a Welshman – a missionary, perhaps, or the son of a missionary? But I was mistaken.

"I am a thoroughbred Khasi," laughed her husband Darwin, a former Chief Commissioner of Meghalaya, and now chairman of the Law Commission.

"My father was the Rev. E.B. Pugh, and I asked Daddy one day how we came by that name. He said his father must have taken it from some tombstone or other, presumably because he liked the sound of it.

"Khasis often do this kind of thing, and the consequences can be hilarious. People used to listen to missionaries or, in the last war, British soldiers speaking English, and would get attracted to the sound of words without having a clue as to their meanings. So sometimes you get rather lovely names, like 'Milky Way' – or 'Whisky': sounds nice and tastes good. But then, again from the war, you run into dull names like 'Control Rate', or the string of boys called 'First Gear', 'Second Gear' and 'Third Gear'.

"I remember the time a missionary was presented with a child at baptism, and when asked what he should christen the boy, was told 'Syphilis'. Not surprisingly, the missionary refused, and gave the child a name of his own choosing, but I believe the parents went on calling their boy 'Syphilis'. The same kind of problem arose with the parents who wanted to call their son 'Vagina'."

All of the women present that lunchtime had been taught at the Welsh Mission Girls' High School (now renamed somewhat lugubriously the Khasi Jaintia Presbyterian – or KJP – Girls' High School), and most of the older ones had served as teachers there. They had lively memories of their teachers, especially Miss Hilda Jones, a Caersws farmer's daughter who, after graduating at Aberystwyth, sailed to India in 1923, and was principal of the school between 1926 and 1944.

"I loved Hilda Jones," said Esther. "Some people thought she was domineering and despotic, but I didn't find her like that. She was a great lover of music. She introduced us to action songs, dressing up and pageants. It was Hilda Jones who recommended my name, when I was eight years old, to the Sunday school in . . . that, er, place in Wales I can spell but can't pronounce – "

"Llanidloes?"

"That's right. The children there raised money to support the cost of my education. I used to write to the secretary of the Guild in, er, that place . . . Miss Alma Morgan, and she always used to send me something for Christmas. One year she sent me two handkerchiefs – I kept them for years, I didn't dare to use them.

"I am so grateful for all that the Welsh missionaries did for us. Things would have been very different for the Khasis if they hadn't come – we could have become Hindus or Muslims."

Millionora, though, was not a fan of Hilda Jones. "Far too strict," she remarked, before returning to her work in the kitchen with a *"hei di ho, di hei di hei di ho, a'r gwynt i'r drws bob bore . . . "*

Esther admitted that there was sometimes an imperious aloofness about the missionaries.

"I remember going with two or three other girls to the house of our teacher, Miss Annetta Jones, to see about some homework. We knocked at the door, and as we entered we began looking

around the various chairs in her living room to see which ones
we should sit on – when Miss Jones said to us, as if it was the
most obvious thing in the world, 'Sit on the floor'."

39

The Khasis, who think westerners have a pitiably casual attitude
to nomenclature, give serious consideration to the naming of
their children.

They choose above all names that are euphonious; if a name
embodies some desirable quality of character, or is associated
with someone famous or a prestigious profession or some thing
of loveliness, so much the better, but first it should sound well.
Perhaps a traditional name such as Kynpham (inspirer of
confidence) will do, or something less conventional: Lyngksiar
(gilded) or Mewanrap (God help) or Dalarympei (protect the
hearth) or Aridapha (so it's you!). A man is normally prefixed as
'U' So-and-so, which is roughly equivalent to 'Mr.', or, among
family and friends, 'Bah' (brother); a woman is 'Ka' (Ms.) or
'Kong' (sister).

When the missionaries arrived in the Hills, bringing with
them the English language (and a word or two of Welsh: older
Khasis still 'cwtsh' their grandchildren), an enticing new word-
hoard rang in Khasi ears. Many, since then, have given their
offspring western names: Ka Mary Jones, U Water Kingdom, U
Overland, U Royal Edward, U Mister Jones, U Mission, Ka Red
Sea, Ka Brindisi (derived from a route often followed by the
missionaries: Calais to Brindisi by train, and thence, through
Suez, by liner), U Oliver Cromwell, U Shakewell Bones, Ka
Parliament, U Seminar, U Grassful, U Probert, Ka Victories, U
Quotient, U Loverwell, Ka Streamlet, U Headstar, Ka
Precioustar, U Regional and the Rev. Mania Lyngdoh.

At baptism Khasis often jettisoned their 'demon given' names
for something more western or biblical. The first child to be
baptised by the Mission in 1852 was christened Ka Salome.
Then there was the boy who was christened U William Lewis,
after Thomas Jones's co-worker: he grew up, naturally, to become

a leading Presbyterian. Another early convert decided to call his firstborn after the secretary of the Society that had brought Christianity to his people: arise U John Roberts. When a visitor to the Hills in the 1880s asked a native teacher why on earth he had christened his two boys Wellington and Washington, the father replied "Because I wanted them both to be good soldiers for Christ."

Parents no doubt feel that choosing a good career name for their child, such as Barrister, Reverend or Abbot, is bound to give the boy a head start in life without necessarily bogging him down in the tedious formalities of having to study for such a handle. And for those with literary or philosophical pretensions, what could be a better advertisement than a name like Wordsworth, Hamlet or Pascal?

Some apparently western names are in fact Khasi names which have been blurred over. In Shillong I met the Rev. Wellburn Manners whose original family name would have been Myner. And Sylvester Dykes (from Dkhar) was one of several Presbyterians who told me about the Rev. Robert Cunville, "Billy Graham's right-hand man", whose name would once have been Khongwir.

Khasi siblings often rhyme and alliterate: Karen and Sharon; Sufficiency and Efficiency; Edify and Modify – known to their pals, of course, as Edi and Modi.

But there must be those who, entranced by the sound of a word, would have chosen differently had they known at the time precisely what it meant – the parents, for instance, of U Atom Bomb, who must have fallen for those eerily mantric words having heard them on the radio soon after August 6, 1945; or the parents who christened their lovely daughters Toilet and Latrine. They could have done worse, I suppose, like the Shillong woman who was named Prostitute, Kong Pro for short.

But three cheers for the garage mechanic who, having had two boys, Piston Rod and Crankshaft, desperately wanted a daughter. At last his wife gave birth to a girl, and he christened her Mobil Oil.

40

One evening Esther and Darwin's daughter Linda, who is assistant director of the state's adult literacy programme, drove me in her jeep to the golf course side of town to meet another 'old timer', Kong Rani Shullai. "She's related to my ex-husband," said Linda, "but she always makes me welcome and I love to visit her. Such spirit, such fantastic energy. She's seventy-six, retired years ago, but she doesn't know the meaning of the word."

It was dark by the time we knocked on Kong Rani's door. "Come in," she beamed. "Come in and welcome. Someone from Wales. What a nice surprise. The Welsh, you know, they made us what we are, they gave us everything, eternal values – values, in these dark days, the Khasis would do well to remember."

This widowed 'old timer', who in youth must have been a considerable beauty, was in no respect one of life's abstainers. She sat us down in her high, spacious living room, then padded into the kitchen, which was plipping with demijohns of pear and rhubarb wine, to fetch us "a little refreshment".

To my request for a beer she responded with not one but two pint bottles of 'Black Label', plonked down, with glass and opener, on the table at my side. Then, nursing a tumbler of brandy in both hands, she settled into an armchair, eager to talk.

She too had been taught by Miss Hilda Jones at the Welsh Mission Girls' High School, remembering her with affection as quite firm and "smelling of, let's be honest about it, perfume and armpit".

Kong Rani, known formally as Mrs. Evelyn Shullai, 'retired' as Inspector of Schools for the Khasi and Jaintia Hills in 1976, and immediately threw herself into voluntary work. A Red Cross activist and a leading figure in the scouts and guides movement, she had represented India at conferences all over the world. Just months ago, at the age of 75, she had opened on her own premises a school for juniors and infants, in which she herself teaches, five days a week. "As long as I am sound in mind and body," she said, "I have a contribution to make."

Kong Rani had cause to feel more threatened than most by the events of recent weeks. Some of the bloodiest atrocities had taken place only a few streets from her house, although the full horror of what had happened was not immediately apparent to her.

"Some non-tribals came running to me for shelter. They were being chased by Khasis who were going to kill them. They were really desperate. I hid them in the bakehouse at the end of my property. Then another man came, at his wits' end with fear, so I pushed him into a chicken coop. We Khasis," she leaned forward, her eyes wide with despair, "what has become of us? I am so ashamed for us . . ." She paused a moment, only the plips of the demijohns breaking the silence.

"Then, hot on the heels of these terrified non-tribals came some Khasi youths. They said they wanted to drink the blood of the men they were after, and demanded to know where I had hidden them. They'd have had to kill me before I'd let them get hold of the men I'd given shelter to – I think they were very close to killing me. Anyway, I denied giving them shelter, and said they could search my house. Perhaps they believed me. Somehow they let it pass, and ran on. Later I learned that just minutes before this happened ten people in our part of town had been massacred – by Khasis.

"Some days afterwards a journalist from *The Shillong Times* came out to see me. They'd heard that I had sheltered these men, and wanted to do a story on it. They'd earlier done an item about a non-Khasi giving shelter to a Khasi, and this, they thought, would make a good balancing piece. I was afraid, not for myself but for my family. Perhaps these people would get my grandchildren. I had to think hard about the journalist's request, but eventually I gave my permission."

After the story appeared in the press some youths came to Kong Rani's house and warned her that they would 'see to her'. So far they had not, and she was hoping the affair would blow over.

41

"Christianity has made us soft," mutters the poet as he joins Desmond and me, and our chauffeur Scott, for the drive to Cherrapunji. Sliding onto the back seat of the Ambassador, he pulls from his pocket a rolled up copy of the *Shillong Times* and points excitedly to an article about the police breaking up a group of Khasi patriots who had been training with guns in a remote part of the Hills.

Kynpham Singh Nongkynrih seems to be in a mixed mood of simmering rage and elation – rage that a steady influx of outsiders is threatening his culture with annihilation, and elation 'that some, at least, of his compatriots are sufficiently daring to want to take up arms and do something about it. This mood, I am to find, is anything but typical of Kynpham who is characterised normally by the dark-eyed sensitivity you might expect in a young lecturer engaged, as he is, in doctoral research on the letters of John Keats. But Fanny Brawne and the music of nightingales are the last things on his mind this morning; Kynpham this morning is more than half in love with easeful terrorism.

"We, the Khasis, were the great warriors, we were the plunderers of the plains," he exclaims. "But look at us now. We don't feel like heroes any more. Just as the British destroyed our capacity to make iron, so they made us children again, helpless to defend ourselves.

"What are we to do when the police take in our young people and beat them so badly about the hands and fingers that they have to eat their food off the prison floor, like lapping dogs, their broken hands worse than useless?

"I rejoice that there are guerilla groups training in the hills. I want there to be violence – it is better to be violent than cowardly. There must be blood and deaths, I want the non-tribals kicked out, they're exploiting the Khasi people, who are very simple. They are totally destroying our way of life."

Desmond, handing round the *kwai* to calm us down, talks of the futility, in today's circumstances, of the officially praised escapist verse of the old school of Khasi poets. "You can't romanticise the beautiful hills and lakes, you can't talk only of rainbows, sanity, the good things of life – you have to talk about the bloodshed, the pain, the people who won't walk any more, the people with secret scars. As Neruda says in his famous poem about the Spanish Civil War, 'Come and see the blood in the streets, come and see the blood in the streets!'"

Outright Khasi separatism seems not to be Kynpham's goal. Only the most militant activists appear to think that cutting adrift from India is the solution to Khasiland's problems. What most seem to want are Khasi-mediated economic, social and political structures that are strong enough to defend and advance their embattled culture.

One such agency, the Seng Khasi (Khasi Association), has long been in place. It sprang out of a major cultural revival that erupted at the turn of the century and represented, for the first time, a coherent and purposeful challenge to the influence of Christianity and the missionaries' sway over intellectual and cultural affairs. Still active nearly a century later, the Seng Khasi · exists to promote the indigenous faith and culture and to combat the newer religion's 'alien' cultural forms.

Some of the movement's leading writers, notably Rabon Singh and Radhon Singh Berry, were disenchanted Christians who had abandoned the faith. The former mission teacher Rabon Singh, who complains in one poem that thanks to the Christian taboo on alcohol he cannot drink "even a bottle of rice beer/To wish one another good health", renounced Christianity soon after he had been deputed to accompany the Welsh MP Sir J. Herbert Roberts and entourage on a tour of the Hills. The patronising and dismissive attitudes expressed towards Khasi culture by visitors and missionaries alike disgusted him.

But even the non- or indeed anti-Christians of the Seng Khasi will readily acknowledge the positive aspects of the missionaries' presence among them. Kynpham, for instance, describes Thomas Jones as "both a bane and a boon. We all revere him not as a saint but as the father of Khasi alphabets, the man who gave us our written word.

"If Thomas Jones and the Welsh missionaries had not come, we might have been totally influenced by the Bengali culture. He kept our language alive, otherwise we would have ended up reading and writing in Bengali, or perhaps in English only."

The road south to Cherra is almost deserted, a telling indicator of the steady decline of what was once an important regional centre.

We pass through the village of Mylliem which is full of blacksmiths, hammering sweatily in the smoke of their thatched four-poster shelters; the air, acrid with coal fumes, is sweetly percussive with the tippety tap of iron on iron. It's a scene that seems hardly to have changed in the century and a half since Hooker was in the Hills. He too found "the tinkling sound of the hammers from the distant forges on all sides . . . singularly musical and pleasing; they fell on the ear like 'bells upon the wind', each ring being exquisitely melodious, and chiming harmoniously with the others."

A little over half way there, the road begins its perilous glide along the rim of the great Cherra gorge that yawns dramatically to our left, intersected here and there by lesser gorges, and echoed by wave on wave of parallel gorges, their long crests repeated, like a green Grand Canyon, as far to the east as the eye can see. I am glad that Scott rather than Mohammed is at the wheel. The drop is almost vertical, and the bottom, thousands of feet below us, is invisible.

"Two things are certain when a car goes over the top here," says Desmond. "Death. And the impossibility of recovering the bodies. When a Christian's car goes over, they hold the funeral here on the roadside. They sing a hymn, the minister says a few prayers, then they hurl a wooden cross down into the gorge."

We pull over once or twice to take in the view and to savour, in the traffic-free silence, the honeyed breeze wafting up to us from the oceanic jungle. On the opposite slopes you can just about trace some of the zigzag paths that are the sole means of access to dozens of largely hidden gorge settlements. The odd wisp of smoke twirling from the treetops gives a couple of them away. And we can make out the little tin-roofed Bethels of two or three of the larger villages, perhaps three and a half thousand

134

feet below us. The church is invariably a village's most prominent building.

The approach to Cherra from the mountainous north is as sensational, in its way, as the approach from the southern flatlands – as thrilling as that moment for a child when, after a long journey, the family car breasts the final rise, and there below is the blue and dazzling wonder of the sea. At about the same time as Cherra comes into view, so too, beyond the little hilltop town, does the vast, blue-green expanse of the Bangladesh plain which, if you didn't know better, you'd swear was the Bay of Bengal itself. No doubt there was a time when waves disbanded on the shingle at the bottom of Cherra's towering limestone cliffs, but, in recent millenia, they have been breaking on a swampy coast two hundred humid miles to the south of here. Although, in the rainy season, such is the flooding of Bangladesh that it must look from these heights as if a long-absent tide has made a sudden, devastating return.

Sohra is the Khasi name for the town. It was the approximating Brits who, unable or disinclined to pronounce 'Sohra' as other than 'Sho-ra', tacked the suffix 'poonjee' (capital) onto the word, and presided over 'Sho-ra Poonjee''s gradual mutation into Cherrapunji or, familiarly, Cherra.

Although famous as the wettest place in the world, Cherra, in the pleasant 'winter' months, is so dry that water shortages, if not actual drought, are a serious problem. The Cherra tableland is criss-crossed with shallow water courses, and its infertile cover is so sandy that any rainfall is rapidly channelled away into the ravines that surround it on almost every side. Mud, in Cherra, is never seen.

On the edge of town, we pull up briefly in the lee of the Rama Krishna Mission, whose long red roof with its huge white letters dominates the northern approach. Kypham leads us down a rubbly bank to look at some box-cromlechs, so compact that they are almost lost in the shin-high grass. Khasi cromlechs come in many shapes and sizes, and are found, with standing stones, almost everywhere – on hilltops and in forests, jutting out of the roadside tarmac, dotted around the campus of the university. These box-cromlechs, not much more than a cubic

135

foot in volume, and clustered rather unusually in a kind of cemetery, are apparently the smallest in the Hills.

Orthodox Khasis continue to dispose of their dead according to the ancient rituals which, if followed to the letter, are highly elaborate.

Following the sacrifice of goats and chickens, and the divinatory breaking of eggs, the body is placed on a pyre of logs, and four arrows are fired – north, south, east, west – to frighten away the demons that are believed to throng a funeral, bent on hindering the deceased's spirit from joining the ancestors. As the flames consume the corpse, family and friends gather round to throw *kwai* onto the fire, chanting *"Khublei khie leit bam kwai sha iing u Blei ho"* ("Goodbye, go and eat *kwai* in the House of God"). When the ashes are cold, the uncalcined bones are gathered into an earthenware vessel and kept in the home for at least a year, after which they are placed, with sacrificial offerings, under a small, round-stone cromlech known as the *mawshieng* (family stone).

A second ceremony follows, perhaps long afterwards, when the family is able to afford it. The bones are transferred, amid much rejoicing, dancing and animal sacrifice, from the family cromlech to the *mawbah*, the cromlech of the dead person's natal clan. These celebrations can last up to nine days. An important feature of both the first and second interment is the placing of food and drink on top or in front of the cromlech, to refresh the deceased on his or her long journey home to the nine Khasi clans in Heaven. It is only when the bones are deposited in the clan cromlech with all due ceremony that the dead person's spirit will cease its restless wandering of the Hills, and is considered to be at rest with the forbears.

Failure to perform the obsequies in the appointed manner is deemed an affront to the ancestors. It is believed that in such cases the spirits of the dead roam the Hills and haunt their relations, plaguing them with endless misfortunes.

Skirting the town itself, and just before Nongsawlia, the district that the missionaries made the nerve-centre of their activities, we come on two stone funeral *ghats*, as big as houses, in the middle of a shallow river. Each was built specifically to cremate a Syiem (chief) of Cherra. These state ceremonials, attended by upwards of 15,000 people, were of such intricacy and expense that often years would elapse – no less than 33 years in one case – between a chief's death and his funeral. Until the time was right for his funeral, the dead chief would be kept in a hollowed-out tree trunk, his body preserved from decay by a process of pickling in liquor and lime juice. An earlier method of preserving corpses, particularly during the rainy season when it's all but impossible to light a fire outdoors, was to embalm them in honey. Natives of Cherra, who did a lively trade in honey, tended to discourage any talk of this technique, for fear that it would undermine confidence in their product. But there were many who, for obvious reasons, would purchase Cherra honey only in the comb, not in the pot.

Cherrapunji, with its declining population of 6,000, seems much more than 35 miles away from overcrowded Shillong. The climate, even in the dry season, feels different, as the southerlies, blowing up from Bangladesh, keep it a degree or two warmer. With hardly any traffic, it is peaceful here and the air – as we reach our hostel on the eastern edge of the Cherra plateau – is sweetly spicy with jungle bloom from the ravine below, and the tang of mimosa. It seems fitting, somehow, that the Shillong newspapers should always arrive in Cherra a day late.

42

At Dain Thlen Falls west of Cherra, a few yards from the ledge over which the river plunges into a narrow, jungly gorge, there's an eerie squiggle, like a fossilised snake, in the otherwise stratiform rock. About twelve feet long and three inches high, it is the mark of the Thlen, the shape-shifting serpent – of orthodox belief and murderous practice – that is propitiated only by human blood.

To the missionaries, and most Western observers, the Khasis' indigenous faith, *Niam Khasi*, amounted to nothing more than aboriginal demon-worship of the crudest kind. They dismissed it out of hand as a religion of despair, and pointed to the Thlen, the demon of demons, as crowning proof of the religion's predatory brutishness.

The Thlen today looks harmless enough. Someone has even built a V-shaped wall a yard or so upstream, to protect its sibilant form from the corrosive currents of the river in spate. But rocks and stones, bounced violently downstream by the monsoon waters, have battered a gaping hole in the apex of the 'V', exposing the friable serpent – already a shadow of its former self – to possible terminal erosion over the next few summers.

As its rocky profile has worn steadily away, so has its lethal influence retreated from village life. "The Thlen now is a metaphor," Kynpham told me. An urbane adherent of *Niam Khasi*, Kynpham feels that Westerners, obsessed with the gruesome sideshows of Khasi belief and custom, have wilfully misrepresented the essence of his faith. Nevertheless, the Thlen is a 'metaphor' whose appetites can still splash bloody headlines across the front pages of the local press.

According to the legend, it was from a cave near the falls that the gigantic snake would slither forth to ambush people on their way to market. If they were a party of ten farmers, he would instantly devour five of them and leave the rest unharmed. The only way you could pass safely through his territory was to go alone, because the Thlen had to leave untouched a half of those who passed by.

So many thousands did the Thlen dispatch that the Khasis, fearing for humanity's survival, called on U Suidnoh, an intrepid loner, to do what he could to rid them of the monster.

U Suidnoh went to the Thlen's cave with a herd of goats, and fed them one by one to the voracious serpent. "Come, old friend, come and open your mouth," U Suidnoh would call into the darkness of the cave, "open your mouth wide for a feast of flesh." And when the Thlen glided, jaws agape, to the entrance of his cave, U Suidnoh would fling a huge lump of meat into the serpent's mouth.

U Suidnoh and the Thlen grew daily more intimate. When he was sure of the serpent's confidence, U Suidnoh prepared a furnace and heated a lump of iron until it was red hot. Then he called into the cave, "Come, my friend, it's time for your meat."

And when the serpent appeared, his jaws wide open, U Suidnoh hurled the glowing iron straight down the beast's gullet.

The Thlen writhed in its cave with the violence of an earthquake. When its death struggle was finished, the people came and dragged the serpent's carcase to a rock on the dry riverbed, and there they cut him up. The place has been known ever since as Dain Thlen – 'the cutting of the Thlen'. And the large, clear pools that honeycomb the rock are, it is said, the mortars in which they pestled their spices as they set about cooking and eating the creature.

Every last scrap of the demon had to be eaten: if so much as a sliver were left behind, there'd be substance enough for a Thlen to breed again – endlessly.

The people fed full and made a clean sweep of their monstrous repast – everyone, that is, except an old woman who took a piece of Thlen meat home to Cherra for her son. She forgot to give it to him until it was too late and the dead flesh became once more, in the words of Kynpham's poem, "the monster that sought our blood,/only our blood."

The Thlen took up residence in her house, and could not be got rid of. She and her family became the first of the 'Thlen keepers', a sect feared and shunned throughout the Khasi Hills. The demon, which may take the form of a fish or a cat or a leech as well as a snake, attaches itself to property, and has the power to confer great riches upon its host. But its largesse depends on its being supplied from time to time with Khasi blood, although a hank of hair or piece of clothing may sometimes do to be going on with. The Thlen keepers know when the demon is craving blood because it will strike their family with illness or an accident or sudden poverty.

It is time then to hire a murderer, the *nongshonoh* or 'beater', so called because it is with a club and not with an iron weapon that he must kill his victim, iron having been used against the Thlen by U Suidnoh. The *nongshonoh*, who does not have to be a Khasi, fortifies himself with strong liquor, ritually mixes some turmeric with rice, then goes in search of a suitable victim, always a Khasi. Having stalked his prey, he throws the rice over the wretch to confuse him, then clubs him to death. With a pair of silver scissors, the *nongshonoh* cuts off his victim's eyebrows, earlobes, finger nails, toe nails and lips; he uses a silver lancet to pierce the man's nostrils and decants into a bamboo tube the all-important sample of blood.

Meanwhile, back at the Thlen keeper's house, often at the dead of night, preparations are made to receive the propitiatory offerings. All doors are opened, cloths are spread on the floor of the house, and a brass plate is laid on the ground. On this plate, when the *nongshonoh* arrives, is placed the murderer's bloody haul, then a drum is beaten to call the Thlen from its lair, and, as the demon expands, devouring the spirit of its victim, its keepers implore its blessings and a restoration of their health and prosperity.

By the end of the nineteenth century the British authorities, having conquered *thugee* and *suttee* in 'mainland' India, thought they had put an end to human sacrifice in the Khasi and Jaintia Hills. But the Rev. William Morgan Jenkins, from Taibach near Port Talbot, knew this to be a premature assumption.

He was a missionary at Shangpung in the Jaintia Hills when, in 1896, he found himself defending one of his native teachers against the charge of being a Thlen murderer. The teacher, a Christian, had been arrested after the body of a woman had been discovered on a road over which he had travelled early one morning. She had been horribly mutilated, in typical Thlen murder style, and the villagers were convinced that the teacher had been the culprit. The prosecution seems to have been something of a put-up job; Jenkins, cross-examining various witnesses, managed to expose the implausibility of the prosecution case, and so saved his man from the gallows.

Now, one hundred years later, things are supposed to have changed, and the Thlen has become a metaphor. "Of what?" I asked Kynpham.

"It's a metaphor that images the inner treachery of the Khasis," he said. "This treachery of 'our greedy infested pigs at the top,' as I call our leaders in one of my poems, is our curse. Where they should defend Khasi interests, they sell out every time. The Thlen is not a real serpent, it's an image: our leaders are the serpents."

Cherrapunji, ever since that old woman's blunder with the Thlen take-away, is the most notorious area for Thlen keepers. And Kynpham, a native of Cherra, is a member of one of the main clans identified with the dreaded practice. But he is not, he assured me, a Thlen keeper himself.

"You wouldn't tell me if you were, would you?"

"No," he grinned.

43

There are no hotels in Cherrapunji. Our hostel, the Circuit House, is a lodge for touring government officials who have business to attend to in the southern Hills. It's a grand imperial bungalow, with cavernous rooms and Shanks' plumbing in the attached bathrooms. The garden out front, all clipped verges and neat rosebeds, could be a quotation from somewhere in the English Home Counties were it not for the concrete troughs set in the borders to decant the monsoon deluge. All that can be heard, as we gaze over the grassy emptiness that was once home to the Sylhet Light Infantry, is the wind sighing through the garden's Bilat (meaning British) pines and the distant laughter of children.

The 'In Charge' is an aloof black-maned beauty by the name of Rebecca. Desmond had sent her a few poems and a request for accommodation for our little party. Perhaps because Desmond's father is a government official, and business, anyway, is slack – a policeman and his young family seem to be the only other guests – she lets us have a couple of rooms. We don't see much of Rebecca during our stay. God and her shiny new jeep seem to be her main concerns; she appears to have little interest in poetry and even less, alas, in poets.

Our meals are provided by the cook-cum-*chowkidar* Ranjan Das, a tall, rake-thin Bengali, who takes our orders and a few rupees to purchase the necessary provisions, then reappears at the appointed hour with the promised repast. In theory, at least. We find that the system doesn't always work as planned. What Ranjan brings us, when he brings it, is invariably plentiful and delicious, but he has a couple of pastimes which occasion the odd delay: evidence of one of them we can smell on his breath; the other, which possibly explains his skeletal physique, has resulted in him fathering no fewer than fifteen unsettlingly beautiful daughters.

It being dark by five, we would spend the long evenings chatting over bottles of Black Label beer. One subject of which I was in need of a clearer understanding was the nature of orthodox Khasi religion, which even sympathetic outsiders consistently misconstrue. "You must understand," Kynpham had admonished me in a letter, "that we have our own non-pagan faith and that that faith has nothing to do with either animism or ancestor worship as the missionaries and others routinely claimed."

The missionaries, in fact, were normally much less restrained than this in their contemptuously dismissive characterisations of *Niam Khasi* or, to use its full name, *Ka Niam Tip Briew Tip Blei* (the religion which knows God and humankind). "The Khasi faith, as in the rest of mountainous India, is devil-worship, which, except for Fetishism, is the basest of religions," wrote the Rev. Griffith Hughes in 1890. "There is not a gleam of hope or joy, or comfort in it," declared the Rev. William Morgan Jenkins. "It cries 'give, give, give,' and has nothing to give in return . . . Such is the belief of the people in evil spirits, that they are completely under the influence of the priests, and spend large sums of money in order to secure their favour." The Mission's historian John Hughes Morris, transfixed by accounts of Thlen murders, described the religion of the Hill tribes, in contrast to Hinduism, as "nothing but the crudest superstition" and "a crude form of demonology".

What the missionaries perceived of Khasi religion no doubt reminded them all too vividly of the subterranean beliefs in magic, evil spirits, supernatural forces, witches, soothsayers and *dynion hysbys* that were rife in Wales – and not only among the illiterate – until well into the nineteenth century, despite all the efforts of resurgent Christianity to root them.

The missionaries' ignorance of Khasi beliefs was wilful. In their zealous demonisation of the old religion and everything associated with it they succeeded in overlooking entirely *Niam Khasi's* points of contact with Christian beliefs, an oversight which today's proponents of 'indigenisation' hold responsible, ironically, for retarding the development of Christianity in the longer term. Notwithstanding the missionaries' sweeping excoriations of the old faith, the Khasi people, long impervious to the Hinduism and Islam that surrounded them on all sides, found themselves responding readily to aspects of Christianity that struck curiously familiar chords.

Far from worshipping serpents or demons or a pantheon of deities, orthodox Khasis believe in Providence and they worship – in their hearts and their homes, rather than in churches – one God only. The worship of idols or graven images is specifically forsworn: no one on earth has actually set eyes on U Blei (God), so, they argue, no-one can know what *U Blei* looks like. They are enjoined to obey three simple yet all-embracing commandments: know man, know God, earn righteousness.

They believe that humankind, in its original innocence, was without sin and had direct intercourse with God – heaven and earth being linked to each other by the 'forbidden tree' or 'golden ladder'. But man, in his hubristic interference with the natural order, had severed that link and brought about a catastrophic fall from grace. Suffering humanity had been redeemed, however, by the cockerel's selfless act of intercession.

"It could well be," suggested Kynpham, "that the Khasis were attune to certain similarities between our religion and Christianity. People took to Christianity, more than any other outside religion, because it teaches love and simplicity, and accords well with our instinctively democratic way of life.

"But there are differences too. We don't believe in Hell – Hell was introduced here by the Christians. We believe in Heaven, because we are a celestial race. We believe that whether good or bad, a person will normally go to Heaven. Especially good people may even become angels. But people who are really evil when they die are doomed to roam the earth eternally as evil spirits, and their families will try to propitiate those spirits to protect themselves from evil."

And the claims of ancestor worship?

143

"The Welsh missionaries were misled by our rituals. They observed that whenever a person dies we burn his body, then we collect the bones and place them in a cromlech, and they assumed that this amounted to ancestor worship. But we do not worship the ancestors, we simply respect the dead. Nor do we worship the rooster, as they so often claimed. The rooster – which, after all, is the favourite dish in our feasts – is a mediator only. It was after our people cut down the great tree that we resorted to sacrificing the rooster to look for signs from God as to the outcome of our enterprises."

When the Seng Khasi was formed towards the end of the nineteenth century, one of its leading intellectuals, the former mission teacher Rabon Singh who had renounced Christianity, addressed himself to the codification of Khasi religion. He argued that although *Niam Khasi* was in essence monotheistic it had been contaminated by a tendency to incorporate lesser deities, by rituals to appease evil spirits and by ceremonies to propitiate ancestors. He attempted to systematise Khasi theology and remove such anomalies. Later theologians have suggested that a main reason for the 'corruption' of Khasi religion, and for its being mistaken for mere animism or demon-worship, is that until Christianity arrived in the Hills the Khasis lacked a conception of God as a loving and caring deity with whom one can develop a personal relationship. The very remoteness of the Khasis' 'faceless' God led them, particularly in times of crisis, to the somewhat heretical adoption of demons and spirits as objects of worship and sacrifice. Some have gone so far as to claim that in its unadulterated form Khasi religion is Christianity without Christ and the Bible.

"Christianity," mutters Kynpham shaking his head. "The only way they could tame the Khasis was to introduce Christianity to make us soft. All this business about turning the other cheek . . . We used to be a very strong people who never put up with any nonsense. Always we retaliated, but since we stopped retaliating we have come to our present sorry state.

"Soso Tham said that no one should rejoice that the white man has gone away, because worse is to come in the form of the black man, the Indian. He predicted that the Khasis would end up as house servants of the black man, and it's happening now all the time. They talk to our people as if they are animals. The Indian intention is to draw everyone into the mainsteam. We don't want this. It is monoculture.

"If there are people who won't allow us to live as we want to live, we will not allow them to live in our land."

44

'Slap', as the Khasis call rain, the only 'slap' of my sojourn in the world's wettest place, had drummed all night on the corrugated roof of the Circuit House, but by morning the sandy ground of Cherra was as dry as if the deluge had been the figment of a dream.

The only trace of the night's downpour was a thick mist bundling into clouds in the eastern gorges whose topmost levels hung like long black islands in a spectral sea. Hoping that the sun, which already had us sweating, would soon evaporate the fog, we set off in the Ambassador to have a look at Bangladesh.

We stopped on the way to take in Mawsmai Falls which, at 1,800 feet, are India's biggest. At first there was nothing to be seen at the 'viewpoint' except a huge sump of fog and, perched on its rim, a weather-stained rotunda that declared itself a visitors' centre and restaurant; this was closed, had never in fact been opened, the money to complete its construction having soaked away like Cherrapunji rain.

The development of tourism, which Khasi officialdom thinks of as a desirable 'smokeless industry', is hamstrung not only by the formidable complications of obtaining a 'Restricted Area Permit' but by a range of 'infrastructural desiderata'. There are no hotels outside Shillong; there is only one bank in the entire state that will cash a traveller's cheque, taking at least an hour to do so; the ambitiously designated 'national highways' are clogged with coal trucks and subject to spectacular jams that can last two or three days; the only major airport – outside the state, at Guwahati – is too small for international jetliners; and in Shillong, even without a curfew, there's not a taxi to be had after

145

about 8 p.m.: the only revellers with a satisfying night-life are the pye-dogs that yowl through the city's abandoned streets in lager-loutish packs.

Sooner, no doubt, rather than later the authorities will slot some of these vital missing pieces into the touristic jigsaw and many a tripper-friendly lure besides: interpretation centres at the sacred groves; bloodless simulations of goat sacrifices; Thomas Jones heritage trails for charter-flight parties of *Merched y Wawr*. For the Khasis seem poised to blunder into the same kind of dollar-grabbing, identity-sapping tourism that has nullified 'exotic' cultures all over the world. Perhaps there is such a thing as benign tourism, but few Khasis appear to be alert to the dangers inherent in the American Express model which they seem doomed to pursue with the suicidal gusto of a turkey yearning for Christmas.

I came to think of my daily bucket of cold water in the Prakash as a kind of surety against begging on the city streets. The day they install hot baths and showers to make the hotel ready for big-spending guests, will be the day, regardless of the Khasis' deep aversion to begging, that the hustlers and panhandlers hit the streets of Shillong,

Shortly after our arrival at the observation point, the fog began to clear and Mawsmai Falls, the fourth highest in the world, shouldered into view on the other side of a vast amphitheatrical bowl. Being the dry season, there were no more than two or three streams cascading in a rainbow mist down the pinky-brown, gargantuan cliff that filled the whole of our northern horizon, their thunder all but stolen by the factory-like drone that welled up from millions of cicadas in the forest below.

As the fog rolled eastward down the gorge, we could make out, in the brilliant fizz of jungle greens, the occasional village clearing, each with its dominating red-roofed chapel.

"No roads, no electricity, no police down there," said Desmond, "and as hot as hell, with plenty of tigers drifting up from the plains in the monsoon season. Even the Indian army would have reservations about going in there. But these gorge dwellers are strong – stupendous calves, mighty biceps. Every bag of cement, every sheet of tin for their houses and their churches they have had to carry themselves down these sheer slopes. Sometimes after a day in Sohra they're quite drunk, but you never hear of them falling."

Mawsmai, like most waterfalls in the Khasi Hills, has a tale to tell of a tragic woman's death. Sngi Thiang, which means 'Sweet Sun', was a captivating Cherra beauty who determined to marry her childhood sweetheart. The boy, though handsome, was an orphan, and her unfeeling parents, concerned only with the financial aspects of the match, refused to let her marry him, forcing her instead into an arranged marriage with a rich man. Tyrannised and broken hearted, Sngi Thiang ran to the precipice at Mawsmai and threw herself to the rocky pools below.

A mile further on, we paused to view the gorge from a different angle, just below the level of the road that snakes along its southern side. There, on a bushy ledge, we found a reed hut on stilts, no more than eight feet by four, which was home to a young mother and her three children. They were scouring their gleaming metal pots on a verandah constructed, for easy washing, of widely spaced bamboo slats. Khasi women, no matter how humble and smoke-blackened their surroundings, take pride in shining their cooking utensils until they blaze like silver.

She told us she had come up from the village of Laitiam ('Free from Weeping') at the bottom of the gorge to try to make a better life for herself – it could be as hot as 50 degrees Celsius down there, and was far from healthy. She and her children had taken just a couple of days to build their little hut which would last them until the next monsoon, by which time, she hoped, they'd have found enough work to build themselves something better on the outskirts of Sohra.

The next hairpin bend should have brought us face to face with the plains of Sylhet, but we gazed, as from an aircraft, on a prairie of cloud. Then, suddenly, there was a break in the cover, and we peered down through a tube in the mist to catch a watery green eyeful of Bangladesh.

By the time we reached the Mottrop viewpoint the mist was rapidly dispersing. We parked the car and stepped down to a balustrade on a charred lip of rock from which a languid stream, pecked by scores of lustrous dragon flies, or 'water fuckers' as the Khasis call them, plunged giddily away to a destination lost in thick jungle far below. The noise here was deafening – not of the waterfall but of the cicadas known as *niang bein-bein*, 'the deriding insect'; these black-and-lime-striped ventriloquists have an extraordinary repertoire of mechanical sounds, from a rock-piercing drill to the seamless whine of a jumbo turbine: close your eyes and you could be standing on a building site in the middle of an international airport.

Rearing up in front of us is a blackened free-standing column of limestone, shaped like an upended basket, or *trop* , that has been designed for a Khasi of mythic proportions – in the days, no doubt, when there were giants in these hills.

And beyond the grass-tufted *trop*, for as far south, east and west as the eye can see, stretch the pastel lowlands of Bangladesh. The town of Sylhet and the river Surma are some twenty miles in front of us, lost in the haze, but the smokestacks of the cement works in Chattuck are clearly visible; so too are some darker dabs of green – the wooded 'islands' that stand clear, normally, of the monsoon inundation. Even in the dry season huge swathes of the country lie under shallow inland seas that glare like tarnished copper through the grey distances. The sixty-seven rivers that lattice Bangladesh carry three trillion tons of silt to the ocean every year, a rate of erosion that is increasing annually, thanks to acute deforestation of the rivers' headwaters and the destruction of Bangladesh's own forests by her rapidly expanding population.

"The monsoon takes our topsoil away and gives it to the Bangladeshis," says Kynpham. "It is they who farm the best of our land!"

This is indeed a landscape for giants, vouchsafing to fussy, self-absorbed, modern hurrying man an experience of terrestrial space, of geographical immensity that few people, in whole lifetimes, are privileged to undergo.

The phenomenal rainfall of Cherra, which dismayed even the webfooted Welsh, is explained by the way in which the Khasi mountains erupt violently from the featureless plains, unmediated by a region of precursory foothills. Accustomed to an annual average at home of no more than four or five feet, the missionaries found that even the most sodden place in Wales, Crib Goch in Eryri with its fourteen feet of rain a year, was in an entirely inferior league of dampness to Cherrapunji's forty or fifty feet. In 1974 Cherra's total rainfall was no less than eighty feet.

What happens is that the south-west monsoon, at its height between June and August, blows up the Indian Ocean and across the flood plains of Bengal, swollen with ever-increasing tonnages of moisture. Suddenly, after thousands of miles of smooth, uninterrupted sailing, these bloated monsoon clouds are confronted with a wall of limestone nearly five thousand feet high. Rising in order to cross this barrier, the clouds, rapidly cooling, jettison their load: and rain, the husband of the earth, as the Khasis see it, comes down to lie with his bride.

The Bangladeshis, who have to cope with the issue of this encounter, view things differently. As a Bengali poet once wrote at monsoon time, "The Mother of Bengal is enjoying her shower-bath every day at Cherrapunji".

The Khasis and the Bengalis, the edgiest of neighbours, rarely see eye to eye.

Desmond recalls the old days when Khasi raiding parties used to descend on the Bengalis to ransack their villages and abduct their women. "Any family name with 'Khar' in it, such as Dkhar, or my own name, Kharmawphlang, suggests that sometime in the past that family was married into by a woman they had stolen from the plains. Dkhar is the word we use for a non-Khasi whom we've adopted into our tribe. She is fully integrated and becomes after marriage the first mother of a new Khasi clan."

And Kynpham recalls a time when most of the territory visible to us today belonged to the hillfolk. "South-east of here was the kingdom of Jaintiapur, a region of the Pnars or Jaintia people. They were extremely Hindu, even believing in human sacrifice, but the Rajah of Jaintiapur was in all respects a Pnar."

"Today it's part of Bangladesh," says Desmond. "We even had an outlet to the sea once, but now it's gone. We've lost a vast tract of land to Bangladesh – it has simply been deleted."

Partition in 1947 led to tens of thousands of ethnic Khasis, most of them Pnars, being stranded in what became, at that moment, East Pakistan. Kynpham thinks that perhaps a quarter of all Khasis live now in Bangaladesh. Growing betel nut and *pan*, and fencing off their communities in their own '*Khasipunji*'s, they dream of a return one day to the Khasi mountain fold. They have even established an outpost of the Khasi Jaintia Presbyterian Synod.

Partition also dealt a blow to the Khasi economy, from which it has never fully recovered. Overnight, the whole of Assam lost her usual trade routes to Calcutta and the wider world; it was the Khasis who bore the brunt of this loss, as the new international border cut them adrift from their traditional markets in the plains. There were the farmers of Mawlong, for instance, a village across the ravine immediately to our right: they had grown rich on the cultivation of oranges, but they found themselves abruptly deprived of an outlet for their produce. Conversely, rice, an import from the plains and a staple of the Khasi diet, was suddenly inaccessible to the people of the southern Hills. The price of food rocketed throughout the land, and many died of hunger. As they watched their now unsaleable fruits wither on the vine, the farmers turned in desperation to intensified cultivation of the areca (betel) nut. But it takes an areca ten years to mature, and the poverty, as they waited for their trees to grow, was pitiful.

The Indian Government's much talked-about border fence might do something to stanch the influx of 'economic refugees' but small traders in the immediate vicinity of the frontier, who these days manage to do business across it with few restraints, want the barriers to remain political rather than physical.

Kynpham believes the fence plan has little to do with keeping Bangladeshis out of India. "Delhi wants that fence in order to trap the region's militant outfits and prevent foreign aid from reaching them. That way, they hope to neutralize the hillmen and pave the way for a peaceful settlement of the Hills by Hindus. Far-fetched as it may sound, such a conspiracy unfortunately exists. Recently a letter signed by an official of the BJP spilled out the whole sinister plan. Writing to his bosses in Delhi, he welcomed the planned Hindu colonisation of the Hills and bragged that in places like Shillong the job was almost done."

Not far below us the river Wahrew, having boiled through miles of rocky gorge, sprawls out near the village of Majai to take its ease on the alluvial plain. The Bangladesh border, cutting across the river there, is marked clearly by half a dozen concrete posts standing sentry in the sand. Thomas Jones, say the locals, would no doubt have left his footprints in the sand at Majai as he trudged towards the base of the supernal colossus that he and his delicate bride would have to scale before reaching their journey's end.

As my friends and I wound back towards the plateau, we crossed and recrossed the famous bridle path of David Scott, its flagstones still more or less holding their ground, on which the Joneses would have walked, in driving rain, the last few miles to Cherrapunji.

45

The Khasi word *phareng*, meaning 'white foreigner', came into the language from the trade the Khasis conducted with the Arabs, who tended to refer to all white people as 'Franks'.

And as the Arabs gave the Khasis a word, so the Khasis gave the Arabs something – a fruit.

For centuries oranges have been the main produce of the warm southern slopes of the Khasi Hills. These thin-skinned, small and exceptionally succulent Khasi oranges are considered the finest in India. They proved irresistible, apparently, to the Arabs, whose traders imported them to the markets of Syria. And there, during the Crusades, the 'Franks' discovered them, and, similarly palate-smitten, carried them back to their Christian homelands.

Soon the fruit groves of southern Europe, as far as the hills of Spain, were pendulous with Khasi oranges.

46

There is no sign of "the mother of breakfasts" that Ranjan, the Circuit House cook, had promised us round about midnight when, fuelled by half a bottle of whisky that Desmond had smuggled to him down his Y-fronts, our chef had delivered, almost into our laps, "the mother of all dinners". So I walk out to take a closer look at a monument that certain young Khasis would cheerfully put a bomb under – the memorial to their 'conqueror', David Scott.

This grandiloquent obelisk presides, like some forlorn quotation from Calcutta's South Park Street Cemetery, over a typical clutter of concrete houses, their walls streaked with rust from steel reinforcement rods sticking out at crazy angles from their flat roofs. On some marshy ground nearby there's a flurry of activity, and I can see, getting nearer, that a family group has just completed the slaughter of a cow. The adults and older children, having skinned the animal, are hacking her carcase into marketable chunks; a small girl squeezes the shit from a tangle of intestines before washing them out in a stream.

It has been said that had David Scott exercised his talents in a more prominent theatre of Empire, rather than amid the obscure jungles of the north-east, he would occupy a place in history alongside the likes of Malcolm, Elphinstone and Metcalfe. It is an estimation of Scott's imperial worth shared by various friends and pious contemporaries who persuaded the authorities to erect a permanent memorial to the man – a tribute rarely paid by the Company to one of its servants. Scott's claim to monumental fame is set out in a fulsome inscription – all but the lower lines of which have proved, for once, to be beyond the reach of the collectors of lead inlay:

In Memory of
DAVID SCOTT.
Agent to the Governor General
of the North-East Frontier of Bengal,
and Commissioner of Revenue and Circuit
in the Districts of Assam,
North-Eastern parts of Rungapore, Sheerpore & Sylhet.
Died 20th August 1831
aged 45 years and 3 months.

This monument is erected by order of the
Supreme Government as a public
and lasting record of its consideration
for the personal character of the deceased,
and of its estimation of the emininent services
rendered by him in the
administration of the extensive territory
committed to his charge. By his demise
the Government has been deprived of
a most zealous, able and intelligent servant,
whose loss it deeply laments, while his name
will be held in grateful remembrance
and veneration by the native population
to whom he was justly endeared
by his impartial dispensation of justice,
his kind and conciliatory manners,
and his constant and unwearied endeavours
to promote their happiness
and welfare.

It is as well, perhaps, that when the monument was unveiled the poor bloody 'natives', still smarting from Scott's "constant and unwearied endeavours to promote their happiness", were unable to read this vapouring encomium.

It was Europe's pursuit of black pepper that first drove her merchant adventurers to India. Cochin, Travancore – the names of the distant pepper kingdoms had long made tantalising music in the ears of European traders as they struck deals with the spice traffickers of the Middle East. Then Vasco da Gama's pioneering voyage from Portugal to India at the end of the fifteenth century made it possible, at last, to bypass the middlemen of the Islamic world and sail direct to the fount of the hot black prize. Another name that ensorcelled those adventurers was 'Cossiyah' or 'Kasya', a mysterious mountain fastness where the word for pepper, which grew there in abundance, meant 'the black prince'.

The 'Cossiyahs', as things turned out, were among the last people in the subcontinent to submit to the colonisers' might.

The British became 'neighbours' to the Khasis in 1765 when the East India Company, following the defeat of the Mughal Emperor Shah Alam II, helped themselves to Bengal, Bihar and Orissa. In the process, and with an insouciance typical of the British Empire, they 'absent mindedly' helped themselves to hundreds of square miles in the plains of Sylhet and Assam that belonged – it seems to have escaped their notice – to the Khasi Jaintias. The British were surprised and rather hurt, therefore, when their mountaineer neighbours, armed with bows and arrows, descended on the plains in a murderous fury – which they were wont to do with distressing regularity. It seemed such ungracious behaviour, particularly in the light of British willingness to provide the Khasis with a ready market for their limestone and iron, their honey and wax, their silk, their ivory, their oranges, their – why, had it not been for the neighbourly solicitude of John Company these ingenuous hillmen would have fallen, like lambs to the knife, into the venal clutches of the French and other foreigners. It was high time, no doubt, that these feisty little upstarts were persuaded to show some gratitude.

A British force therefore 'visited' one or two Khasi Jaintia strongholds in the plains "to convince them of their insignificance", and forts were thrown up along the base of the Hills not only to 'contain' the raiders but to keep the interfering French, Greeks and Armenians at bay: the Hills were ripe for the Company's picking, and the last thing the British wanted was any gun-running Parly-voo beating them to it.

The British policy of non-intervention in the Hills was finally abandoned in 1824 when it became apparent that the Burmese, whose army had already occupied Assam and Manipur, were about to invade Bengal. Something had to be done. Enter at this juncture the Scotsman Major David Scott who, as Agent to the Governor-General on the North-East Frontier of Bengal, marched deep into the Jaintia Hills to root out a detachment of Burmese who were heading from Assam in the direction of Sylhet.

His mission accomplished, Scott returned to the Hills soon afterwards, firstly to persuade the Rajah of Jaintia that if he knew what was good for him he'd accept the Company's 'protection' or be treated as an enemy, and secondly to survey the Hills, with a view to constructing a short-cut straight across them. Such a road would transform north-south communications in the region: troops and Company personnel travelling between the Surma and Brahmaputra valleys, instead of having to endure a thirty-day river journey that took them on a 400-mile westerly loop around the Garo Hills, would face a journey of only 125 miles.

David Scott, who had studied under William Carey and others at Fort William College in Calcutta, was a Company man through and through. Unmarried, and considered therefore well-suited to a life on the storm-tossed frontiers of Empire, he returned home not once during his whole career in India.

Work on Scott's first cross-country route, through the Jaintia Hills, was abandoned after three years. It was during the construction of the second, linking Sylhet with Barduar in Assam, that the Anglo-Khasi War broke out – as a result, according to the Brits, of, more or less, an unfortunate misunderstanding. It is not an interpretation of history shared by the Khasis.

Most British accounts, taking their cue from R.B. Pemberton's contemporary *Report on the Eastern Frontier of British India*, suggest that the conflict was occasioned merely by "the false and foolish speech of a Bengalee Chupprassee, who, in a dispute with the Cassyas, . . . had threatened them with his master's [i.e. Scott's] vengeance, and had plainly told them that it entered into his master's plans to subject them to taxation, the same as the inhabitants of the plains."

Perhaps this 'indiscretion' passed some Chupprassee's lips, perhaps it didn't. Either way, the Khasis by now had seen enough of the British to draw their own conclusions about their 'neighbour''s colonising intentions, without being in need of enlightenment from some irascible peon.

Scott had employed a combination of threats, economic blockade, bribes of land in the plains and political chicanery to 'negotiate' a route for his bridle path and free passage along it. One of his more pressageful manoeuvres was to get the heir to the Syiemship of Khadsawphra, whose capital was the strategically important village of Nongkhlaw, replaced by his 'own' contender, the commanding and princely Tirot Singh, whose uncle was the Syiem of Mawmluh, a village near Cherra. Still in his early twenties at the time of his accession in 1826, Tirot Singh proved to be anything but a Company stooge: within less than three years, the Owain Glyndŵr of the Khasis had declared war on his people's oppressor.

The causes of war, in addition to the very real prospect of taxation, were numerous: the annexation of Khasi territory in the plains; the Company's attempts to control trade; the ominous growth of Scott's two power bases, at Cherrapunji in the south and Nongkhlaw in the north, which were closing on the Hills like the bosses of a huge clamp; the imperious behaviour of Scott's men toward the Khasis; and Scott's demand that the Khasi Syiems combine with him against Tirot Singh's greatest ally, Bormanik Syiem, who had pulled off a Twm Siôn Cati-style raid on a party of Company revenue officers.

But what perhaps rankled most with Tirot Singh was the way in which Scott had double-crossed him over his Hima's (or state's) holdings at Barduar, just inside Assam. Scott had offered to cede this purloined territory back to Tirot Singh, on condition that the Company be allowed to build its road through Tirot's Hima of Khadsawphra. Now, according to the Khasi tradition of democracy, this was not a decision that Tirot Singh was at liberty to make: his people would have to determine the matter at a state durbar.

This parliament was a tense, drawn-out affair, and, for the British who witnessed it, an edifying introduction to Khasi oratory.

"Utterly ignorant of the habits and manners of these people," wrote Scott's Assistant, Captain White, in a memoir, "conceive of my astonishment when five or six hundred warriors came bounding along the hills armed with two-handed swords, bows and quivers, and arrayed in the picturesque garb of the Cassyas, resembling the Roman toga . . . A circle having been formed [on a hill at Nongkhlaw]. . ., the Rajah [i.e. the Syiem] proceeded to explain the object of the meeting, and requested the different orators to express their sentiments on the proposition of the British Government. The leading orator, on the part of the opposition, immediately . . . commenced a long harangue in condemnation of the measure, expressed in a continuous flow of language, accompanied with much animation of manner and appropriate gesticulation. This was replied to by an orator of the Rajah's party; and in this manner the ball was kept rolling till evening. I was struck with astonishment at the order and decorum which characterised these debates. No shouts of exultation, or indecent attempts to put down the orator of the opposite party; on the contrary, every speaker was fairly heard out. I have often witnessed the debates in St. Stephen's Chapel but those of the Cassya Parliament appeared to me to be conducted with more dignity of manner . . . At this time, as far as I could understand, the Government appeared to be lodged in a widely extended Aristocracy; but since then, subsequent inquiries have shown that it was of a much more Republican cast, the Rajah, and the leading men, possessing very little control over the people . . . "

Towards evening, David Scott, impatient for a resolution, ordered a dozen bottles of rum to be sent up the hill, a catalyst to debate which he had employed with profit in the neighbouring Garo Hills. But, noted White, "the liquor was returned with a message saying that they would not drink spirits until they had come to the point at issue."

The durbar closed at midnight the following day, and a treaty, couched in English only, was concluded between David

Scott and Tirot Singh. To what extent the Khasis understood the document must remain in doubt, for the interpreter was probably Harry Inglis, the piratical magnate who in due course would engineer the downfall of both Tirot Singh and Thomas Jones; Inglis was hardly the trustiest of brokers. As far as the Khasis were concerned, their Syiem had put his mark to an agreement that the Company, in exchange for permission to construct a road through the Hima of Khadsawphra, would restore Barduar to Tirot's Hima.

Scott's convict navvies began work on the road immediately, but Tirot Singh waited in vain for the restoration of Barduar.

The first offensive of the war, the so-called Nongkhlaw massacre, took all but one of the British completely by surprise. On the morning of 4 April, 1829, Tirot Sing and about five hundred warriors descended on David Scott's bungalow at Nongkhlaw, Tirot and his fellow Syiems having decided at a secret meeting to drive the British from the Hills. But the Agent to the Governor General was not at home, and the Khasis had to deal instead with two young lieutenants, Philip Burlton and Richard Bedingfield, who, exhausted and sick after years spent mapping the Brahmaputra, were convalescing under Scott's roof.

Bedingfield, who had come out of the house unarmed, was asked by the Khasis if the British intended to establish themselves permanently in the Hills. Before he had prevaricated his way through an answer, the enraged mob fell upon him and, after tying his hands behind his back and cutting the tendons of his legs, they riddled him with arrows until his corpse bristled like a porcupine. Then they cut off his head, placed it on a rock, and laid siege to the bungalow. Burlton, who had remained helplessly inside with a guard of sepoys, managed to hold out until the early hours of the following morning when the Khasis set fire to the bungalow. He and about sixty sepoys made a dash towards Guwahati but they were soon overtaken: one of the first to die was Burlton, cut down while attempting to extract an arrow from his wrist. Only ten of the sepoys managed to reach Assam.

On a hillock near the market at Nongkhlaw stands a dilapidated, weed-covered stone pile which is on the verge of being sundered by the roots of a pipal tree. It is a monument, as its now vanished inscription used to proclaim, "Sacred to the memory of Lieutenants Bedingfield and Burlton, Bengal Artillery, who were barbarously murdered by the Cossyas of Nunklow . . ." The monument also honours "H. Beadon, Esq., Assistant Surgeon, who was killed on 25 of May, 1829, whilst nobly avenging their death". There is no mention of the fifty or more sepoys who also lost their lives.

The one Britisher who seems to have been forewarned of the Nongkhlaw massacre was its intended chief victim. Ask a Khasi how David Scott caught wind of the conspiracy, and he'll reply drily *"Wad ia ka briew"* – *cherchez la femme* . . . For it was none other than Tirot Singh's own mother, Ka Ksan, who told the Major that the Syiems had hatched a plot to kill him: David Scott, the Khasis believe, was Ka Ksan's lover. Without warning his compatriots of the mortal danger they were in, Scott slipped away from Nongkhlaw the day before the rising, and made his way to Sylhet. There he raised an army which he sent back into the Hills to put down the insurgents: the Anglo-Khasi war had begun in earnest.

That Tirot Singh's own mother, the *Syiem-sad* ('queen mother') of the kingdom, should have betrayed not only her son but her people as a whole, is a wound that still festers in the Khasi imagination.

"Had David Scott not escaped," Kynpham told me, "I don't think the British would have won the war, because David Scott was the only one among them who knew the lie of our land. The treachery of woman!"

Although Governor General Lord Bentinck in the far metropolis pooh-pooed the war as a mere "bow and arrow insurrection", it is a tribute to Khasi resolve that in spite of suffering atrocities that have shocked military historians ever since, Tirot Singh's forces held out against the British for nearly four years, and it was to be a further six years before the 'pacification' of the Khasis was considered, in 1839, to be complete.

The Khasis fought a guerilla war of ambush and surprise, with frequent raids into the plains. Wet weather suited the

159

Khasis best, as it had the medieval Welsh in their wars against the English: the rains severely hampered the enemy's mobility and rendered useless their flintlock muskets which depended on dry gunpowder. The 'sophisticated' weaponry of the British was no match, in such conditions, for the Khasi bow and arrow.

The British, imposing a trade blockade on the Hills, attempted to starve the Khasis into submission. It was also routine British practice to set fire to Khasi villages, and to seize or destroy all property and livestock, in the expectation that such tactics would frighten neighbouring communities into switching sides. The policy is set forth with disarming candour in a letter written by Scott to George Swinton, Chief Secretary of Government at Fort William: "I considered it proper as the only means of punishment in our power to authorise the destruction of houses in [Mylliem] and the adjoining hamlets, in consequence of the adoption of which measures, a disposition begins to be shown by the lower order of the people to separate from their chiefs and afford their aid towards the discovery of their places of retreat situated in caves among rocks."

But Scott's efforts to divide and rule were only fitfully successful, and the British, despairing of ever forcing the Khasis into a settlement, began to adopt more desperate measures. In 1831 they unleashed on their foe a certain Ensign David Brodie and his column of light irregulars who swept ferociously from one end of the region to the other, beating up and burning village after village.

The university historian Professor Imdad Hussain finds Brodie's report on these operations "a sickening journal of warfare directed against defenceless women and children. It would have been the basis for his indictment by military courts had he not been under the orders of the civilian authorities."

Eventually this naked terrorism began to pay off, and some of the alliances between the Khasi chiefs started to unravel: one by one the Syiems in the southern Hills were compelled to come to terms with the British. The treaties of abject surrender they were obliged to sign make pathetic reading.

Most of the surrendering chieftains were pardoned, but the Government was determined that "the liberty which implies impunity" should not be extended to Tirot Singh. Harry Inglis, by now a captain in the Sylhet Light Infantry, was charged with the job of winding him in.

In January 1833 Inglis negotiated, through a go-between, for Tirot Singh's surrender, on condition that the Syiem's life be spared. The two men subsequently met in person to formalise the arrangement: Tirot Singh solemnised the pledge by licking salt from the blade of a sword, which was his tribe's way of swearing an oath. Inglis also licked salt – then he turned and ordered his soldiers to arrest the rebel.

The Syiem's life was indeed spared, but he spent the rest of his days as a prisoner in Dhaka. Tradition has it that when he was offered his Syiemship back, on strictly British terms, Tirot Singh told his captors: "I would rather die in this prison like a king than sit on the throne like a slave." He died on July 17, 1835.

A lumpenly ugly stone monument to his memory was raised at Mairang in 1954; a happier reminder of Tirot Singh is the state holiday that the Khasis enjoy on the fourth of every April, the date of the Nongkhlaw rising.

A song of lamentation composed by the wife of U Mon, one of Tirot Singh's generals, expresses better than any historical account the hardship and misery of those war years:

> O the anguish I have suffered
> Because of Mon's obsession.
> No more does he care for the family,
> And the world to me is sad and dreary.
> The thatch is a shambles,
> Our clothes are in tatters,
> For the master is away from here.
> Cold the wind that moans
> Around the hut of Mon,
> Furious its moan, rageful its moan
> Through these cracked walls.
> The children cry in fear,
> The women moan in tears.
> Where is there not woe,
> Where is there not wailing?

It's small wonder that David Scott, a corpulent and bibulous workaholic with a heart condition, was so determined to establish a 'sanatarium' in the Hills. He liked nothing better than to "eat the European air" of the Khasi Hills, as he put it, but the salubrious zephyrs of Cherrapunji were not enough in themselves to save him from an early grave.

Although seriously incapacitated by ill health in his last years, he rarely let his ailments interfere with his administrative and military duties, which entailed long, hard journeys on the back of a horse – his bridle path was not intended for wheeled vehicles. The heart disease could cause violent palpitations, and made it difficult sometimes for him to walk. "I fear for the worst," he wrote to George Swinton. "Something of consequence must, I apprehend, have happened to the structure of the heart itself, the motion being now very different from what it was, and the throbbing consisting rather in a general movement of the whole body than in the direct beating of the heart . . . I cannot sleep, I am troubled with frequent sickness at stomach, and am exhausted with the least exertion."

Friends in Calcutta recommended the usual 'cure', a sea journey, but by then Scott was too ill to leave his bed in Cherrapunji. His last words, on August 20, 1831, were: "I wish you, gentlemen, to bear witness to Government that I am no longer able to conduct the affairs of the country."

His doctor, who immediately conducted a post-mortem on the swollen and horribly discoloured body, was astonished, on examining Scott's heart, that his patient had survived for so long. "On attempting to pass my fingers along the aorta," he wrote, "I found it obstructed . . . by a bony substance and on examination found all the valves of the aorta ossified, and the vessel itself almost totally blocked up by a honeycomb-like bony substance . . . "

Scott was buried the same evening on a hillock in Nongsawlia alongside his comrade-in-arms Ensign Brodie who had died of malaria at Nongkhlaw five months earlier. These two harriers of the Khasis, deprived by their early deaths of the satisfaction of seeing Tirot Singh delivered to a jail in Dhaka with only a blanket to cover his nakedness, were the first of many colonial gentlefolk to be buried in the little Anglican burial ground. The cemetery is crowded now and long abandoned to the grasses which sway above the low wall that rings it like a coronet. The rain that drove many a Company wallah to suicide has effaced all but a few of the tombs' inscriptions.

As for Scott's bridle path, you may still stumble on odd stretches of it, a little overgrown sometimes, but, as it curves uphill, solid enough to host a fleeting vision of the fat Major himself, dismounting from his grey mare to relieve her of his weight, then plodding along in her wake, holding fast to her tail with both hands.

47

In spite of Cherra's rain, Thomas Jones, a skilled miller, cooper, wheelwright, stone mason, carpenter and farm worker, addressed himself vigorously to practicalities.

He believed – as William Carey and, indeed, David Scott had believed – that the missionary was under an obligation to combine the work of proselytisation with instruction in agriculture and the mechanical arts. He set out to make himself useful to the Khasis, in order to improve their material lot, and, through demonstrated love, to identify the benefits of good works with those of 'good news'. His commitment to the Khasis' material welfare, in the pursuit of which he showed himself to be far in advance of most mid-nineteenth century missionaries, would eventually bring him into conflict both with his co-workers in the field and the directors in Liverpool.

Just as the iron-forging Celts introduced Europe to most of the basic tools that are in use all over the world today, so this Montgomeryshire Celt, with his new implements and novel methods, began a technological revolution among the Khasis.

He showed them how to use a rip saw to win planks from a tree trunk, instead of hacking at the wood with adzes to fashion just one crude board. The Rev. Duari Ropmay reconstructed the scene in his 1940 history of the Presbyterian church: "When they beheld the missionary's tools, particularly his saw, the people's wonder knew no bounds. They had never in their lives seen such tools. About fifty to a hundred spectators gathered round as he began to saw. 'How can he possibly do it?' they exclaimed. But when he finished, they jumped, danced and shouted in excitement like children."

He furnished them with an almanac which demonstrated how their eight-day week related to the seven-day week of the Europeans, and taught them accounting, so that Khasi traders and porters would be less at the mercy of wily merchants from the plains.

He improved their methods of growing potatoes. He taught them the crafts of blacksmith and mason, showing them how to dress the grey sandstone of the Cherra table-land, and how to build houses with it themselves, instead of employing Bengali bricklayers.

He even – Khasi rumour is persistent, though church histories make few boasts of it – taught them how to distil alcohol. Now what, considering that the very word for 'sin' in Khasi is *pop*, was a Welsh Calvinistic Methodist missionary doing distilling booze and, stranger still, inducting his flock into the diablerie?

One explanation, which seems to confuse brewing with distilling, is that he felt the Khasi brewers of rice-beer were not doing the business they might be doing with the soldiers of the Sylhet Light Infantry. Here indeed was an infinitely porous market: the soldiers and convalescents at Cherrapunji were inclined to boredom, particularly during the rainy season, and drinking, with the smoking of opium and *ganja*, was about their only pastime. David Scott had had occasion to complain about this in a letter to his friend George Swinton: "Captain Broadhurst [the commandant] cannot trust anyone of them without risk of them all getting drunk . . ., the Cossya being hale fellows and having no objection to giving them a glass of grog in the very penetralia of their houses." (The unfortunate Broadhurst was prone himself to occasional sorties in the land of pink elephants, and had to be relieved of his command after forcing one of his men to drink urine.) The missionary, according to this theory, saw that the Khasis would do a brisker trade if they could offer a somewhat tastier and stronger tipple – which he alone had the wizardry to perfect.

Another theory is that Thomas Jones, alarmed at the risks to health of the Khasis' traditional brewing methods, introduced them to the still, and persuaded them to adopt more hygienic techniques of liquor production.

A health motive is also behind what seems to represent, from a Calvinistic Methodist point of view, the most felicitous explanation. In Cherrapunji I met an old man who, as a boy, had met an old man who had told him that Thomas Jones's massive fillip to the booze industry was entirely unintended. Although not trained as a doctor, he would have found himself resorting to rudimentary medical practices to cure simple ailments, often in competition with the local egg-breaker whose divinations were intended to exorcise an invalid's demons. According to my contact's contact, who as a young man had actually known Thomas Jones, people sometimes came to the missionary with festering wounds that had been dressed by some medicine-man with nothing more than mud. What was called for was an efficacious antiseptic, so the resourceful missionary improvised a retort and started distilling alcohol – for strictly medicinal purposes, naturally. It wasn't long, of course, before the Khasis found out that this strangely cold liquid that worked such wonders on the outer man, could also perform hot-heeled somersaults and many a curious turn for the inner.

Like the Celtic saints of old, Thomas Jones soon acquired in the land of his mission an illustrious reputation for wisdom, dedication, inventiveness and a power to work seeming miracles. But unlike the Company sahebs who kept themselves aloof from the natives, this Welsh *phareng* moved cheerfully among them, and quickly earned their affection. "He is like God and can do everything," commented a Khasi observer.

48

The limekilns tucked into a moonscape of white slag at the edge of the Cherra moorland, with clouds of lung-pickling coal smoke gusting from under their thatched canopies, look just as the limekilns of Wales must have looked a century and more ago.

This is no coincidence, for Thomas Jones is remembered still as the man who revolutionised the Khasi lime industry.

Nowhere in India produces better quality limestone than the Khasi Hills. Reputedly 96% pure lime, it has been quarried here since the time of the Mughals. It is rendered into a paste for consumption with *kwai*, but it is as a constituent of cement that it is most in demand. Perhaps in recognition of its importance to the British, who stuck Calcutta together with Khasi lime, cement is known hereabouts as *khyndaw Bilat*, 'British soil'.

Before Thomas Jones arrived in the Hills, the Khasis used wood to burn their limestone or exported it direct to Chattuck and the delta towns of Bengal, where reed-fuelled kilns would take up to fourteen days to oxidise a furnace-full of stone. Today the hills of Cherra, "once rich with deep green camouflage", to quote one of Kynpham's poems, "gape like rat-bitten potatoes", thanks to the manner in which, for centuries, their forests were heedlessly plundered to feed the fires of industry. As the woodland retreated from the plateau and fuel-foraging expeditions had to range further and further afield, smelting iron with charcoal or burning limestone with wood came to be a time-consuming, wasteful business.

What transformed the lime industry was Thomas Jones's recommendation that coal be used in the kilns instead of wood. Coal-mining, fundamental to the industrial revolution that had made Wales the iron-making capital of the world, was in its infancy in the Khasi Hills.

They say that coal was first discovered there in about 1813 or 1814 by some other Jones who was sent by the Government to explore the Sylhet frontier for minerals. But presumably because the British had yet to hatch an excuse for barging into the Khasi Hills, nothing seems to have been done about the find until 1832 when the Anglo-Khasi War looked at last to be going the Government's way. With scarcely disguised glee, a British investigator described the extensive Cherra seam as "of the very finest quality, being largely impregnated with bituminous matter, easily converted into coke, and leaving scarcely any ashes or earthy residue. This supply which may be wrought with the greatest facility . . . might be estimated to meet the demand of ages; but it is ascertained that the mineral exists in all parts of the hills in profuse abundance."

A contributor to the *Asiatic Journal* in 1836 concluded after a visit to the Hills that Cherrapunji had everything – minerals, water- and wind-power, rich food supplies, able-bodied labourers – that might be needed to build "a new Sheffield . . ., as populous and thriving as its English counterpart, in the very heart of hills whose existence has scarcely been thought of . . . " All that seemed to be lacking were a few missionaries to bring religious enlightenment to the "docile, tractable" workforce

It was not until 1840, the year before Thomas Jones's arrival, that Cherra coal began to be mined in earnest – by a man who, with his son-in-law Harry Inglis, was to become the missionary's sworn enemy: the Political Agent to the Khasi Hills, Captain Lister.

The Khasis found that burning lime with coal saved time and money: the changes urged on them by Thomas Jones reduced their costs by a third. It must have struck the Welshman as bitterly ironic, therefore, that the party who profited most from his improvements was not the Khasis who actually owned, quarried and burnt the lime but Harry Inglis who, through various shifty leasehold manoeuvres, came to control every quarry in the southern Hills, and most other productive enterprises as well. Until the 1880s, when the Government broke his company's monopoly, Inglis & Co. made a fortune from lime, there being no competitor in the whole of Bengal: in the 1850s the profit from his lime interests alone was around £100,000 a year.

The best of Cherra's coal was worked out within a hundred years, although miners still dig for the low-grade duff that remains, usually within a few feet of the surface. There's a pastoral quietude to the scrubby downland of the Cherra plateau – a few cows chewing the less than luscious cud, a boy with a silvery cullender scouring the couch-grass for the hairy black caterpillers that Khasis like to boil and eat. But a stroll on one of these ridges, like a stroll round Orme's Head or on the edge of Merthyr, is in fact a journey through a post-industrial landscape: to your left, a pile of stones that was once a small furnace; and here, look – you're about to step on it – a nugget of smelted ore, from the days before the British killed off the Khasi iron industry. Then – bmwff! – there's the muffled crump of an underground explosion, and as you drop down the other side of the rise you see where it came from: a one-man bell-pit burrowed into the side of the hill, with a rough little pyramid of coal-dust piled at its mouth.

This is the stuff they burn the limestone with. Perhaps in Thomas Jones's time they used the newly-discovered high-grade coal in their kilns, but in other respects the procedures seem basically as he established them, and the workers, I imagine, are not much better off than they were in Inglis's exploitative heyday.

In the big quarry near Mawsmai, women as well as men labour for as long as it's light, tapping away with chisels, bars and sledges high up on the cliff-face, or looming through the poisonous smokes below, neck muscles fanning out beneath headstraps as their foreheads strain against the leaden weight of their conical baskets.

There are no machines, so plenty of jobs. But: a stone-breaker at the quarry earns 100 rupees a week (£2), and he will die, if not as the result of an accident then probably of cancer, some 30 years sooner than most other Khasis, at the age of about 40.

49

The nugget of Khasi iron that I keep in a matchbox makes me think of a mermaid. For according to legend it was a woman descended from a mermaid who introduced the Khasis to the art of smelting iron. It made them rich.

Of the mermaid herself little is known. She is thought to have come to the Jaintia Hills from somewhere beyond the Kopili river, which is in Assam, about thirty miles north-east of the Hills, and an awful long way from the sea. She found a husband in the Hills, and the Jaintia people came to call her and her children Lalu, after the earthen jar in which, to their amazement, she was able to accommodate herself. She is regarded as the first ancestress of the extensive Diengdoh clan.

The mermaid's family prospered in the Hills until a civil war broke out, driving them back across the Kopili river. They flourished there for several generations, then a plague fell on the land and wiped out all but one of the Lalus, a woman by the name of Ka Iaw-Iaw. As the sole inheritor of the family's wealth, she was much lusted after, and had to flee from her suitors' avaricous attentions to the Jaintia Hills. At Jowai she married into the family of a *lyngdoh* (priest) who had given her shelter, but the boys from beyond the Kopili came after her. Again she took flight, heading west into the Khasi Hills, until she came to a place called Sohphohkynrum, not far from Nongkrem.

Here she established a village and a market, and built a furnace to smelt iron. Soon she was forging daos and axes, arrowheads and swords, and exporting her wares to the plains; it was the beginning of a long and lucrative Khasi tradition.

The country for miles around Nongkrem, so puzzlingly strewn with thousands of granite boulders as big as houses, is witness to the extent of the iron industry in the central Hills. What geological process, I wondered, could possibly account for such a profusion of monadnocks, with scarcely room between them for a brassica patch or a reed hut? The iron-workers, I learnt, had had as big a hand as nature in the sculpting of this giant's pincushion of a landscape. As they dug out from the slopes the softer, ore-bearing rock, so they removed the 'cement' that bound the harder rocks together: the boulders one by one detached themselves, rolled downhill and crashed to a halt, like megaton marbles, on the levels below.

Huge quantities of pig-iron, in rough spheroid lumps, were carried daily by basket to Assam and the Sylhet plain. The Bengali blacksmiths, who forged it into clamps for the boatbuilding industry, preferred the malleability of Khasi iron to the hardness of British iron. It was decided by the imperialists, therefore, that steps would have to be taken to protect the British market by undercutting the price of the Khasi product.

By the 1850s the Khasis were exporting less than a thousand tons a year. Forty years later British protectionism had succeeded in reducing the Khasi iron industry to little more than a memory, as rusty and inert as the Khasi cannon in the State museum.

50

As Thomas Jones taught the Khasis new mechanical crafts, so they taught him their language.

It wasn't easy, because there was no written language to guide him, but the Welshman proved a fast learner. He hired two young Khasis who, as students in the 1830s of the Baptist Missionary Alexander Lish, could speak a little English, and as he went about his work he would pick up a tool or point to some utensil, name it in English and ask them to provide him with the Khasi equivalent.

"After learning how to pronounce things correctly," he reported to the directors, "I would write them down in alphabetical order, and everything I could gather about the grammar of their language I'd make an ordered note of. I would also write down English sentences with literal translations above." Often he invited the numerous lookers-on at his wonder-working demonstrations to pronounce Khasi words for him, "but sometimes one person's pronunciation differed from that of another, and I would have to work out for myself which was the correct one."

Although within six months he had enough Khasi to hold a conversation and begin preaching in the language, he was hesitant about the texts he was working on, such as a Khasi primer and his translation of the child's catechism *Rhodd Mam* (A Mother's Gift). He had not yet familiarised himself with the various dialects of Khasi – of which today there are eleven – and hoped to arrive at a 'standard' version of the language that would be acceptable to all. "When I have done that," he wrote, "and prepared a Grammar and a Dictionary, I'll be ready to say that I have mastered the language."

Of India's 800 languages, Khasi stands isolated in its mountain fastness as the sole representative of the Mon-Khmer group of languages. It has some tenuous link with the Munda language family of central India, but its closest relatives are to be found to the south-east, in Burma, Laos, Vietnam, Thailand, Kampuchea – and it differs from all its cousins in that it is the only Mon-Khmer language to distinguish its nouns as either masculine or feminine, with feminine nouns greatly predominating. The names of stars and the moon, mountains, stones, plants and fruits are masculine; those of rivers, lakes, places, the sun and all abstract nouns are feminine.

"Their language," opined Hooker, "is disagreeably nasal and guttural . . ." Thomas Oldhams, a visitor with a more sympathetic ear, wrote a long chapter on "The Language and Ethnology of The Khasi" in his *On the Geological Structure of Part of the Khasi Hills* (1854). He found that "the very varied and remarkable intonations of voice used freely by the Khasis, and the unceasing tendency to the juxtaposition and composition of words in order to express complex ideas, render this language a peculiarly expressive one . . . The constant recurrence of half-suppressed, half-uttered chest-tones, and the frequent elevation and depression of the voice, though not unmusical, give a peculiar jerking character to the sounds, and a kind of unfinished or incompleted tone to the words, (somewhat like the sudden stopping of the vibrations of a musical string with the hand)."

A characteristic that must have helped the early missionaries in their understanding of the language was the Khasis' strongly gestural manner of speech. "The Khasis also in common with most half-civilized tribes are excellent pantomimists," noted Oldhams. "The expressive and easy action, with which they accompanied the description of any occurrence, or the relation of any story, has often excited my admiration. In fact, after a very few weeks' residence, I could in a great degree understand their recital of such occurrences, although not a word of the language they used was intelligible."

In contrast to the rushing, unbroken flow of Bengali, Khasi is notably more monosyllabic and onomatopoeic – *miaw* (cat), *slap* (rain), *rkhie* (laugh), *shit* (hot), *hoh* (cough) – though no less musical: if Bengali is like the Brahmaputra in flood, Khasi is like sunlight dancing on the surface of a lake. It is a language, like Welsh, with a wonderfully inventive facility for compound words: the word for 'West', *ka sepngi*, means 'towards the fading day'; 'eternity', *ka bymjiwkut*, is 'the never ending'; 'to ride', *shong kulai*, is 'to sit horse'; 'tobacco', *dumasla*, is 'smoke leaf'; 'fog', *lyoh khyndew*, is 'cloud that comes from earth'. They have many words for particularising the weather – but the word for 'snow', *ior*, used to be unknown to the people of Cherra, where snow has never fallen.

Missionaries are sometimes accused, not without justification, of ignoring or undermining the customs and arts of the lightless heathen they land among: in the Khasi Hills, as elsewhere in the world, 'soldiers of the Cross' derided and proscribed indigenous music, dance, ritual, dress and sport. But in the matter of language – the channel through which light may strike a path to the benighted soul – missionaries have normally shown themselves to be diligent and constructive. The number of unwritten languages in the world is so great that, even at the end of the twentieth century, more grammars of unwritten languages are being compiled by missionaries than by linguists.

The missionaries' care for minority languages was often at odds with the homogenising inclinations of Empire. "Learn the blighters English (or at least Bengali or Hindustani), and bring these recalcitrant oddities more securely under our sway," was, more or less, officialdom's attitude to the baffling array of 'small peoples' the Empire found itself disposing, from Wales to Manipur.

In spite of the failure of the Bengali-script bibles associated with Serampore's earlier missions, most authorities continued to advocate perseverance with the project of reducing the Khasi language to Bengali letters. To Thomas Jones this was folly because, he said, "after years of labour and enormous expense, not one Khasi has been able to read a page of the books that [Alexander Lish] produced . . ." As tenacious as he was inventive, he made up his mind that the Roman script was a more suitable medium for the Khasi language, not only because it had many fewer letters but because the Khasis "regard Bengali letters with superstitious terror, believing beyond the shadow of a doubt that if they try to form a letter they'll be stricken on the spot with blindness, or some fatal disease."

One of the few in Calcutta to support Thomas Jones's controversial experiment was the influential Scottish missionary Dr. Alexander Duff. "I applaud entirely your decision to publish your translations using Roman letters," he wrote. "In an area such as yours, where the natives have no letters whatsoever of their own, to have attempted to use winding, shapeless, costly and flawed letters like the Bengali, rather than the Roman alphabet, which is so clear and shapely . . . is to raise ramparts against the coming of the Truth to the land. No, our aim is constantly to ease rather than hinder the dissemination of true knowledge of all kinds: and one way of doing this is to support everywhere the use of Roman letters, rather than the native alphabets which are associated with all kinds of idol worship."

Not the least contentious aspect of the Jones project was his decision to use Welsh orthography. The Khasi alphabet has undergone several modifications since Thomas Jones's time – his Welsh 'c', for instance, has been replaced by a 'k'. But it is still pronounced much as the alphabet is pronounced in Wales. "We marvel," wrote an anonymous contributor to the Thomas Jones jubilee programme in 1991, "at the scholarship of Thomas Jones who was able to tune in to the peculiar sounds of Khasi and match these with the alphabet, thus rendering the writing of

Khasi more or less phonetic." Although each alphabet has certain sounds that the other lacks – Khasi, for instance, has a Spanish-style 'ñ' – a Welsh speaker would have little difficulty sounding Khasi words, and would feel at home with the Khasi 'ng', the 'w' that performs as a vowel, and the 'y' that is sounded in words such as *mynta* ('now') just as the 'y' in 'Dyfed' or '*cyngor*' is sounded. I doubt, though, that a Khasi would make much headway with Welsh: there is nothing in their language to prepare them for the tender mercies of 'll', 'ch' and 'dd'.

The Khasi alphabet's Welsh flavour caused a degree of strangulated dudgeon among the team-captains of Empire. Sir Charles Eliot, Chief Commissioner of Assam, complained in 1884 that "The Welsh missionaries in the Khasi Hills . . . have unfortunately proceeded on the wrong tack. Not only are all the Khasi religious and educational books printed in Roman character, but the transliteration is so barbarous and uncouth that it requires the reader to learn Welsh in order to know how the words are to be pronounced."

There was division too in the Welsh camp. Some of the directors in Liverpool were hostile to Thomas Jones's handling of written Khasi, and for a while after his death the debate rumbled on. The Rev. William Pryse (1820-1869), who drew on Thomas Jones's research to complete his *Introduction to the Khasi Language*, declared himself against not only the Roman script but, in the longer term, the Khasi language itself. "It is obvious," he wrote in his preface, "that such a small and uninfluential tribe will not be able to retain characters different from those of the larger nations and the plains which surround their hills. Should the Khasia tribe be ever brought under the influence of education, civilization and commercial intercourse, the Bengali character must supplant the Roman at a not very distant day. For the sake of the Khasis that would be very desirable. Nor would it be less desirable for the Bengali language to supplant all the hill dialects of the North-East Frontier."

The English authors of the infamous *Blue Books* on the state of education among Pryse's own "small and uninfluential tribe" would have applauded the good Reverend's sentiments; so, later, might Matthew Arnold who desired, in the name of modern civilisation, "The fusion of all the inhabitants of these [British] islands into one homogeneous, English-speaking whole," and the disappearance, therefore, the sooner the better, of the Welsh language (*On the Study of Celtic Literature*, 1867). The Rev. Pryse, who spent only a few months in the Hills before moving down to Sylhet to establish a mission field on the plains, was harmoniously in accord with the prevailing Establishment antipathy to 'minority cultures'; fortunately for the Khasis, most of his compatriots in the field were not, and they resisted Government pressure and financial incentives to set up Bengali-medium schools.

Early in 1842 Thomas Jones published for use in the mission's three schools his *First Khasi Reader* and *Rhodd Mam*. These, the first publications in the tribe's own language, mark the modest beginnings of Khasi literature.

Where the Bengali alphabet had failed, the Welshman's script began to take root. Its success would lead eventually to the adoption of Roman rather than Bengali letters by the neighbouring Garo, Mizo and Naga peoples who, like the Khasi Jaintias, have come to value their own alphabet as a badge of tribal identity.

More by accident than by design, then, it was *Ka Ktien Sohra* (the speech of Cherra) that established itself as literary touchstone and chief of the Khasi dialects – simply because Cherrapunji happened to be the missionaries' home base in the Hills. The accident is said by linguists to be a happy one, for Cherra, with its famously euphonious dialect, is renowned as the capital of Khasi oratory.

Today, all natives of the Hills speak either Khasi or Pnar (the Jaintia people's 'sister' tongue), and about half of them are able to read and write their own language. But it is a language under stress: since 1973 campaigners have been trying to establish official status for the language, calling on central government to add Khasi to the list of recognised languages in the Eighth Schedule to the Constitution of India. Without such recognition a language has few statutory defences against the depredations suffered by minority languages worldwide including, as in Wales, a steady influx of cocky incomers who don't or won't speak it. English, understood by only a minority of the people, remains the official language of the state of Meghalaya.

Yet Khasi has proved remarkably resilient, partly because it has adapted to change by borrowing unashamedly from other languages. Efforts have been made to popularise compound phrases for certain modern inventions – *ka kor ring sur na jngai* ('a machine draw sound from afar') for 'radio', or *ka lieng suin* ('a boat sky') for 'aeroplane' – but these confections usually failed to catch on: the people were happier with *redjo* and *eroplen*.

Kitab, the word for 'book', a thing unknown to the Khasis since the flood that stole their script away, is a borrowing from Hindi. But when Thomas Jones arrived in the Hills they ceased to think of books as something foreign: he equipped them with what they needed to write their own *kitab*.

51

Even the Khasis had doubts, initially, about the value of a Khasi-centred education, Bengali being the language of commerce in the region. They were quick to realise, however, that the adoption of Roman letters gave them access to another powerful, money-making language.

The children of some of the richer Khasis constantly badgered Thomas Jones for English lessons. "If we could only speak English," they pleaded, "we could earn a living anywhere."

He reasoned that, their mercenary motives notwithstanding, a knowledge of English might well benefit the Mission, "because if it pleases the Lord to change their hearts, some command of the English language would be an excellent qualification for them to become teachers or preachers of the gospel." He ordered a selection of books from the Christian Book Society, and was soon teaching some of the Khasis English.

By 1911 there were more readers and writers of English in the Khasi Hills than anywhere else in Assam. The lack of official status for Khasi means that all students have to take their exams in the supposed *lingua franca*, therefore educated Khasis invariably speak good English, and even those with little schooling may have a useful smattering.

One evening, in the rural 'streets' of lower Cherra, I hailed a taxi crammed with tired miners smelling of earth and rice beer. Astonished, at first, to find a hairy white man squeezing in beside them, one or two of them were soon trying out their English on me, and translating their friends' questions. A man who'd caught a couple of trout asked what sort of fish we had in Wales, and were there tigers in our jungles? And his elderly pal, who was complaining about the trout dripping on his trousers, wanted to know if Bala and Trefecca still existed.

52

In September 1841, as the monsoon began to give way to lighter 'puja showers', Thomas and Anne Jones were able to move out of their cramped quarters in the Lewins' house to a bungalow of their own.

To be based, still, in the military cantonment and identified in Khasi eyes with their conquerors was far from ideal, but at least in their own Mission House the Joneses had more room for conducting their increasingly popular literacy classes. Within a few months three of their students were sufficiently literate for the missionary to consider using them as teachers in the schools he was planning to open.

There can be no doubt that Thomas Jones and other missionaries learned invaluable lessons from the remarkable success of Griffith Jones's Circulating Schools which, over the course of the eighteenth century, made Wales arguably the most literate country in Europe.

There is also the possibility that Griffith Jones's experience suggested to Thomas Jones a model of a more personal kind. For Griffith Jones had himself, as a young man, felt a keen ambition to travel to India as a missionary, but had eventually decided against it, believing that his own benighted countrymen were in greater need of his energies than non-Christians elsewhere. We know that when offered a missionary posting in South Africa

177

Thomas Jones turned it down; it was in India, and only India – he was quite adamant, if not stubborn about it – that he wished to serve. Might he not have felt that now the spiritual condition of the Welsh had been transformed he was relieved of the long-standing imperative to combat heathenism at home, and free at last to take up the international challenge that had presented itself only briefly to the great evangelist of literacy all those years before?

In a letter which sets out the principles on which the work of the Mission would proceed for years to come, he hints at an indebtedness to Griffith Jones's procedures and acknowledges the usefulness to his mission of the programme devised for Welsh Sunday Schools by Thomas Charles, Bala.

"The only plan which appears to me likely to answer a good purpose," he wrote, "is to establish schools in the various villages, to teach the Khasis – children and adults – to read their own language; and to instruct them in the principles of the Christian religion: or in other words, to give them the same kind of instruction as is given in our Sunday Schools at home, and not to introduce any other feature, except what may be necessary to draw the children to the schools, or to train native teachers; and to make use of the natives to teach their fellow-countrymen to read . . . In this way we shall not only bring up the young people in the knowledge of Gospel doctrines, but we shall also teach them to read; and when we shall have translated and printed the Holy Scriptures into their language, we shall have some, at least, in every family, able to read them, and I may add, able to understand them also; and I would regard this as an important step towards their evangelisation."

Having calculated that it would cost Rs 50 to build a simple one-room school, and perhaps Rs 8 a month to pay a teacher, he appealed to friends at home for the necessary funds. Early in 1842 he was able to open his first three schools – in the nearby villages of Mawsmai and Mawmluh, and in Cherrapunji itself.

For the next fifty years the education of the Khasis would be entirely in the hands of Welsh chapel-goers and their missionaries in the field.

53

The oldest surviving school building, though not all of it is the Thomas Jones original, is the one in upper Cherra, a few yards away from the market – where the missionaries used to preach, provocatively, in the shadow of a venerable monolith.

Built of local grey sandstone, it's a solid, purposeful little *bwthyn* that seems still to declare, in spite of a sheet of blue plastic flapping at a window, that it is here to stay. And there's no mistaking the hand of a real craftsman – U Saheb Jones himself? – in the confident curve of the dressed stone wall that borders the street.

But these days it's somebody's home. The school, still run by the Presbyterians, has moved across the road to a building behind the chapel that resembles a dilapidated outhouse on a west Wales farm, sunlight streaming through gaps in its corrugated roof. A storm a few weeks ago had ripped off most of the roof and blown it down into the gorge, the teacher explains, and she's awaiting the completion of repairs.

The kids, aged from about five to eleven, go crazy when they see my camera, whooping, waving, laughing and thumping each other for good posing positions. The teacher calls her thirty gigglers to order behind their long narrow benches for a couple of more formal shots. They find the whole thing hilarious, apart from a tearful tot cowering behind one of the bigger boys – it's the first time he's seen a white man.

The school is typical of hundreds of little tin-shack academies all over the Hills, and, I imagine, not dissimilar in its spartan simplicity – the bare walls, the chanted lessons, the individual writing slates – to the schools established by the first missionaries. Their schools, of which there were about four hundred by the turn of the century, were normally about 20' by 11', with grass roofs and reed-and-daub walls. Built by the villagers themselves, they often doubled as churches.

The Khasis could not, initially, see the point of these schools. They argued that having swallowed their book at the time of the great flood, they already carried inside themselves all the knowledge they could possibly need – what benefit to them was all this book learning? The immediate benefit, replied the missionaries, was sixpence for every child who managed to master the first two pages of Thomas Jones's *First Khasi Reader*. Yes, until about 1849, it was largely through bribery that Khasi boys were taught to read.

There was even greater resistance to the notion of educating girls. But teaching them to knit and sew – of which the Khasis knew nothing until Welsh womanhood arrived among them – was found to be relatively uncontentious. Chatting, as they knitted, about this and that, sooner or later they would find themselves talking about their pretty names, and how beautiful they looked when written down. Gradually the girls too began to read: by about 1904 a Government census was acknowledging that thanks to the work of the Welsh Mission the Khasi Jaintia Hills was the only part of India where female education could be said to exist.

At that time the number of boys at school outnumbered the girls by two to one, but today, as this little school in Cherra shows, the balance has tilted the other way.

As the teacher lines her charges up outside for another picture, it's noticeable, as it often is in other schools, that the girls tend to be more smartly turned out than the boys. Scruffy girls are rare, but the boys – barefoot, sometimes, their trousers well-worn, their shirts a mite grimy – can look a little neglected. The Khasi inclination to favour the female begins at an early age.

54

Meat. In Cherra market there is plenty of meat – hocks of cow, slabs of pig, streamers of gut, oesophagi, brain, liver, tongue and what Desmond calls the shit-pipes, a highly popular dish.

A vegetarian Khasi is as eccentric a number as a teetotal Welsh rugby fan, but Desmond tries to be one.

"Shall I tell you how they slaughter pigs? They get a stick like a broom-handle, wrap a thick, tight wad of cloth round one end, then they ram it down the pig's throat so that it suffocates . . . and therefore no blood is wasted."

A tale is told of the Diko people, a cannibal sub-tribe of the west Khasi Hills.

The first missionary to beat a path to their remote fastness near the Garo Hills was also the first white man they had ever encountered. The Welshman, having been shown to what he took to be the seat of honour in the centre of the village, tried to engage the Diko chief in conversation, but he was distracted by one of the villagers who kept prowling round, unable to take his eyes off him.

"Why is that man staring at me?" asked the missionary.

"Because," said the chief, "he is the food inspector."

55

In addition to the friendship of the Lewins, Thomas Jones also enjoyed the lively company of Lieut. Henry Yule (1820-1889), a witty young Scotsman who would later become famous as Sir Henry Yule the geographer.

Yule was also a poet (sometimes in Scots), an artist and fine draftsman, a keen observer of social and political affairs and a champion of philanthropic causes. He is probably best remembered as the author of *Hobson Jobson* (1886), a richly entertaining glossary of Anglo-Indian words and phrases culled from books, diaries, letters and his own experience of India. Yule reminds us of the scores of words – loot, thug, jodhpur, veranda, sandals, shampoo, dungarees, dinghy, mufti, curry, bungalow, khaki, shufty, pyjamas, shawl, pukka, gymkhana, juggernaut – that have crept into English from the Indian languages, or colonialist mishearings of those languages. The expression chosen for the book's title, meaning any kind of native festivity, is itself a frivolous re-rendering of the Shia Muslims' harrowing cry *"Ya Hussein, Ya Hassan!"*

Young Henry, whose father was an East India Company man, had passed from Chatham to the Bengal Engineers; his first posting in India was to the Khasi Hills where the help he gave

181

Thomas Jones's embryonic mission included financial support of some boys in the Cherra school, and companionship on the odd foray into the interior.

At the beginning of November, 1842 Thomas Jones headed east on an eight-day exploration of the Jaintia Hills with both Lewin and Yule, who was about the only officer at Cherrapunji to have troubled to learn Khasi, Hindi being the *lingua franca* of the predominantly sepoy army. Thomas Jones wanted to investigate the possibilities of opening schools in the region, but the triumvirate was spurned by the War people of the southern Jaintia Hills who had lately suffered the punitive burning of their villages by their new British overlords.

As the Welshman, the Scotsman and the Englishman rode north, their reception seemed to improve. In a letter home the missionary describes how he intervened in the usual market-day revelry of a certain village to deliver a sermon against alcohol.

"I spoke to them on the evils of drunkenness, and urged them to repent and seek forgiveness. They assented to the truth of my remarks, and I succeeded in drawing a large number away from the old woman who sold the drink, and to these I preached the Gospel. Many of them listened attentively . . ., especially one man, who asked anxiously several times if God would pardon his sins. The idea of a full and free pardon appeared too great a thing for him to believe. The next morning a large congregation assembled, and I placed before them simply the principal doctrines of the Gospel. The greater number of the people sat on the ground, and they listened with great seriousness and deep feeling; but when I began to declare to them the plan of salvation through the death of Christ, they suddenly jumped to their feet, as one man, and put their faces as near mine as they could, as if they would meet the words as they fell from my lips. Their tears flowed freely, and they showed their approval of the words spoken much in the same way as would a warm and responsive Welsh congregation."

The Jaintia people seemed ready to trade in the bottle for the bible, but in the absence of the new missionaries he was urging the directors to send him, Thomas Jones was powerless to extend his mission's influence into the interior. Supporters among Cherrapunji's British community such as Lewin and Yule were few, and their commitment was necessarily part-time.

Yule, in any case, would leave the Khasi Hills altogether a few months later, for marriage to his cousin, Anna Marie, and a glittering career as the protégé of Lord Dalhousie charged with the direction of his great scheme for an Indian railway system.

56

"Drink is the curse of Khasia," lamented one J. Herbert Roberts who spent three weeks in the Hills during his 1884-5 World Tour. "The drunkenness here, as everywhere else, impoverishes the drinkers, ruins their health, and reduces their families to hunger and wretchedness . . . Consider for a moment what would be the result if the Christian world were able to remove this curse, and teach man to look on drunkenness as a sin before God."

His compatriots in the Hills, whose devout labours he eulogises in *Ymweliad â Bryniau Khasia*, waged unremitting war against the demon drink, a war that is still being waged – officially, at any rate – by the native inheritors of Yr Hen Gorff's teetotalitarian tradition. Victory in this unequal contest remains as hard to bring into focus as the dark side of the moon.

Of all the strict conditions for church membership – observation of the Sabbath, the absolute refusal of 'pagan' beliefs and practices, a sound grasp of the scriptures, the adoption of a clean and pure way of life – none was more zealously pursued than total abstention from alcohol. These Presbyterians, complained one poor old backslider, had "so many sins!" Their rules and regulations were enough, great Jesus, to turn a man to Unitarianism – or back to the booze.

The church's fundamentalist taboo on alcohol, flying against centuries of Khasi custom, must often have proved counter-productive, rendering doubly and dangerously attractive an activity that had long been an integrated feature of daily life. Too many straight-backed tea-sipping sessions with earnest pillars of the Church could indeed, I found, provoke a devilishly

183

purposeful day's-end thirst that required three or four (rather than the usual two) bottles of Black Label to assuage.

"Consumption of liquor is injurious to health," warned the garish label on the bottle of 'He-Man – Ultra Super Strong Beer" I had sometimes to buy when the booze shop near the Prakash ran out of the more palatable middle-strength beers. A lifetime on "He-Man", would prove, no doubt, to be newtish and brief, but the majority of Indian commercial beers are wholesome and tasty. Unfortunately for most Khasis, they are, at Rs.26 (50p) a bottle, prohibitively expensive. A determined but hard-up drinker who finds that even the traditional rice or millet-beer is out of his pocket's reach is likely to fall prey to the vendor of headbanging *kiadsaw* which is infinitely more injurious to body and mind than "He-Man" or "Volcano".

Kiadsaw is basically rice-beer which has been watered down then re-fermented – with dead rats, snakes and insects, limestone, dry-cell batteries, newspapers . . . anything to give the brew that extra, fatal kick. This illegal mind-rot costs about Rs.50 a barrel to make, and sells at a profit of 300 to 400%, making the booze-sharks among the richest people in the Khasi Hills, with houses and property all over the place.

They say that *kiadsaw* is consumed by possibly a quarter of the population. After two or three years an habitual drinker is likely to start losing his eyesight, and then, soon afterwards, his life – while still, perhaps, in his early twenties. Many Khasis believe that alcohol is the greatest social menace to their nation.

"The first question we ask when someone dies is 'Was it drink that killed him?'" said Kynpham, as we wandered back from Dain Thlen Falls in the brassy light of late afternoon.

I had been swimming in, and drinking from, the deep and clear 'mortar' pools that pock the shallow riverbed near the falls' edge. Things were going well – good interviews and discussions, useful photographs, numinous locations, warm and enriching new friendships: we were tired but happy – Desmond, Kynpham, Scott and I – as we ambled back across the undulating moorland towards the ford, a couple of miles distant, where the track had run out and we'd had to leave the car.

"We shouldn't have left the car unguarded," said Kynpham. "We should have asked Scott to stay by it."

"Have faith, Kynpham, have faith," said Desmond.

I wanted to sample some rice-beer, and we'd been looking out for one of the little booze shops that Desmond said dotted these upland wastes. With no roads and few traces of human habitation, it seemed unpromising territory for a pub, but there, as we rounded the foot of a grassy knoll, was the hostelry we'd been hoping for, a reed and bamboo hut, no more than twelve feet long by eight wide, roofed with blue plastic sheeting and some balding thatch.

For so thinly populated a wilderness, the shop, full to its smoke-twirling doorway with peasants and miners, was doing a lively trade. Desmond handed a few rupees into the warm darkness, and out, within seconds, came a recycled whisky bottle stoppered with a twist of banana leaf, and a request that we drink its contents on the premises, rather than take it away: they had to have the bottle back.

We stood outside, taking swigs in turn from the chip-mouthed bottle, and feasting our eyes on a glorious stand of pandanus palms, turned orangey-green by the setting sun, on the other side of the loudly rushing Dain Thlen stream. The air was cooling now, and the cloudy rice brew, tasting more like saki than beer, slid like velvet fire to the body's core. Among the half dozen customers who drifted in and out were two barefoot young boozers; though they asked somewhat desperately for a drink, they had no money to pay for it, and were turned away.

Slumped comatose against a stack of firewood was another young man. A lumbering black sow snuffled up to him and prodded his cheeks with her wet snout. He began to stir; then, rubbing his face, he sat up and blinked out on a world at whose blurry centre – surely his eyes were playing tricks? – was a large hairy white man. He shook his head vigorously, staggered to his feet and shuffled around me in open-mouthed disbelief.

"What the hell is this?" he muttered (Desmond provided the translation).

"Look at his eyes," he called to the drinkers in the hut. "They're not dark like ours . . . do you reckon he can see with such pale eyes? Do you think they work?"

He lurched back to the woodpile and fell back into a doze.

We drained the bottle and moved on, exchanging a cheery *"Khublei, bah"* (Greetings, brother) with a small boy we met along the way.

Approaching the ford where we'd left the car, we noticed two young men running off on the opposite bank – the same lads, thought Kynpham, we'd seen turned away from the booze shop. Then we saw that a quarter-light had been smashed and the car broken into.

"I knew we should have left Scott with the car," said Kynpham, distressed to find his bag stolen.

Desmond too had lost a bag, and some medicines and tablets. My own bag, with passport, money and – disaster of disasters – all my films and notebooks, was also missing. As I cursed myself to hell and back for the spectacular folly of leaving these irreplaceable things in an unguarded car in the middle of nowhere, Scott reached under the front seat and pulled out . . . Jenkins's shoulder bag, contents intact: he'd managed to stash at least some of our things before leaving the car, and evidently we'd surprised the thieves before they'd had time to make a thorough search.

"After them, boys," said Desmond.

We ran up to a dingy little cowshed on a nearby rise, flushing out the two thieves. They darted into the thick undergrowth of the almost sheer riverbank. There, we felt sure, they'd lie low until sunset, then steal away under cover of dark. We had less than twenty minutes' worth of light to find them and the things they'd stolen which included, in Kynpham's bag, some important papers, his favourite shirt and a treasured muffler that his girlfriend had made for him.

What we wanted was someone positioned on the opposite bank, to look out for movement in the bushes below us. Some peasants wending homeward with their billhooks and daos joined eagerly in the fray, 'spotting' for us from the opposite bank, and raining sticks and stones on the bushes to try to force the thieves to break cover. Two of these workers waded across the river and dived into the undergrowth like a pair of terriers.

Just as the last of the afterglow disappeared from the black horizon, and our cause seemed lost, three of the peasants appeared with one of the thieves. Emboldened by nightfall, he'd attempted to sneak back to the cowshed where he and his pal had hidden some of their haul, but the peasants had caught him as he ran from the bushes towards the shed. They'd missed his partner, but he'd given them his name.

"Please be merciful, sir," he said to me in good English. "I have been through college, but I have no job, I have no money."

"Yes, you've spent it all on alcohol," said Kynpham.

The thief, who couldn't have been more than twenty and was shivering with fear, was sent into the cowshed to recover what he'd hidden there in the dry dung – Desmond's leather bag, some of the medicaments, Kynpham's papers; most of his clothes, and the precious muffler, were still unaccounted for.

What were we to do with the wretched lad? The peasants were all for beating him up on the spot.

"They say that he has brought shame on our people by treating a visitor in this way," explained Kynpham. "They are very angry with him."

When Desmond forbade them their rough justice, they argued that we should hand him over to the police, knowing full well, said Desmond, that the beating he'd receive at the police station would be far worse than anything that might be meted out here.

It was decided eventually to hand him over to the District Council, which had law-enforcing powers and usually gave miscreants a fairer hearing than they'd get from the State-controlled police system. We all, including the thief and about five of the peasants, piled into the Ambassador and, with a great clattering of hooks and axes, bounced slowly towards Cherrapunji.

The headman was 'out of station', so we trooped round to the home of his general secretary. He invited us in to his polished front room, full of brass crucifixes and Christian mottoes, and bade all except the culprit sit down, while the kwai was handed round and the relevant particulars noted, and the secretary's wide-eyed children worked up the courage, nudging and giggling among themselves, to offer the bearded *phareng* an orange.

"What do you think they'll do with the guy?" I asked Desmond as we left.

"They'll lock him up overnight, and he'll appear before the District Council sometime tomorrow."

We heard later that his accomplice had been caught, and both had been made to clean Cherra market for a month, with a notice on their backs explaining the reasons for their punishment.

57

Opium they outlawed. Alcohol they anathematised. *Kwai* they frowned on, but tolerated grudgingly. Tobacco, however, was something else.

Most missionaries were inveterate pipe smokers, and heartily encouraged their young pastors in the habit. One evangelist of the briar is well remembered for the initiation homily he routinely delivered to intending ministers.

"This pipe," the old missionary would declare to his Khasi novices, "is the pipe of three important things. It is the pipe of concentration. It is the pipe of meditation. It is the pipe of fellowship. And if you want to be a minister in my church you had better learn to smoke it."

The Presbyterians, whose ministers tend to this day to be mettlesome pipemen, have long been known as 'the smoking church'.

58

Pride of place above the *sêt fawr* in Nongsawlia Mission Compound church is given to a weighty marble plaque (someone stole the original brass one) to the memory of the Rev. William Lewis (1814-1891), Thomas Jones's first missionary co-worker. Like his plaque, Lewis seems to have been a somewhat ponderous stickler, fundamentally uneasy with Jones's emphasis on raising the Khasis' standard of living.

The two had been students together at Bala; Thomas had also been friendly with Lewis's wife, Mary (née Roberts, 1817-1896), with whose family he and other secessionist supporters had lodged during the showdown at Llanfair Caereinion in April 1840. Thomas and Mary were 'friendly', probably, in no more than the platonic sense, although Merfyn Jones suggests in his novel, for reasons of dramatic tension (and somewhat to the raised eyebrows of less imaginative Presbyterians), that there smouldered in Mary a passion for Tom – "the most important person to me on this earth" – that dared not speak its name, except in letters to her confidante in Llanfair.

William Lewis was born in Manchester to parents who had come to the city from Montgomeryshire. In his boyhood, during which he worked in a warehouse and in the clerking department of an engineering firm, he became friendly with another Manchester Welsh lad (and gifted plodder) who was to earn modest renown as the Rev. Dr. John Parry of Bala, first editor of *Y Gwyddoniadur Cymreig*, the encylopaedia whose nine thousand pages make it the longest work ever composed in Welsh. The missionary spirit burned powerfully in both their adolescent breasts, although only William would fulfil a shared ambition to carry the gospel overseas. Seeing the Welsh around them falling into squalorous poverty and irreligious ways, they and their friends set out to redirect their compatriots in Manchester along the paths of grace. In winter William would get up at five in the morning to light the fire in his local chapel's stove, so that the building would be warm for those attending the seven o'clock prayer meeting. And, giving his services free, he started a night school in the chapel gallery to teach young people writing, arithmetic and the rudiments of English grammar; the school also, of course, funnelled fresh recruits into the chapel's Sunday school and congregation. Here was a system he'd put to good use in Khasia.

He attended the Calvinistic Methodists' Coleg y Bala, with his friend Parry, Thomas Jones and James Williams (who would inaugurate the Church's comparatively unsuccessful Mission to

189

Britanny in July, 1842), and in 1841 offered himself to the new society in Liverpool as a missionary candidate.

He married Mary Roberts in June, 1842, the month before they sailed to India. Mary, no less fired by missionary zeal than her husband, and probably the greater intellect, was born in Meidrim, Carmarthenshire, but her father's job as excise officer led the family round half a dozen Welsh towns, including Llanidloes and Llanfair, before they settled, for a while, in Tywyn, Meirionydd. Her Baptist mother, forever talking of "Carey, Marshman and Ward", instilled a missionary fervour in the girl at an early age, and Mary never forgot the impression made on her, aged about ten, by the still young but ailing missionary Evan Evans who came back from South Africa to Llanidloes to die.

Like William in Manchester, Mary also ran a little school, and did much else in Tywyn to serve the Methodist cause. When the time came for her to leave Tywyn with her new husband, "She felt for a moment her spirit faint away inside her," according to the Rev. Griffith Ellis's short biography of William Lewis, "but thinking of the pitiful condition of the pagans, and the love that God showed to his Son, she found the strength to make the sacrifice." Indeed, she and William, no less gravely apprehensive than the Joneses who had preceded them, "made every sacrifice willingly in order to put the Gospel within the grasp of the yellow-skinned pagans of Bryniau Khasia."

They and a third missionary, Dr. Owen Richards (1813-1886), sailed from Liverpool on 16 July, 1842 aboard a ship called the *Malabar*.

Dr. Richards, whose stay in the Khasi Hills was destined by a certain *folie d'amour* to be a brief one, had with him his six-year-old son, Owen Charles, who was the great-grandson of Thomas Charles, Bala. Richards, a Cardiganshire man of reputedly exceptional medical abilities, had married Maria Charles, a grand-daughter of the venerable Methodist patriarch and a sister of the wife of Coleg y Bala's principal, Lewis Edwards; Maria had died in 1836, leaving him with just the one child.

The potential for conflict between Thomas Jones and William Lewis may have been apparent in their student days at Bala. Waiting for Lewis on his arrival in Calcutta on 24 November, 1842 was a letter from Principal Edwards that hints at the danger of a possible rift between them.

"Well, my dear friend," his former teacher writes in English, "you are at last . . . a missionary in India . . ., entering upon your labours with holy zeal, with deep earnestness, with unflinching integrity of purpose and with firm faith in the promise of God. Expect great things, and you will do great things . . . 'Love one another'. I have perfect confidence in you all. But still, I cannot forget that there were quarrels and divisions among the Apostles. Some deference ought to be paid to Jones as the oldest. But should any difference arise, remember that you are Presbyterians, and that all causes should be decided by the majority. It is very well to have this rule in case of necessity, but at the same time I hope it will not be needed, and that you will always be one in your views as well as feelings . . . "

These were prescient remarks. The two young pioneers were to be constantly at odds over the extent to which the Mission should concern itself with the physical well-being of the Khasis. William Lewis, subscribing to the conventional wisdom of the times, believed that a missionary, putting spiritual needs before those of the body, should be first and foremost a preacher and evangelist. Thomas Jones, a 'theologian of liberation' as he would surely be considered today, felt that priority should be given to improving the Khasis' economic and material conditions – the work of converting them to Christianity would develop from such a foundation in due course.

Most of the Mission's directors would have inclined to the Lewis view, but there existed elsewhere a number of missionary societies in which Thomas Jones's socially committed missionary practice would not have been considered eccentric – although how conscious he was of their work is not known. Switzerland's Basel Mission, for instance, was dedicated from its inception in 1815 to the material advancement of the people it sought to convert, a majority of whom, in southern India, came from the most impoverished classes. It established various enterprises to promote the manufacture and sale of commodities such as tiles and textiles, without, apparently, compromising its spiritual integrity.

After a few days in Calcutta, the new missionaries set off for the Hills, spending Christmas on their little country boats in the swampy Bengal plain. On 2 January, 1843 they reached Cherrapunji: Thomas and Ann Jones, alone in the field for eighteen months, had the help at last for which they had urgently petitioned – and a playmate, perhaps, for their new daughter, Anne Jane. The future was looking bright for the fledgeling Mission, but there were dark and baneful days ahead.

59

Relations at first were cordial. A bungalow had been found for the Lewises, and Richards and his son moved in, for the time being, with the Joneses. The newcomers were fortunate to have arrived in Cherra in the dry season. While Anne Jones, pasty and feeble much of the time, tended her baby daughter and read the bible, the others could spend their days outside, enjoying the cool, sunny weather of the Cherra tableland.

Thomas Jones had been feeling despondent about his progress so far. "I am sorry to say," he wrote to the directors after eighteen months in the field, "that I am nowhere near to doing what I wanted and expected to do . . . My wife has been really ill, and there has been no-one to look after her but myself." The monsoon had severely hampered him, and the printer in Calcutta had been late delivering his translation of *Rhodd Mam*. Nevertheless, there had been some achievements.

"I have found out the best way of corresponding and sending messages between this place and Calcutta; I have gained a certain amount of knowledge of the people and their country . . .; [the new missionaries] will be able to take advantage of what I have learned about and written in the language, so that they may learn in a day what it cost me a month of labour to learn; a few teachers have been instructed, and books have been prepared; . . . two schools have been built, and one is under construction; and there are at least two men showing every indication that the truths of the gospel are having a serious effect on their minds."

With three full-time co-workers, Thomas Jones looked forward to a dramatic expansion of the Mission's activities. He led Lewis and Richards on an expedition into the Jaintia Hills, from which they concluded that one of their number should be stationed at Jowai. But thanks to Dr. Richards' brusque summoning back to Wales in March 1844, for misdeeds the Mission's historian J.H. Morris cannot bring himself to name, the Jowai plan was abandoned, and the entire Mission came close to ignominious collapse.

What unCalvinistic capers gave rise to such scandal – with whom, perhaps, and how many, even? Morris says only that the decision to recall Richards and 'dissolve the connection' with him "was fully justified by the evidence presented at the time, and indisputably confirmed by subsequent events" – declining to smirch our imaginations with even a hint of that 'evidence'.

Merfyn Jones, taking a novelist's inventive stab at the truth, suggests in *Ar Fryniau'r Glaw* that Richards got into trouble because he kept "undesirable company" with the military base's drink and dance set. But what seems to have happened is that the thirty-year-old doctor took a lusty shine to Lieutenant Lewin's elder daughter Jane, who could have been no more than fifteen or sixteen at the time: on his declining to marry the girl, there was a violent quarrel between Richards and her outraged father, which spilled over into the wider community.

Morris, for whom the consequences of the affair are easier to contemplate than its causes, found it "painful to record that . . . a great storm, which threatened, indeed, the existence of the Mission, was raised by influential friends of Dr. Richards, not only in Wales but also on the Mission field."

Evidently Lewin, who had been a generous and active patron of the Mission, succeeded in rallying significant local support to his injured side, with the result that "the natives, influenced by European sympathisers, [avoided] all intercourse with the missionaries who remained, and [withdrew] their children from the schools."

For several months, as the disgraced Richards and little Owen Charles sailed homeward, the Presbyterians' mission ship lay becalmed by boycott.

On his arrival in Wales, Richards turned his back entirely on Calvinistic Methodism, set himself up in Bala as a general practitioner, and married a local widow. Owen Charles died young, in 1856; it would be another thirty years before father joined son in the churchyard at Llanycil.

Following Richards's removal from Cherrapunji, Lewin seems in time to have forgiven the offence caused his family, remaining a friend of the Mission to the (not far distant) end of his days. Jane is believed to have been sent to stay for a while with her brother Edward in the Punjab.

In England years later, Jane's cousin T.H. Lewin, the soldier-administrator of what is now Mizoram, fell in love with her, but to no avail. Whatever it was that passed between Jane and Dr. Richards in far away Cherra may account, in part, for her reportedly wistful disposition in after life. An abidingly religious woman, she spent her last days being pushed around Tunbridge Wells in a bath chair, where she died after a fall in 1914. She never married.

60

"The worst feature in the manners of the people, and one likely to be a serious obstacle to the missionary is the laxity of their marriages, indeed divorce is so frequent that their unions can hardly be honoured with the name of marriage." So declared Lieutenant Yule in his "Notes on the Kasia Hills and People".

If the missionaries looked askance at the mating procedures of the natives, the Khasis must have observed with some bemusement the mincing proprieties of European courtship rituals. They had, and still have, their own solemn marital codes, but they remain, even the Christians among them, refreshingly down-to-earth in affairs of the heart.

194

Desmond told me one evening in the Circuit House of "festivals of drinking and freedom" that take place in the northern Hills.

"They drink plenty of rice beer, then the girls and boys pair off and disappear into the jungle for a fuck. The girl reports back the next day on how things went. If she didn't like it too well with this particular guy, she'll have a go with someone else, and so on, until she finds one who does satisfy her."

"What if she gets pregnant by a man who isn't the one she finally settles for?" I asked.

"It doesn't matter," said Desmond, "because there is no possessive attitude towards 'my seed'. And if she doesn't settle for any of the guys, but ends up pregnant, nobody minds, because in Khasi society there is no such thing as illegitimacy."

Dowries and arranged marriages are also alien to Khasi custom. While monogamy tends to be the norm, there are some distinctive variations on the theme. It is traditional among non-Christian Jaintias, for instance, that husband and wife do not live together: he is forever a gentleman caller at his mother-in-law's house. And it used to be the custom in certain areas for a married man to contract an informal relationship with another woman, although this 'stolen wife' could not be from the same village as his original wife. The Khasis' belief in love matches freely entered into is reflected in an old saying: "You don't instruct your children from the waist down, only from the waist up."

There is however one instruction about which there can be no equivocation: when you 'marry', which may mean simply 'move in with', you must choose a partner from outside your own clan. The penalty for breaking this *sang*, or taboo – for Christians and non-Christians alike – is to be ostracised and driven out of the community; *sang*-breakers, when they die, are refused the usual obsequies, and their bones are denied a place in the clan cromlech.

Both partners retain their own names, but, this being a matrilineal society, all children take the family name of the mother. It is still very much the custom that after marriage the man moves into the woman's family home: there are rarely any

195

baby-sitting problems, and when you're ill or old there is always someone to look after you.

If you get on with your mother-in-law and the rest of your wife's family – and there could be ten or twenty of them in a three-bungalow compound – it is an arrangement that works well. But I met many young men who, after a few beers and a promise from me that I would not divulge their names, were relieved to articulate to an outsider an explosive sense of frustration. They are fed up with a social system in which, they feel, the women are automatically favoured and the men are largely disregarded. Any suggestion that, ironically, their discontent might mirror the frustrations felt by many women in patriarchal societies does little to mollify their pain and pent-up rage.

"Western feminists come here and they see our matrilineal society as some kind of paradise," said one tipsy desperado. "But they never ask the men how they feel. I've had enough, I can tell you, of the matrilineal system. My sister got all the attention when I lived at home, and now that I've gone to live with my wife's family it's even worse. I'm just a nobody there. What's to become of me if she chucks me out? I can't go back to my parents' place, because my sister's got married and there's no room for me any more. Where am I to go?

"I'm not saying we should do away with the matrilineal system, but we should certainly do something to change it – so that men don't feel so . . . disposable."

Christianity's institutionalisation of marriage has made divorce a more complicated matter than it was in the old days, when a woman could go through so many changes of husband that her children might well be ignorant of their fathers' names. But divorce is still common and relatively easy. When a couple have decided to split up they simply inform their respective clans, whose elders then meet in the open air and agree forthwith to a dissolution of the marriage.

So impressed were the Jaintias by the number of divorces notched up, generations ago, by a certain Ka Kampatwat that when she died they erected near Sutnga a group of stones to her memory. There were thirty stones in all – a monolith for every husband that, one after another, she restlessly discarded.

61

For nearly three years the Mission was housed on the military station at Saitsohpen. It was not until the summer of 1844 that the missionaries were able to distance themselves, at last, from the swagger and excess of the Sylhet Light Infantry, by establishing an independent Mission Compound beyond the army's pale.

They set themselves up at Nongsawlia, meaning 'red well' – "Ffynnon Goch", as the Welsh sometimes called it among themselves – which was situated in an unconsciously symbolic position midway between the colonisers, at Saitsohpen, and the colonised, in Sohra village.

At the end of 1843, Thomas Jones had obtained permission from the Syiem of Sohra, or Cherra, to build new mission premises on a hillock at Nongsawlia, thanks largely to growing sympathy for the Christian cause from the Syiem's nephew and heir, Bor Singh.

There's not a trace today of the school and two houses that were built under Thomas Jones's direction. A sketch of 1846 shows a cluster of thatched, single-storey buildings, not unlike bungaloid versions of the 'black and white' houses of his native Montgomeryshire. They could almost be prototypes of the ubiquitous 'Assam bungalow' whose tin roofs and wide verandahs are so characteristic of Indian hill stations, but they lack the extended eaves that are normally considered essential deflectors of the monsoon's bluster.

From this unpromising triad of windowed haystacks, the Welsh built up a classical Mission Compound which would become the model for those in Shillong and Jowai, and, in due course, the Bala of north-east India.

The Compound, looking much as it did when the Welsh departed in 1969, is best viewed in its entirety from atop the steep knoll that has served since the 1840s as the Presbyterian

197

cemetery. It is flanked to the north by a huge inlet of the Cherra gorge, the massive wall of its far side streaked by waterfalls as thin, from this distance, as disembodied nerves. Lift your eyes from that puff of cloud drifting vaguely towards Burma hundreds of feet below us, and you'll light on a hefty shoulder of the Cherra tableland spread with long, low, whitewashed buildings: these are the student hostels and lecturers' quarters, the Normal or teachers' training college, and, further 'inland', the secondary school. Across the road from the school, as you turn your gaze gradually southward, are the ample red roofs of the Theological College, the black corrugations of the primary school, the broad frontage of an old missionary's bungalow, and the white bell-tower of the church. Scroll your eyes against the glare beaming from the direction of Bangladesh, and the Bilat pines that flame darkly here and there lend this hillocky backwater a Tuscan feel – a sensation augumented by the Italianate facia of Cherra's Roman Catholic church high on the ridge behind us.

The church in Nongsawlia is older, of course, than that Catholic church, but it is not the missionaries' original. All that remains of the Mission's first church is a patch of reddish rubble, just below the brow of the cemetery hill. No one seems to know precisely when the church was built, but the moment of its destruction can be pinpointed to the minute: 5 p.m. on Saturday, June 12, 1897, when the biggest earthquake in living memory devastated the region.

62

It killed a total of 1,542 people and, as it literally redesigned the area's mountain landscape, reduced to dust and splinters every church, school, hospital and mission house the Welsh had built, both in the Hills and down in Sylhet. Miraculously, as they saw it, none of the Welsh community was killed, but of the 916 Khasi Jaintias who died, 600 were from Cherrapunji and neighbouring villages. Many more died later of hunger and disease.

In mission compounds all over the Hills that Saturday afternoon, the Welsh were taking tea; some, no doubt, were putting the final touches to the sermons they'd be preaching the following morning. Providence, Destiny, Judgement, those bywords of Empire, might have offered themselves as subject matter, for this was Jubilee Year, and in ten days' time, on June 22, there would be rejoicing throughout the Empire as the Great White Queen celebrated her fiftieth year on the imperial throne. The Rev. Robert Evans, the musical farmer's son from Aberffraw who is remembered still as the man who taught the Khasis tonic sol-fa, was at home in his bungalow at Mawphlang, savouring a lull in the monsoon deluge that had drummed on his roof for most of the day. There were no advance tremors to warn of the impending catastrophe.

"This time the danger was everywhere and instantly upon us," he wrote in *Y Ddaeargryn yn Khasia a'i Heffeithiau.* "Quarter of a minute made the biggest change possible to every building in the land; and even the face of the land itself was hugely altered. At the end of this short period, all stone buildings were in ruins, and every wooden house had been twisted and turned, into every imaginable shape, until it was entirely unfit for habitation. Hundreds of thousands of tons of earth were carried away in colossal landslips, falling hundreds of feet with the sound of deafening thunder . . .

"After the first great shake, which continued for some minutes came to an end, we had a short, dreamy respite of about a minute, during which we could look around us, and take in the damage that had been done . . . We thought now the worst was over . . . but very soon the earth started to shake and roar in so fierce a manner that it seemed it would flatten every house that it had not yet fully destroyed. The earth was somewhat like a child having convulsions. It would hurl itself about with indomitable strength, and then quieten down for a short while. It roared with every shake like a wounded beast in tortuous pain; indeed, it was as if all the beasts of the earth were howling together."

Night was beginning to fall, and the sky was clouding over again, but the terrifying antics of the earth's crust were all too visible.

"The surface of the earth was like the surface of the sea in a storm, lifted up by waves, so that no-one could stand on their feet. It would have been bad enough to see these waves coming from one direction, but they were being pushed and shoved at us from all directions . . . And casting our eyes about for a moment over the surrounding country, we'd see the earth torn open to the horizon, like a great curtain in a strong wind; and the highest hills looked as if they were pursuing each other, trying with one surge to tumble over one another."

There were smaller quakes through the night and hundreds of tremors in the weeks that followed. Hillsides that had once been covered with grass or forest were stripped in seconds of soil and vegetation: they looked like vast quarries, and the acres below them resembled crudely ploughed land. The Government despatched a surveyor to assess changes in the landscape: he reported that one mountain had had so many rocks shaken from its summit that it was now many feet lower than it had formerly been; another had been lifted many scores of feet higher than it had stood before, and a lake had formed nearby where previously there had been none. The surveyor's superiors found his observations so bizarre that they sent the presumed incompetent back to the Hills and told him to take his measurements again, but he reported back with the same results.

The Emperor of Japan also sent an expert. This distinguished professor, noting the way in which stone walls had been not simply demolished, but scattered over a distance of several feet, calculated that the earthquake had sent a shock-wave through the Hills that had jerked everything forwards at least ten inches, and then jerked it back ten inches – a cataclysmic whiplash movement which no stone structure could possibly survive.

In material terms, the earthquake was a catastrophe for the Mission: it lost 21 missionaries' houses, 30 chapels, two hospitals, 250 schools and its Theological College. But spiritually, it built as it destroyed, driving hundreds of dismayed and battered Khasis into the arms of the Church.

"I incline strongly to the belief that perfecting His people and saving souls was God's great purpose in this earthquake," wrote the Rev. Robert Evans. "There were in Khasia many who had heard the Gospel and had recognised its truth, but who had not obeyed the call . . . had not heard clearly enough to want to abandon their old faith and their sins, and profess Christ as their Saviour. There was the need to do something big, in order to get them to realise the presence and the sanctity of God. This was done by the earthquake, and many [of these waverers] were fearful in their hearts, until they turned their minds to the Gospel and a life in the service of Christ."

In the months that followed, some two thousand Khasis became Calvinistic Methodists.

The poet Robin Ngangom has written of the "tremendous fear/of the earthshaker/who turns violently in his sleep . . .", but prior to 1897 the Khasis seem to have been relatively unconcerned about the frequent minor shakings that the restless Himalayan massif inflicts on their Hills. Cherra had had two mildly damaging earthquakes in 1851, and Shillong had suffered a couple of shocks in the 1860s. These certainly rattled the Europeans in their stone houses, but the Khasis, in their light and pliable wooden huts, seemed to the missionaries remarkably unperturbed. In the many stories the Khasis told of events that happened three or more generations ago, there appeared to be no recollection of any particularly destructive earthquakes; and the presence, for longer than anyone could remember, of monoliths as high as twelve, fourteen or even twenty-seven feet suggested that there could not have been a really serious earthquake in the Hills for perhaps hundreds of years.

But the quake of '97, which toppled several of these stone giants, violently altered perceptions; as a landmark year by which, for instance, people used to reckon their ages, it dwells like a scar in the Khasi mind. While there may not, indeed, have been anything like it in living memory, there is at least one long-standing Khasi taboo that hints, after all, at some deep collective consciousness of the dangers of earthquakes: the prohibition in Khasi religion against building a house with stone walls on all four sides. Perhaps centuries ago, even before their

201

arrival in these Hills, the Khasis learned from some seismic catastrophe that to surround yourself with stone in earthquake country is to box yourself into a potential tomb.

After the earthquake, the use of bricks and stone in residential buildings was carefully avoided: houses built of planks and reeds daubed with plaster sprang up all over Shillong.

But with an influx of non-tribals and an absence lately of any sharp reminders from mother Earth, the protective reflexes of tribal consciousness are not what they were, at least in the towns: bricks and concrete and killer buildings rule.

63

If the Khasis have escaped major earthquakes in recent years, and find themselves beyond the reach of the floods that annually overwhelm their neighbours, they are long accustomed to murderous landslides.

We were talking at sundown of Ka Likai's story, perched like ants on the edge of the chasm whose mare's-tail waterfall, thundering almost inaudibly into a pool a third of a mile below us, bears the tragic burden of Likai's name. Opposite us, the western side of the gorge was by now a wall of darkness broken only by a pinky wisp of smoke drifting sunward from some hutment buried deep in the jungle.

Ka Likai lived upstream from here, in the village of Rangjyrteh. Her husband, who was a porter, died after carrying a load of iron to Sylhet, leaving her with a baby girl, and no money. So she, like many women, also became a carrier of iron, plying daily between Rangjyrteh and the village of Mawmluh, and leaving her baby in the care of others.

"You should get a man," they told her, "The child needs a father."

So she got herself a man, a man who proved a monster.

Resentful of the love and attention she lavished on her baby, he killed the girl one day when Ka Likai was out carrying iron, chopped up the body and made a curry from the flesh. The head and the bones he threw away, but he forgot to dispose of the fingers.

Ka Likai returned, tired and hungry, to an empty house. Where was her baby – with a neighbour, perhaps, or out with her new father? The smell of the curry set her mouth watering. She would eat, then look for her little one.

The curried pork – or was it chicken? – her husband had left her was delicious. She decided to round off the meal with some *kwai*.

But it wasn't only *kwai* that she found in her *kwai* basket – there were fingers there, the severed fingers of her own sweet child. She ran screaming through the village, brandishing a dao at anyone who tried to stop her. She ran and ran until, as Kynpham's poem says

> ... she reached that bald spot
> from where she threw herself
> into the only thing she knew
> could give her peace.

Yes, we were talking at dusk of Ka Likai, when suddenly from the jungle below us there came a crack like the crack of a mighty branch breaking, then the panicky thumping of an unimaginably huge bag of spuds being spilled.

"A landslide," said Kynpham. "Please look the other way: we never look in the direction of a landslide . . . otherwise, God forbid, a mother or a father might die."

64

Having established themselves at Nongsawlia, the missionaries decided on a rough division of labour. The Lewises, with the help of Anne Jones when her health permitted, would take charge of the schools; Thomas Jones would concentrate on translating the scriptures.

Any Welsh missionary would have been keenly aware of the importance of a bible in the vernacular, not only to the growth of Christianity but to the sustenance of an entire culture. Had it not been for Bishop William Morgan's translation of the bible into Welsh in the sixteenth century, the Reformation in Wales would have foundered, and the Welsh language, bereft of the revitalisation and enhanced status accorded it by Morgan's bible, would doubtless have gone the way of Cornish and Manx.

The example of William Morgan, who undertook his herculean task at Llanrhaeadr-ym-Mochnant, no more than ten miles away from Thomas Jones's birthplace, would not have been lost on the missionary at Cherrapunji as he laboured, like Morgan, far from libraries and centres of learning, to translate the scriptures into the language of the people. And on the river journey to distant Calcutta, where he would stay to see his translations through the press, he must often have thought of William Morgan making a similarly arduous trip to London, to deal there, for months on end, with compositors who knew not a word of the language in which they were printing the holy texts.

To the early missionaries, translating the Bible proved a major distraction from the work of evangelisation, but it was a principle of central importance to Protestant missions that Christians should have a bible in their hands in their own language as soon as humanly possible. Throughout the nineteenth century, it was the Protestants rather than the Catholics who led the field as translators, more than trebling – to about 300 – the number of languages into which the bible had been wholly or partly translated.

When, early in 1842, Thomas Jones inaugurated Khasi literature with the publication of his *First Khasi Reader* and his translation of *Rhodd Mam*, he had already started translating the *New Testament*. And in 1843 he saw through the press nine chapters of Thomas Charles's catechism and doctrinal compendium *Yr Hyfforddwr*. Two years later he compiled the first small collection of hymns.

"As for the hymns," reported Thomas Jones to his directors, "we haven't made a great effort to render them with *cynghanedd* – our concern has been to get them to make good sense, that has been the main thing . . . In a word, there is in them everything necessary to show forth the truths of the gospel in song, and we are as fond of them here as you at home are fond of the hymns of Williams and Watts. Writing hymns in *cynghanedd* is work for future years."

In addition to translations of favourite Welsh hymns the collection included Thomas Jones's own "Ki Lok Jong Nga Ki La Leit Noh" (My friends have gone on before) which the Rev. William Pryse, in his *Introduction to the Khasi Language* (1855), hails as "the best specimen, perhaps, of Khasia poetry" – not that the competition could have been particularly ferocious: at the time of composition, the hymn was also, perhaps, the only specimen of written Khasia poetry. But it has stood the test of time, and is still sung at Khasi funerals. Several other hymns, one with a Cherrapunji flavour, another on the theme of Sabbatarian observance, are said to have been written by Thomas Jones, but to this day confusion abounds as to who wrote what in the Khasi hymnbook.

What is beyond debate, from the profusion of Joneses, Lewises, Robertses, Griffithses, Thomases, Evanses and Williamses listed in its prefatory pages as translators and/or originators, is that the Khasi hymnbook is very much a work of the Welsh. Of more than 500 hymns in the latest edition, published in 1964, only a handful were composed by Khasis.

But the chief literary endeavour of the missionaries was the translation of the bible. In February 1846 Thomas Jones returned from Calcutta, after several months at the Baptist Mission Press, with not only a full translation of *Yr Hyfforddwr* but one thousand copies of the *Gospel of Matthew*, the only book of the *New Testament* he managed to complete before his expulsion from the Church and early death.

The work he began was carried on, with rather less flair and competence, but with dogged determination, by William and Mary Lewis. Looking back over a long life, Mary Lewis wrote in 1893, "The most taxing period for us was the time we spent as missionaries. My dear husband would rise every day between four and five in the morning, and he never went to bed before midnight."

A formidable obstacle to the Lewises, as to any translator, was the Khasi language's dearth of abstract words and phrases suitable for the articulation of religious emotion. They and their successors had to invent many new words and terms, with sometimes incomprehensible results. As William Salesbury was to the early Welsh bible, so to some extent was William Lewis to the Khasi: his translations, though not without merit, were found to be flawed in several respects, and difficult for many readers to understand.

Sickness and exhaustion drove the Lewises back to Wales in 1860, but in spite of recurring ill-health they continued to work on the *New Testament* at their home in Wrecsam – undeterred even when a fire at the printing house in London destroyed all their manuscripts: they simply started again, from scratch. After a decade's labour, the Lewises' *New Testament* was published by the Bible Society in London in 1871, and sent out to the Khasis.

It was as if the lost book of ancient legend had been returned to them. By the time J. Herbert Roberts visited the Hills on his Grand Tour in 1888, the *New Testament*, in a revised edition, was a potent force in the life of the tribe.

"Think of these Khasis, never having seen a book of any kind before, managing to learn to read in a short time, and having the New Testament in their possession!" wrote Roberts in *Ymweliad â Bryniau Khasia*. "How great their respect for the book as they study it, searching in it for the words of eternal life. They carry the Testament around with them in their pockets all the time, so that they can dip into it at any moment of leisure, and pass on its wonderful story to whatever compatriots they encounter. It is the Guide-book of their lives, the fount of all truth to them; you often see many of them sitting round the fire of an evening, reading chapter after chapter, as the *hwyl* mounts. Quote a verse from the New Testament in a debate with a Khasi, and he will argue with you no further, for he will accept the authority of that verse. It is hardly a mystery that Christianity has this kind of hold on them. They are more familiar with the life of Christ than with the life of anyone else, because this is the only life that they have read about: Palestine is the only country they have seen described on paper; they hold in their thoughts a living picture of that land, and take the greatest interest in it. Their conversation is peppered with Biblical references. We would be the last to suggest that the literature of the Khasis should be confined to the Bible only, the best of good books as it is, but we can't be too thankful that it was the Testament that the Khasis' eyes first looked on when their minds awoke from the long sleep of ignorance, and opened their senses to a world of thought of whose like they had never before dreamed."

The missionaries in the field who had corrected the Lewises' *New Testament* were themselves busily translating the *Old Testament*. Of those whose names are recorded as contributing translators – Griffith Hughes, T. Jerman Jones, John Jones, Robert Evans, C.L. Stephens, Hugh Roberts, Griffith Griffiths – no one surpassed in talent and commitment the Rev. Dr. John Roberts, the former quarryman from Corris, who single-handedly translated twenty-three books of the *Old Testament* – over two thirds of the total.

As overseer of the entire project, Roberts had the satisfaction of guiding the finished bible through the press in 1891. Bishop Morgan and company took three quarters of a century to translate the bible into Welsh; even at the end of the nineteenth century, this was still considered by the Bible Society the normal gestation period for a full translation of the bible. But the Welsh in the Khasi Hills had taken only fifty years to do the job. The bible they gave the Khasis, like our own William Morgan version, set a standard of literary excellence for poets and writers for generations to come.

It also clamped a set of blinkers on their heads. Just as Welsh literature was overwhelmingly religious and didactic for two or three hundred years after the translation of the bible, so, for the first forty years, would Khasi literature be almost exclusively Christian and moralistic in character.

65

A day in the life of Thomas Jones would have been structured according to the 'classical' pattern of missionary activity pursued from Nongsawlia's 'classical' Mission Compound: evangelisation, education, translation, medication.

We can imagine him, leaving Anne and little Anne Jane to their slumbers, rising perhaps an hour before dawn and calling their Khasi servant girl to light a coal fire – for warmth in the winter; to keep the rotting dampness at bay during the torrential summer. He might settle down then to the translation of a hymn or a few verses of *Matthew*, ambling to the doorway from time to time in the hope, perhaps, of finding in the mist out there the word he wanted, a mist so thick he could hardly make out the Lewises' bungalow just a few yards away. There might just be time, with Anne out of bed now and boiling the rice for breakfast, to write yet another letter to the directors in Liverpool, urging them to send him, with all speed, a replacement for Dr. Richards whose medical skills, irrespective of the trouble caused by his personal indiscretions, had proved one of the Mission's most persuasive assets.

His chest feels stiff – from an accident some weeks ago – and deep breathing still hurts him. He had been exploring the jungle on his mule, on the look-out for plants he might use to make medicines, when the animal had slipped, dislodging his rider. The fall had broken several of the missionary's ribs.

After breakfast, the Joneses and the Lewises assemble in the schoolroom with the twenty or so Khasis who have been showing a keen interest in Christianity; there are by now, mid 1845, three if not four of them who are close to asking for baptism. This would be a momentous breakthrough, but the temptation must be resisted to push them into too hasty a decision. There are readings in Khasi from Thomas Jones's *New Testament* translations, followed by prayers.

By the time the prayers have finished, the pupils have arrived for their lessons. Anne, pregnant a third time, is once again too poorly to take her classes; her world seems to have narrowed in recent months to little more than her room, her bible, and her God. So Thomas, who had hoped to spend the next few hours on his translations, stands in for her: reading, arithmetic and, to round off the morning, a new hymn.

He eats his lunchtime curry alone. Anne, weak and pallid, and in almost constant pain, is trying to rest on her bed, much to the irritation of Anne Jane, who wants her mother to play with her. Before Thomas can finish his meal, the daughter of U Jonkha appears in the missionary's doorway. Would the Saheb come quickly? Her father is sick, and calling for the white man's medicine – the family think it's his only hope.

Here's a promising change of heart, thinks the missionary, as he steps into the steaming, post-deluge afternoon with the ragged little girl. U Jonkha's family had turned him from their door only a week ago, determined that the old rituals of disembowelling roosters and smashing eggs would cure the patient. Naturally, they had not.

At U Jonkha's house, the missionary finds the patient considerably sicker than when he had last been allowed to see him, but he believes that frequent doses of the potion usually dispensed in such cases should improve the man's condition in a day or two. Before leaving the house, he instructs the entire family in matters of cleanliness and hygiene, advising them to wash U Jonkha and to keep his room and all vessels free from dirt.

The hot, hard work of the afternoon is preaching at Cherra market, in the very shadow of the pagan monoliths. The large flat stone in front of them serves very well as a pulpit. Two or three of those who come regularly to the prayer meetings at the Compound are there waiting for him: together they sing a hymn that, floating out above the hubbub of buying and selling, soon draws a crowd. There are thousands here every market day, many of whom, coming from remote gorge villages, have never seen a white man: they stare at the missionary, intrigued. Many more have never heard a white man speak Khasi, and are astonished not only that Thomas Jones is able to speak their language with ease, but that he seems to understand so many of their ways.

"Is it not the case," he asks his audience, his eyes sweeping intently from one side of the crowd to the other, "Is it not the case that whenever you sacrifice a rooster you say to the being you worship, 'We sacrifice to thee, o spirit, because we have not yet received the book that is to come from the West'? I tell you today that the book has come from the West, and if you come with us and read the book, the darkness you are lost in will melt away, and you will have light, the light of eternal salvation . . ."

And so on for much of the afternoon, with many a wry interjection from sceptical listeners – "Who is this Jesus you speak of? Is he an Englishman? Does he eat *kwai*?" – until the missionary and his supporters conclude with a hymn:

> Enlarge Thou the bounds of Thy kingdom,
>   And gather all them that are Thine;
> Reveal'd by Thine infinite merit
>   To Zion, O Saviour divine!
> May Antichrist's kingdom be riven,
>   O hasten, O hasten the day,
> When Salem's fair city from heaven
>   On earth be established alway.

Back home again, as Mary Lewis entertains little Anne Jane, in order to give her mother a chance to sleep, Thomas spends two hours on the *Matthew* translation. Then three of those who say they are considering baptism – a man and his wife, and a lad of seventeen – come to the Compound for further discussions, in William Lewis's bungalow, with the two missionaries.

The day ends, after so many hours concentrating on the Khasi language, with Thomas and Anne Jones saying their prayers in Welsh, and hoping for a night's sleep untroubled by the tigers that had come up from the gorge last week and ransacked the Compound's livestock shed.

Anne Jones, rarely free from sickness and discomfort during her four years in the Hills, seems never to have recovered fully from the serious illness she suffered in Calcutta. The stress on her already enfeebled body of a monsoon pregnancy, together with the exertions of childbirth, left her lethally exhausted. "For the last six weeks," wrote Thomas Jones, "her torment has been grievous."

The bed in which, on 12 August, 1845, she gave birth to a son was ten days later her deathbed. Weak and feverish, she had grown increasingly delirious. "When unconscious she would cry out incessantly for the 'little man with soft hands'," wrote Griffith Ellis in his biography of William Lewis. "Some minutes before she died she recovered consciousness and declared that she was perfectly at peace and was going to Christ."

She died at 2.30 in the morning of August 22, and was buried at five o'clock that afternoon in "a pleasant glade near the missionary houses". Hers was the first grave in what would become a crowded Presbyterian cemetery.

"Here is something new and strange in the history of our little mission," wrote William Lewis after the funeral. "It is as if the Lord is making us at home, for we have somewhere now to bury our dead."

There could have been no question, I suppose, of casting her adrift among the Anglicans, including David Scott, who were already ploughed under on the hillock across the way.

There is nothing to be seen today either of the 'pleasant glade' or of the grave itself. It is presumed to have been destroyed in the great earthquake, although other pre-earthquake tombs survive. No one knows precisely where on the hill Anne Jones was laid to rest, but a committee has been formed to raise the money to erect a monument, on what they think is the likeliest spot, to the first Welsh woman to work – and die – in the Khasi Hills.

The church below is hemmed in by monuments: to the missionaries who served here, to the Rev. and Mrs. Thomas

Jones, to Thomas Jones on his own. A plan to name the main Sohra-Shillong road after the first missionary fell foul of recent electoral upheavals, but local supporters of the scheme are convinced that the Thomas Jones Memorial Highway is only a government or two away.

67

Thomas Jones, in poor health himself, was left with a small girl and baby son to care for.

His letters home edge close to a debilitating sense of despair: "There's no need for me to describe to you the discomfort of my situation, being left with two small children, and all around me these godless natives." And in another letter he explains how he misses Anne's prayers for him "because I hardly ever left the house without her going to her room to pray for God's protection and grace for me, and such is my sense of loss that I feel a measure of fear and uncertainty in everything I do."

It appears that only ten days or so after Anne's death a doctor on the military base advised a trip to Calcutta for the sake of his health. Given Calcutta's foully insalubrious climate, this seems as whimsical a prescription as a fortnight's breather in Mexico City for a miner with emphysema . . . unless the change of air was urged on him as much for psychological as physical motives. Tormenting himself with blame, perhaps, for choosing a way of life that had inflicted years of pain on his wife and driven her to an early grave, and fearing for his sanity in a place notorious for monsoon suicides, he might have clutched at a month or two in the busy metropolis as his only hope.

Whatever the reasoning, Thomas Jones was sufficiently in need of that change to strike out immediately for Calcutta, leaving his two children in the care of William and Mary Lewis. He'd be gone for the best part of six months, and would never set eyes on his son again.

By the time he arrived in Calcutta, towards the end of September, the monsoon had all but rained itself out. Recuperating steadily, he found the strength in due course to resume his translating and proof-reading tasks, but he had not been long in the capital when news came down from Cherrapunji that his little son had died a few weeks earlier, and been buried alongside his mother.

68

It was the end of February, 1846 before Thomas Jones returned to the Hills. He brought with him not only the published *Hyfforddwr* and *Matthew* translations, but two new missionaries, the Rev. Daniel and Mrs. Ann Jones whose ship, the *Cordelia*, had arrived in Calcutta on January 24.

Daniel Jones, born in 1813, was the son of the popular poet (and prolific parent: seventeen children) Edward Jones (1761-1836) of Maes-y-plwm, Denbighshire, whose abundantly alliterative carols, hymns and elegies were known throughout Wales. Determined from an early age to become a missionary, Daniel was only fifteen when he made a solemn covenant in writing to "devote myself entirely to God". From Coleg y Bala he went to London for a course of training in missionary school work, and was subsequently ordained at Bala. After a spell with the Home Mission at Rossett, near Wrecsam, he married a Miss Ann Evans in July, 1845 and sailed with her to India two months later.

Thomas and the two new Joneses were greeted on their arrival in Cherrapunji with news long awaited by both the Mission's workers in the field and its supporters at home: two Khasis, having steadfastly embraced the faith, would be baptised within a matter of days.

The slough of Despond was at last behind them, and the palace Beautiful surely lay ahead – or so the missionaries might forgivably have imagined.

Such was the violence meted out to the first converts by their enraged families that they were forced to seek shelter in one of the Mission houses. In the decades that followed, many converts, fearing persecution in their own communities, were encouraged by the missionaries to take up permanent residence in an ever-expanding Mission Compound, a practice that fostered a 'mission compound mentality' characterised by the enthusiastic adoption of Welsh ways and wholesale rejection of Khasi traditions.

Two of the four to whom William Lewis had given shelter during Thomas Jones's absence, U Amor and U Rujon, were baptised on Sunday, 8 March, 1846.

"O, what a wonderful service!" wrote Lewis, who conducted the baptism. "To describe my feelings on this remarkable occasion is beyond my ability. Suffice it to say that they were a mixture of great joy and fear, such that I was deprived, in some measure, of any facility of thought or speech. The service passed by more quietly than many had expected, for we had thought news of it would have travelled like lightning from the place. It's true there was a wild and sinister look on the faces of some of those present; and when the water was applied to the converts, the watchers bent their heads, unable to witness the proceedings. The candidates were questioned closely on their command of doctrine; and they gave short but perfectly clear answers, confirming their replies, in many cases, by quoting verses of scripture."

There were those in Wales for whom the cost of the Mission, in terms of money spent, life lost and scandal unleashed, was unacceptably high. "You'd think sometimes," wrote William Lewis in response to his critics' impatient expectations, "that there are people at home who imagine that we can both sow and reap on the selfsame day." In fact the missionaries had achieved more in such circumstances than was usual, because a virgin mission field's first conversions do not normally come for ten or twelve years. They had done well, therefore, to notch up two baptisms after less than five years.

The trickle of converts (a total of 19 by 1849; 158 by 1861) had started to flow. It would grow steadily into a stream (307 by 1866), and then, unstoppably, a flood.

70

"Are you Mr. Jones from Wales?" asked an old lady as I walked down the main street of Mawmluh, a village near Cherra renowned for its huge cement factory and, among Christians, for Ka Nabon, the most famous of the missionaries' converts. We had come to see her memorial.

"Not Jones, exactly," I replied, surprised that rumours of my presence seemed to have preceded me, "but it's near enough and yes, I am from Wales."

"Then will you please tell the wonderful people of Wales," she said, giving me a hug that she wanted conveyed to the rest of the nation, "that we are so grateful for all that they have done for our people. They gave us everything – a written language and literature, schools, hospitals, our Christian religion. The lives of our people would have been so different if the Welsh had never come to our Hills. God bless you all."

I didn't have the heart to tell her that 'the wonderful people of Wales' – most of them, at any rate – had never heard of the Khasi Hills. Nor could I pluck up the courage to confess that as an atheist turned agnostic with vague Buddhist leanings and a history of hangovers, I was far too miserable a sinner to take any credit for the wondrous deeds of my Calvinistic compatriots.

She introduced herself as Mrs. Nesidoh Roy Diengdoh, wife of the late Mr. D. Roy, elder of Mawmluh church. A retired school teacher, she too had been a pupil of Miss Hilda Jones in Shillong. "And I am so pleased and proud," she said, "that next year my son, Mr. Peace Leader Diengdoh of Laitumkhrah, will be leading his choir on a tour of Wales."

After more hugs and handshakes, and a snapshot of Mrs. Diengdoh leaning against our car chewing kwai, we walked back

215

to the beginning of the village and Ka Nabon's grey sandstone monument. The moor here was as dense with megaliths as Carnac in Brittany. Somewhere among them must have been the '*maw mluh*' (salt stone) itself, after which the village was named: at that spot, in the distant past, a truce had been solemnised, in traditional style, by the licking of salt from the blade of a sword, and a stone had been erected as witness to the fact. A few yards away from Nabon's monument, in a shallow bowl of the moorland, was a heap of rocks supporting a hand-painted foundation stone which had been unveiled a year earlier by the Rev. Ednyfed Thomas. This was to be the Ka Nabon memorial school.

Ka Nabon Sawian (?1831-1857) was the first Khasi woman to embrace Christianity, and, as her monument declares, she "endured much persecution" for her faith,

Born in Mawmluh to a family of zealous believers in *Niam Khasi*, Nabon was no more than fifteen or sixteen when, as a pupil in the Cherra school, she decided to become a Christian. In spite of this being a matrilineal society, the education of women was considered at that time a scandalous proposition. Nabon's family, however, raised no objection to her attending Mrs. Lewis's classes, where she learned to read and write both Khasi and English. But when, towards the end of 1847, she declared her intention to convert to Christianity her family objected violently, and locked her in the house, forbidding her to return to Cherra.

She managed to escape and ran, weeping, to Mrs. Lewis at Nongsawlia, hotly pursued by her enraged mother. When her mother caught up with her at the Mission Compound she pulled a knife from the folds of her dress, swearing she'd kill Nabon rather than see her turn to Christianity.

The Lewises took the threat seriously, and consented to Nabon's desperate pleas for shelter from the wrath of her family and friends who had by now gathered, shouting and waving their fists, outside the Mission house.

During the next few weeks Nabon's mother tried all manner of ploys – seductive bribery, violent intimidation, suicide threats – to lure the girl away from Nongsawlia. Her family threatened time and again to kill William Lewis, and on several occasions large, noisy crowds gathered at the Compound in a murderously dangerous mood. But Nabon held steadfastly to her new faith.

Then, one day when Nabon went up to the market in Cherra, she happened to meet her mother who, feigning a conciliatory sweetness, tricked her into going home with her to Mawmluh, "just for one night". But as soon as they arrived at the house, she was locked up and guards were put to watch over her. The family let it be known that they would kill the girl if she attempted to return to the Mission Station. The Lewises, convinced Nabon's murder was imminent, called on Colonel F.G. Lister, David Scott's successor as governor of the Hills, to come to the girl's rescue.

Lister (who, it is worth noting, was the father-in-law of Thomas Jones's arch enemy Harry Inglis) put a native translator of the Cherra court on the job. He sent him to Mawmluh with two of the Christian converts to enquire of Nabon, face to face, whether she wanted to stay in the village or return to the Mission Compound.

A furious mob surrounded the house as soon as the triumvirate arrived, threatening the Lewises and their agents with fearful retribution. And when Nabon opted to return to the Mission Compound, the crowd went berserk, shouting and wailing and rolling in the dust. Nabon's mother fell to the ground, tore her hair, threw dust on her head, ripped her silver earrings through the flesh of her lobes and slashed at herself with a knife.

Then, reported William Lewis later, one of the converts fell to his knees, covered his face with his hands and prayed to the Good Shepherd to strengthen and protect this little lamb of His fold from the cruel wolves that surrounded her.

And to everyone's astonishment, Ka Nabon walked calmly and fearlessly through the frenzied crowd, and made her way from Mawmluh back to the Lewises at Nongsawlia.

The violent persecution, and even murder, of Christian converts continued haphazardly for decades to come, but after the events at Mawmluh, Nabon's family family left her alone, and she was baptised on July 16, 1848. The Khasi Christians –

and their Welsh patrons thousands of miles away – now had a native epic of faith and endurance to match the exemplary tale, told them so often by the missionaries, of Mary Jones and her bible.

71

In spite or perhaps because of his sojourn in Calcutta, Thomas Jones's ill-health rumbled on. Twice in 1846 he went down to Sylhet to escape the harm which, according to the advice of an eminent physician in Sylhet, was being done to his system by the water in Cherrapunji.

The towns of the swampy Surma plain were as hot and humid as Calcutta, but they were found to be curiously fever- and ague-free, although no one could explain why a region that looked as if it should be rampantly malarial should prove to be so healthy.

On his visits to Sylhet the missionary probably stayed at the home of a friend by the name of Stainforth, who was Judge of Sylhet. As the owner of land in the Hills, Judge Stainforth would soon find himself a player in the crisis that was looming for Thomas Jones.

72

It is at this point in the story that Thomas Jones, in contracting his supposedly 'injudicious' second marriage, begins to turn into the subject of legend.

That marriage, together with his involvement in certain commercial activities, would lead to his expulsion from the Church: what, therefore, had been so 'injudicious' about it? A cover-up, or at least a great desire to drop a curtain of forgetfulness over the later career of Thomas Jones, has tended to fuel the propagation of some fruity explanations for the first missionary's fall from official grace.

From Church accounts we gather only that his second bride was considered unsuitably youthful (he was by now thirty-six), and that she was 'a lady called Miss Cattell of Cherra'. Merfyn Jones, with a novelist's licence, makes her out to be a pretty Eurasian girl associated with the military station's 'drink and dance set' – the same frolicsome crew, his fiction suggests, that led the disgraced Dr. Richards astray. Given the prejudice of that era against 'miscegenation', the missionary's 'going native' by marrying a 'half-caste' would doubtless have been sufficient in itself to warrant dismissal. But was his second wife a Eurasian? Was she even, in the European understanding of the term, his wife?

The Khasis like to think she was a Khasi. There is a lively tradition that she was a member of the War sub-tribe from the village of Shella, some fifteen miles south-west of Cherra. And if Cattell, assuming that was her name, doesn't look particularly Khasi, it could, some say, be an anglicisation of 'Ka (the female honorific) Tel'. Others, settling for second-best, concede that perhaps she was only half Khasi, with a native mother and a European father.

The more I enquired, the deeper Miss Cattell floated off into the mists of speculation. Surely there'd be some official documentation, a ledger somewhere with some facts? "The earthquake," they'd shrug, "it destroyed so much."

One of my most generous suppliers of information was the university historian Dr. David Syiemlieh who, every few days, would drop off at the Prakash a bulging carrier bag of books, journals and old government reports. The curfew gave me five or six hours a day to trawl these carefully selected documents for clues. In one of the government papers, Judge A.J.M. Mills's *Report on the Khasi and Jaintia Hills, 1853*, I stumbled on the name of a certain E.B. Cattell, one of several "credible, educated and respectable Englishmen" who had reportedly fallen foul of the nefarious thuggery of Harry Inglis and been driven from the region, in 1853, in circumstances similar to those in which, as we shall see, Thomas Jones was harried from the Hills in 1848.

I wondered if this could be Miss Cattell's father, but, reading on, it became likelier that it was her brother: there was a reference to his having known Cherrapunji from boyhood.

This long and baroquely repetitive report anatomizes just one of more than thirty grossly corrupt cases brought by the Inglis-controlled Cherra court against Inglis's competitors, Messrs. Duncan and Gibson, and their servants, "merely to instil terror, and harass them". Inglis, intent on absolute control of trade in the Hills, set about appropriating a quarry run by Messrs. Duncan and Gibson at Choon Cherra. Cattell, who worked for Duncan and Gibson, was arrested and intimidated by the 'Cherra authorities'; then he was assaulted by Inglis's men who capsized a boat he was travelling in, and pushed him overboard nearly causing him to drown; but the court at Cherra, far from apprehending the perpetrators of this violence, issued warrants for the arrest of Cattell and others, accusing them, fantastically, of assaulting and attempting to drown Inglis's men. Cattell, having refused the court's summons, found his house at Lakadong beseiged by Inglis's armed police, and, fearing for his life, "prudently fled by night without being able to stop to take leave of his family at Cherra."

The report concludes that "if the Government leaves matters as they are they are only maintaining a political agency, with above half a regiment of infantry, with police, for the sole use and profit of one individual [i.e. Inglis] . . ." It was surely with Thomas Jones in mind, as well as Cattell and his similarly terrorised colleagues, that one of the report's contributors envisioned a worsening of the situation in which "Some Englishman will perhaps come here whose English spirits will not brook his property being illegally seized before his eyes; his servants being imprisoned merely because they served him, and being bullied in his own house by a ruffian police . . ., and finally being hunted down like a jackal and irretrievably ruined; [thinking perhaps] that having lost all his earthly goods and suffered multiplied indignities, besides that his life is of very little value, he will resist to the death and blood will be shed." Blood, as we shall see, had already been shed, but being Khasi blood it was of the wrong nationality to threaten Inglis's satrapy with exposure in the Indian and British press.

The report makes frequent references to the travails of 'Mr. Jones', and his death is mentioned at least twice. But his wife is referred to only as 'his lady', and no direct connection with E.B. Cattell is made. There is, however, this intriguing sentence.

"Any of the statements concerning Mr. Jones or Mr. Cattell, which I have alluded to . . . can be easily verified at Cherra, by enquiring of Mr. Jones, who is residing there at present, as also Mr. Cattell's mother and other members of his family."

Now, wonder-worker as he was considered to be, it was surely beyond the powers even of Thomas Jones to bring about his own resurrection. The report is full of misprints, the most common being letters missing from words. It is almost certainly, therefore, not 'Mr. Jones' to whom the quoted sentence refers, but 'Mrs. Jones'. Given such a reading, would it not be natural to expect to find the widowed Mrs. Jones (née Cattell) living in Cherra with Mr. Cattell's mother – her mother also – and other members of their family?

Inglis's obsessive persecution of E.B. Cattell, who was after all only a servant of Messrs. Duncan and Gibson, begins in this light to make more sense. For Inglis hated and perhaps feared Thomas Jones. There can be little doubt that he would have viewed any challenge to his thuggish regime from the Welshman's upstart brother-in-law as an impudence to be crushed with all the might and guile at his command.

As I wrestled with these and other mysteries many months after my return from India, I received an eager phone call from David Syiemlieh – not in Shillong, now, but at the India Office Library in London.

"Listen carefully, I've only got twenty pence for the phone, and I've got some exciting news for you. I have just discovered Thomas Jones's second marriage certificate. On 16 September, 1846 he married Emma Jane Cattell. And my goodness she was young! Fifteen or fourteen years is the registered age. No wonder the Church wanted to chuck him out. I'll bring it over to Swansea at the weekend."

It was indeed exciting news, and the copy David brought me seemed to confirm much of the above speculation. The 'spinster' Emma Jane Cattell was registered as the daughter of one George Cattell, and the marriage was witnessed by Charles Smith and Maria Smith, and E.B. Cattell (the presumed brother) and S.E. Cattell (another brother, or E.B.'s wife?). The couple were married not by one of Thomas Jones's Presbyterian co-workers, both of whom would almost certainly have opposed the union, but by the Chaplain of Sylhet.

It all sounded a thoroughly British affair, but I couldn't at that stage close the door entirely on the Khasi fancy, if not folk memory, that Emma may have been half Khasi. For I had found out virtually nothing about her mother: then, as now, a British marriage certificate recorded information pertaining to the parties' father only. She may, in western eyes, have been an alarmingly vernal bride, but it was normal for Khasi girls to marry between the ages of fifteen and eighteen.

Then, a few weeks later, David Syiemlieh sent me fresh information that settled the matter – and, alas, robbed the Khasis of the attractive possibility that in marrying the fifteen- or fourteen-year-old Miss Cattell, Thomas Jones went at least half native.

At the India Office in London David had found the marriage certificate of Emma's parents. In Calcutta Cathedral, on 24 December, 1827, George Cattell had married Susan Elizabeth Halford – who, of course, as 'S.E. Cattell' would witness Emma's marriage in 1846. There could be no further doubt: Thomas Jones's second wife was as European, if not English, as they come.

73

Two months after the marriage, Thomas and Emma Jones set out with Daniel Jones and his wife Ann (now heavy with child), Lieutenant Lewin and one of his daughters, a Dr. Mann from the military station and a woman friend, on an expedition to Jowai that would end in disaster.

Daniel and Ann Jones, having learned the language, were ready to extend the Mission's work into the Jaintia Hills; the purpose of the trip was to ascertain the suitability of Jowai as their base.

The party of young adventurers, riding through mountainous country more lushly beautiful than anything they could have experienced at home, seem to have thoroughly enjoyed their nine days together in the gentle November sunlight. On the return journey they took a detour through muddy and uncharted terrain, to explore regions as yet unvisited by the white man.

They returned to Cherra refreshed in spirit – a refreshment of which Daniel Jones, for one, seems to have been in dire need. The night before they had left for Jowai he had written in his diary: "Although we are going on this journey with a religious object in view, I feel myself very carnal and destitute of godly-mindedness . . ." But the day after their return he was able to register an improvement in his spiritual condition: "How great has been God's goodness in protecting us while on this journey, and in the cordial welcome and the pleasant rest on our return! May this stir me anew to live more devotedly and entirely for the glory of my heavenly Father and my Saviour."

They returned also in good physical shape, or so it seemed. But within days the jungle fever struck.

It had been contracted no doubt in the malarial marshlands through which they had wandered on their way home. The first to show symptoms – a rocketing temperature, teeth-rattling shivers – was Daniel Jones. Under Dr. Mann's care, the fever appeared to subside after three days. But in consequence of sitting too long in a cold room, it returned with increased violence, and Daniel Jones died on the morning of December 6 just an hour after his similarly stricken wife, in an adjoining room, had given birth prematurely to a daughter.

The baby died immediately, and was buried the next day, in the same coffin as her thirty-three year-old father, near the grave of Anne Jones.

"Although unknown to each other in this vale of tears," wrote William Lewis in *The Calcutta Christian Observer* (1847), "it is possible that an acquaintance has already commenced between the two, in that bright world of spirits into which both entered at the same time, but of the mysterious nature of which we are comparatively ignorant."

Their tomb, unlike Anne's, still exists, a chunky box of grey sandstone, surmounted by a squat pyramid – the second of many graves to be found today, all over the Hills, of Welsh men, women and children who died sudden and often agonising deaths.

For nearly a week after the birth, Daniel Jones's wife lay in a coma. When at last she regained consciousness it was to discover that both her husband and daughter were dead and had been buried days earlier. Although dangerously ill for some time, she eventually regained sufficient strength to return to Wales. William and Mary Lewis accompanied her to Calcutta where, fortuitously, she found the *Cordelia*, on which she and her husband had sailed to India, preparing to leave for Liverpool.

The ill-fated Jowai expedition claimed a third victim. Two days after Daniel Jones's death, the missionaries' staunch ally William Lewin succumbed to the jungle fever, and was buried in the Anglican cemetery, aged forty. His wife and children returned to the bosom of the Lewin family at Bexley in Kent.

Years later, Lieutenant Lewin's nephew, the renowned soldier-administrator 'Thangliena' (T.H. Lewin), stranded on the plains at Chattuck, would cast a wistful eye towards the last resting place of his esteemed uncle.

"I am now sitting in a little mat hut with a mud floor, having finished my breakfast of rice & eggs & a glass of brandy & water," he wrote to his mother. "Before me stretch the beautiful blue ranges of the Cassya hills where Uncle William & all of them lived & where he poor fellow died. Cherra Poonjee has hidden his topknot in a fleecy white turban of clouds but all the blue wall of hills is streaked with white lines of foam marking where the cascades take their mad leap of four thousand feet into the plains below."

74

"Great and frequent though the trials of the little Mission had now been," wrote J.H. Morris in his history of the Mission, "its cup of sorrow had not yet been filled. Another, and in one sense perhaps, the greatest sorrow of all, followed closely upon those already related. It is unnecessary to record the painful circumstances in detail. Suffice it to say that after contracting an injudicious marriage, in despite of the counsels of his colleagues, Mr. Thomas Jones entered upon a course of proceedings of a commercial character, which the Directors could not but consider derogatory to the character and calling of a missionary."

Here begins our hero's demise.

In spite of recent disasters, 1847 seems to have opened with Thomas Jones determinedly optimistic about the Mission's progress. His letters refer to the potential for new converts, and to a Khasi woman's eagerness to hold services for other local women. These gatherings would evolve into the women's meetings which underpin to this day significant areas of Presbyterian endeavour. Demand for his Matthew translation – "The Khasis in the school are busy learning and reciting it aloud" – was outstripping supply, and a second impression of *Rhodd Mam* was called for. As soon as he received the directors' permission, he would bring out translations of *Rhodd Tad* (A Father's Gift) and the *Cyffes Ffydd* (Confession of Faith), which would be of "the greatest service to the Khasis".

But owing to a sudden change in his circumstances, these plans came to nothing. By April he and his wife had abandoned Cherrapunji for a village called Pomreng some twenty miles to the north-east as the crow flies. It would seem that the long-smouldering antagonism between William Lewis and himself about missionary priorities had burst abruptly into flame, and Thomas Jones, whose practical approach found little favour with his directors either, had decided that the heat generated between the two missionaries made it impossible for them to continue to work together. Their differences were no doubt compounded by the official rebuke Thomas Jones had received for his 'irregular' second marriage, a judgement with which William Lewis would have concurred.

Mary Lewis, writing her memoirs in the 1890s, suggests that relations between Thomas Jones and his fellow missionaries had been tense and difficult for some time. When the split came, Thomas Jones declared he would take with him all the boys who were in the school at Cherra; he would continue their education at Pomreng where, drawing on the agricultural skills he had acquired at home, he would give them some experience of farming.

It appears that he went into partnership with his friend Mr. Stainforth, the Judge of Sylhet, who had a large farm at Pomreng. While Stainforth fulfilled his judicial obligations in the courts of Sylhet, Thomas Jones managed the farm. He also continued to work as a missionary, and preached regularly to the locals, leaving his young wife at home to care for Anne Jane, the daughter from his first marriage, and, in due course, little Thomas, first and sole fruit of the second.

For some months the directors in Liverpool seemed tolerant towards him, but they were insistent that he change his ways. Remembering, as he surely did, what happened to the Rev. Humphrey Gwalchmai at Llanidloes in 1832, he should have been under no illusions as to the depth of their disapproval. Gwalchmai, one of the giants of Calvinistic Methodism, had been minister of Bethel in Llanidloes (where Thomas Jones first 'heard the call' in 1835) until his involvement in a lead-mining enterprise, and subsequent bankruptcy, led to his dismissal from the ministry.

To a generation of leaders raised on the precepts of Methodist grandees such as Thomas Charles and John Elias, Thomas Jones's wayward dabblings in the secular world must have seemed, like those of Gwalchmai, a gross aberration. Their first overseas missionary was 'of the line', connected both theologically and through his Montgomeryshire family to the very wellsprings of Welsh Methodism – yet here he was, betraying himself into a secular English employment at precisely the moment when the Calvinistic Methodists were capturing the whole of Ynys Môn from native irreligion and the Church of England. In moving into a milieu whose ethos was so alien to that of his rapidly expanding denomination, he had broken that line. Furthermore, his reckless marriage to a mere adolescent threatened the Church with a damaging reprise of the Dr. Richards scandal.

In July the Mission Board sent him an ultimatum: unless he could provide them with an unequivocal assurance that he would desist from involvement in any kind of commercial or wordly undertaking, and confine himself to the work for which he had been sent to the Hills, his connection with the Missionary Society would be terminated. As headstrong now as he had been at the time of the showdown with the LMS, Thomas Jones refused to bend to the board's will. The Mission Society, having waited in vain for a favourable response to their ultimatum, formally severed the connection with Thomas Jones on 8 October, 1847.

Far from retiring beaten from the field, he continued to evangelise as he farmed at Pomreng, but the farming was not a success: the tigers ate his stock, and Stainforth lost a considerable sum of money in the venture.

Although Pomreng is mentioned in several missionary accounts as a village situated between Shillong and Jowai, I failed to locate it on any map, nor could I find any Khasi who had heard of the place. But Hooker mentions it in his journals, spelling it 'Pomrang': he stayed there in 1850 "in an excellent bungalow, built by Mr. Stainforth (Judge of Sylhet)." This bungalow, which could well have been Thomas Jones's home a year or so earlier, "occupied the eastern extremity of a lofty spur that overhangs the deep fir-clad valley of the Oongkot, dividing Khasia from Jyntea." Allowing for the wildly discrepant spellings of that era, and synthesising a variety of topographical references to be found in the literature, my Khasi friends and I came to the conclusion that 'Pomreng' is probably the village that is known today as Puriang.

The historian Professor Imdad Hussain said he had heard there were still tea bushes growing wild at Puriang, left over from Thomas Jones's pioneering efforts with that crop. It was not until the 1830s that tea began to be farmed on the plains of Assam, so Thomas Jones's attempts to grow tea in the Hills can be seen as an audacious, if failed, experiment that was long before its time: it's only in recent years that the Khasis have begun to make a success of their few tea plantations.

Perhaps, in addition to Thomas Jones's tea bushes, I could discover at Puriang the site of his homestead. In the 1880s the Rev. Jerman Jones, looking for relics of Thomas Jones at 'Pomreng', found no farm and no fences; but he did find the blackened chimney stack of what had once been his bungalow.

The chances of finding that chimney stack more than a hundred years later were next to nothing, but maybe there'd be someone in the village who could confirm that Puriang was indeed the disgraced missionary's last home in the Hills.

Any trip on the notorious Shillong-Jowai 'national highway' is not lightly undertaken. So numerous, overladen and breakdown-prone are the coal trucks that blatter day and night along this roller-coaster ribbon of potholes, that it is hubristic folly to toy with any notion of an estimated time of return. Traffic jams on the Jowai road, to the glee of locals who find themselves with a captive market for their gold-standard hard boiled eggs, can last not merely for hours but for one or two whole days, involving convoys of anything up to four hundred coal trucks.

Luckily for us (though not for the eggmen), a strike had transformed the snarling, stinking coal route into an almost deserted country lane, snaking its pine-dappled way through a landscape of rounded mountains. They used to remind the missionaries of *mwynder Maldwyn* (the gentleness of Montgomery-shire), but they are altogether more massive than the rolling uplands of mid Wales. Every bend in the road brought us fresh views of broad fertile valleys hundreds of feet below, and beyond, in all directions, huge mountain ranges folded one after another into the blue horizon. We stopped once to take a piss, savouring the homely musk of sun-warmed pine and the melancholy soughing of a stand of firs.

Half an hour later we parked our vehicle on the main road, and set off on foot, up a steep, rough track that would have been

228

negotiable only by jeep. After about a quarter of a mile we passed three pipe-smoking farmers perched on a boulder with their hooks and knives; their conversation faltered as we approached, and they looked down somewhat quizzically on the sweating *phareng*, until a '*Khublei*' ('greetings') from us broke the silence, and broad *kwai*-tinged smiles lit their plum-brown faces.

"*Khublei*," they replied, and waved us onwards when we asked if we were on the right track.

Another quarter of a mile brought us to the top of the hill and the pretty little village of Puriang. The houses, spread either side of the dusty track, were simple wood-frame structures covered with tin sheets or the ubiquitous mustard oil cans that are opened out and beaten flat to make slate-like tiles. Many were painted with tar, to make the most of what heat could be drawn from the winter sun: this blackened tin was the perfect visual foil to the settlement's gardens which were ablaze with flowers and purple vanda orchids. The villagers seemed as easy-going as the three unflustered sentinels we'd passed on the way up, content to watch their rice drying on raffia mats in front of their houses, and to luxuriate in a vast panorama which included the mountains of Cachar, a glimmer or two of the Himalayas and, near at hand, the bundling Jaintia Hills. Here was a landscape, and a way of life, to throw into withering perspective the scurrying paranoia of city life.

Barefoot children from the tin-shed school and some hunters with ancient flintlocks gathered round us, eager to talk. Desmond asked in Khasi about Thomas Jones, and one of the gunmen disappeared among the houses to make further enquiries on our behalf. In the meantime, a beaming young Unitarian minister, with a shoulder bag stuffed with books, introduced himself to us.

"Let me please try out my Welsh on you," he grinned. "*Iechyd da* and *diolch yn fawr*. There. What do think of that? I bet you never expected to hear Welsh in Puriang, did you? I was a student in Manchester a couple of years ago, and I learned from a Welsh friend there how to say a few things in your lovely language."

The Unitarians, he explained, had formed in Jowai in 1887, when their founder, Hajom Kissor Singh Nongbri, rebelled against the Calvinistic Methodism to which he had been converted as a schoolboy. He started a 'liberation movement' to free the Khasis from their blind faith in trinitarianism, hell and a 'foreign' religion that was turning his people away from their cultural roots. The Welshman's church had branded him a heretic, and his movement had suffered all manner of persecution, including the torching of his church and the stoning of his followers' houses.

"They still think of us as heretics," said the Unitarian, "but we are friendly enough with the Presbyterians these days. They are far more numerous than we are, of course. But we have thirty churches and six thousand members in Meghalaya and Assam. Slowly we grow."

Within ten minutes the hunter returned, having consulted an old woman about Thomas Jones. She seemed to have been rather vague, but she had been able to confirm that, yes, Thomas Jones had lived for a time at Puriang. As for tea bushes and blackened chimney stacks, she was sorry to say that she was unable to help us.

Our Unitarian friend was sure we'd find out more if we could stay longer, but the curfew loomed and we had to get back to the city, much as we were tempted to linger in black and blossoming Puriang.

"*Khublei*," called the minister in farewell as we set off down the stony track. "*Khublei* and *iechyd da*."

The flow of letters from Thomas Jones to *Y Drysorfa Ysbrydol* ceases after his expulsion from the Church, so we lose direct contact with him for the last years of his life. There is no record of how he felt about life in Puriang – if Puriang is indeed the village of 'Pomreng' – but it is tempting to imagine that he too felt at home here, and would have settled at Puriang indefinitely, had it not been for his fight to the death with Harry Inglis.

75

Harry Saheb, as the Khasis knew him, was a fabulously loathsome human being. Born at Sylhet in 1803, his mother was reputedly a native plainswoman, and his father, George Inglis, an English merchant adventurer who had come to Sylhet in 1794 at the age of 20, and would remain there until his death in 1850, having founded the commercial dynasty, Inglis & Co., that held the Khasis in thrall for much of the nineteenth century.

The company, formed in 1799, established a monopoly over the coal, limestone and orange trade of the Khasi Hills, and was notorious for its flagrantly corrupt appropriation of military, political and juridical power.

The younger Inglis's knowledge of the Hills and his relationship with some of the Syiems proved invaluable to the British at the time of the Anglo-Khasi War. For his zealous pursuit of the 'insurgents' as an active volunteer, he was rewarded with a commission in the Sylhet Light Infantry; he consolidated his reputation with the authorities by masterminding the entrapment of Tirot Singh.

The interests of his company began to dovetail neatly with those of civil authority when, in 1835, he was appointed as Assistant to the Political Agent, Colonel F.G. Lister – who just happened to be his father-in-law. Lister, successor to David Scott and, therefore, effectively Governor of the Hills, was empowered as magistrate to levy hefty fines and terms of imprisonment of up to two years. As commander of the Sylhet Light Infantry during the Anglo-Khasi War, Lister's name, according to Judge A.J.M. Mills, "struck terror to the hearts of the Khasis." Inglis, as his Assistant, was also entitled to fine offenders and to send them to prison. Inglis and Lister made a formidable, intimidating team.

Together they annexed that part of the kingdom of Jaintia that lay on the Sylhet Plains, and deposed Rajendra Singh, the last of the Rajas of Jaintia. Having destroyed the king's palace, Inglis presided over a division of the spoils, doling out modest sums to his Khasi soldiers and keeping a fortune in booty for himself.

To Khasis and European traders alike, the regime in the Hills was rampantly corrupt and wildly out of control. But so cowed by its power or beholden to it for their livelihoods were they, that no one dared challenge its lawlessness. Thomas Jones, the first to make a stand, was outraged by the extent of Inglis's exploitation and oppression of the Khasis.

"After a poor man and his family have by assiduous industry planted and weeded and taken care of their groves, collected their oranges and taken them to Chuttuck for sale," he wrote, "Mr. Inglis receives the money and gives them one third of the amount realised. Some of them who attempted to sell their own and receive the money themselves have been made severe examples of, by having their houses pulled down and their plantations ripped up and destroyed."

He campaigned vigorously on various fronts against Inglis's rapacious excesses. He complained in person; he complained to the Government; he complained in the courts.

Towards the end of 1848 he joined forces with the deposed Raja of Jaintia, the Syiem of Mylliem and other Khasis to arraign Inglis in court for his oppressive conduct towards them and various acts of bribery. Accusations were also levelled against Lister of partiality to his Assistant (Inglis). As a result of these charges a Government enquiry was held, but the commissioner responsible for deciding the case found the accusers' testimony so improbable that Inglis managed, as ever, to wriggle free of a guilty verdict, his monopolies intact.

"Property one may lose . . . without repining," wrote an increasingly desperate contributor to the Mills report, "but a man's life is a venture which cannot be apportioned or divided; and is lost all on one cast when it runs into danger, and in no part of India does that danger meet him in so fearful and repulsive a form as in Cherra . . . [To] know that from [such dangers] you are protected by no innocence of life, by no courtesy of demeanour, by no liberality, by no justice, by no mercy, by no sacrifice short of your means of livelihood, by no popularity, is a trial which shakes the nerves of the boldest and renders men ready to brave anything anywhere, rather than wither within under the feverish and agonising anxieties of life in the Khasi Hills . . . As far as I am concerned the Cherra court is of no use to me. I have only to incur the displeasure of one individual [i.e. Harry Inglis], and not a muktiar will plead my cause, or a witness give testimony in my behalf, if I paid them Rs. 1,000 for so doing. In fact, . . . the court has lost the confidence of the entire public, consequently the administration of justice has become a nullity, a bye-word, and reproach . . . If the history of the doings in the Cherra hills were succinctly printed in a pamphlet . . . and given publicity to by the English press . . . they would appear to the bulk of mankind too incredible to be believed."

This, and similar depositions, make it plain that the Khasi Hills were an extraordinarily dangerous region for anyone who was even mildly critical of the Cherra 'authorities'. Thomas Jones's courageous defiance of Harry Inglis, and his relentless persecution are a constant point of reference in these reports, as if even here, in the measured bureaucratese of officialdom, the missionary is already something of a legend.

From various scattered references we can piece together the events of his last months.

Of Inglis's hostility to Thomas Jones, following the court case, there can be no doubt. The Mills report refers to "the dread inspired by the vengeance taken on the Khasias who supported Mr. Jones, whose witnesses suffered both in purse and person for the aid they rendered him." Motivation for the persecution of Jones by the Cherra 'authorities' is clear: "escape from the consequences of their own delinquencies absolutely depended upon his extinction."

One such delinquency, which seems to have been the last straw for Thomas Jones, was the barbaric execution, on Inglis's orders, of a Khasi labourer from Khadsawphra. Inglis's henchmen tried three times to hang the man, but after each attempt he remained alive and conscious. It was not until he had been stabbed several times, following the third attempt, that the man at last died. Thomas Jones's outraged protest at this atrocity was the last straw for Inglis also; he resolved to be rid of the meddlesome missionary.

Inglis sent a posse of thugs, otherwise known as the Cherra police, to Jones's house (presumably at Puriang), under the pretext of delivering a letter from the authorities, requesting to know whether he had a licence to reside in the Hills. Then, according to the Mills report, "with threats and menaces that alarmed [Mrs. Jones] for her husband's life, [they] forced the bungalow's doors, although she stood in the verandah in a state of the greatest agony, begging them to desist, with pen, ink, and paper in her hands, offering to give the required answer."

Thomas Jones, clearly in mortal danger, fled for his life. The Rev. Robert Evans, who served in the Hills between 1879 and 1916, described years later how he met an old Khasi who, as a boy, had followed Thomas Jones on his escape through the jungle. Hiding by day and travelling at night, he took several months to reach Guwahati.

There, the Governor of Assam, a Welshman by the name of Colonel Francis Jenkins, secured the destitute missionary a place on a boat sailing down the Brahmaputra in the direction of Calcutta.

Thomas Jones arrived in Calcutta on September 4, 1849, sick and exhausted after his gruelling ordeal in the malarious jungle. He was taken in by the Rev. David Ewart, a missionary of the Free Church of Scotland, and died in Ewart's house twelve days later. He was 39.

"I am thankful that I was enabled to see poor Jones in his last moments, and to show him what kindness we could," wrote Mr. Ewart to the Directors in Liverpool. "One day, while sitting beside him, I ventured to say, 'Do you not regret the disruption of good and harmonious feelings between you and the home Society, and your brother in the Mission? May these feelings not have arisen from the use of too strong language, and the want of proper forbearance?' He admitted that he had been intemperate in his language, and asked whether I thought the differences between him and the Society might not be healed. All I could say was that if it pleased God to raise him up, there were those here who would willingly do everything in their power to bring about a good understanding. I should have rejoiced to attempt this, for though I could not but regard Mr. Jones as having erred in judgement, and as having used hasty and intemperate language to the authorities connected with the home management of the Mission, I know him to have been a man of God, an earnest and zealous missionary. I have good reason to believe that he died as a Christian minister, looking to the one and living Saviour, and trusting in his merits. He several times expressed a desire to live, if it should please God to order it so. He seemed to think that some things wanted explanation. But he was resigned to the will of God!"

Before his burial in the Scottish Cemetery, there would almost certainly have been a funeral service for Thomas Jones in the dazzling white, Hawksmoor-style St. Andrews Church, near the northern end of the Maidan.

The cause of death on his death certificate is left blank. It is normally assumed that he died of a violent attack of the 'miasma' or fever he picked up during his flight through the jungle. But the Mills report declares, twice, that Thomas Jones died "of a broken heart", occasioned by "the multiplied persecutions and indignities he had suffered . . ."

76

As for Inglis, no amount of depositions and damning government reports in the years that followed were able to do him the damage he deserved.

Dozens of cases were brought against him for quite outrageous infractions: the seizure of competitors' goods; violent assault; unlawful arrest; attempted murder; intimidation and bribery; wilful and corrupt perjury; kidnapping competitors' servants; obstructing waterways with elephants and using gangs of clubmen to smash and rob the boats of competitors . . . But such was his control of the legal system that not once did his many accusers have the satisfaction of seeing him nailed. And when Government investigators were sent to report on his activities they invariably contrived, having amassed copious evidence against him, to let him off the hook.

Perhaps these whitewashers were traduced by some veneer of civility he seemed able to affect, for Inglis, according to the Mills report, was said to be in private life "neither destitute of humanity, nor any of the more honourable feelings for which it is vain to search in the generality of his public actions." Many, at the time, appear to have found him plausible. Hooker, for instance, was a guest of Inglis at both Chattuck and Cherra, where he was received "with the greatest hospitality by that gentleman". Writing in 1850, Hooker seems oblivious to the recent persecution of Thomas Jones and Inglis's terrifying vengeance on the Welshman's Khasi supporters, observing blandly that "the trade in cinnamon . . . is much encouraged by the Inglis family, to whose exertions these people are so greatly indebted."

If a man of Hooker's discriminating sensibility could have been so duped, it is not surprising that men of lesser wit should have had the wool pulled over their eyes. Where, I wonder, was William Lewis in all this? On whose side? Was the handsome stone school that Inglis built for the Mission at Shella in about 1850 (overriding local objections), and which he later rebuilt when it was destroyed by flood, a reward for Lewis's 'neutrality' during Thomas Jones's anti-Inglis crusade – and an earnest of the Mission's continuing loyalty to the Inglis regime? There are, as Thomas Jones mused on his deathbed, 'many things wanting explanation'.

The ruins of the palatial house that Inglis built for himself are still to be found, in a leech-infested jungly copse at the eastern rim of the Cherra moorland. Looming eerily through the mist that billows up from the great gorge, this oval, walled enclosure is a desolate, unvisited place; it is known as Kut Madan, 'end of the earth'. Beyond the house itself, with its thick chunks of wall and ferns growing luxuriantly out of ornate fireplaces, is an extensive private cemetery, long abandoned to impenetrable undergrowth. Here, where the vandas flare and black fritillaries bob, lie the bones of Harry Inglis. His, however, is no ordinary grave.

Inglis made a habit of declaring to the Khasi chiefs that he would continue to exercise dominion over all the lands, rights and leaseholds that were his until the day his body was buried in the ground. He died in England, on 31 July, 1860. Ten years later, his son Lionel, fulfilling somewhat belatedly his father's dying wish, brought the embalmed paternal corpse back to Cherrapunji.

And here at Kut Madan, he placed Inglis's body, as the old shyster had instructed, not in the ground but upon the ground, and built a rectangular tomb around it – so that even in death the unburied principal of Inglis & Co. would continue to lord it over the economy of the Hills.

77

And what of the family that Thomas Jones left behind in the Hills – his wife Emma, their little son Thomas Catell Jones, and the boy's older half-sister, Anne Jane, from the missionary's first marriage?

Rumours and distortions abound. In Shillong I met an old academic who asserted cheerfully as he chomped his *kwai* that there were descendants of Thomas Jones all over the Hills . . . not that he could actually name one or provide an address. Perhaps further inquiries and documentary research will bring to light the lost Joneses of Khasia, perhaps not.

All that can be offered for the time being is the inconclusive dotted line that follows. It has been pieced together from fleeting references in government reports, missionary publications and the continuing investigations of David Syiemlieh . . .

Emma Jones, who could have been no more than eighteen when Thomas died, returned to live with her (presumably widowed) mother at Cherra. But sometime between about 1853 and 1855 she remarried: we know this because the Rev. William Pryse refers to her in the preface to his *Introduction to the Khasi Language* (1855). He obtained some of his material, he writes, from "the youthful widow of the late Rev. Thomas Jones (now Mrs. Mackey) . . ."

Their son Thomas seems in time to have married, and fathered at least two children, Halford Cattell Jones and Rachel

237

Cattell Jones, both of whom died within a month of each other in 1897, the year of the earthquake. They were ten and eight respectively. He may have had at least one other daughter, because the inscription on Rachel's grave refers to her as the "eldest daughter of Thomas Cattell Jones".

Anne Jane, the missionary's daughter from his first marriage, was adopted, aged perhaps seven or eight, by the Rev. Pryse and his wife. She helped him develop the Sylhet mission field, and eventually married a man called Brownlow. (The name Brownlow occurs with surprising frequency in Government reports on the area, and was the middle name of Emma's brother, Eugene Brownlow Cattell.) As Mrs. Brownlow, Thomas Jones's daughter was said by the Rev. Griffith Hughes in 1890 to be living at the foot of the Hills; he describes her in *Bryniau Cassia* as one of the *"caredigion"* of the Mission. She seems to have had at least one daughter of her own, and she was also stepmother to her husband's daughter Ellen.

The reputedly Anglo-Indian Ellen, who was born at Cocheela Tea Estate, Cachar, seems to have been the fruit of one of those common liaisons of Empire between European tea-planter (Mr. Brownlow, in this case) and local female. Ellen, like her stepmother, also became a missionary assistant in Sylhet where, in 1907, she married the Rev. John Pengwern Jones (1859-1927).

Pengwern Jones, a native of Llangollen, was a vibrant and sometimes controversial figure. He founded a co-operative bank to keep poor villagers out of the money lenders' clutches; he and his wife opened an orphanage at Maulvi for the unwanted offspring of bachelor teaplanters; and in 1904 he staged a grand Eisteddfod in Sylhet, the first ever seen in India. The competitions ranged from sharpening a pencil and composing a song to threading a needle and describing an elephant.

Our last sighting of a true descendant of Thomas Jones, until further research clarifies some of this muddle, would seem to be of one of his grand-daughters. When Ellen Pengwern Jones died in about 1925, it appears that her sister, who must have been Anne Jane's biological daughter, came to Maulvi to help the ailing missionary look after the twenty or thirty children in his care. Miss Brownlow – Thomas Jones's grand-daughter – was sitting up with the bed-ridden missionary one night when a thunderbolt tore through the grass roof of the bungalow and set it on fire. No-one was hurt in the blaze, but the building was destroyed. So too, by the end of the year, was the sick and sorrowing missionary, who died and was buried in Shillong.

78

It was time to get serious about UFOs.

Bah Bling had left a note at the Circuit House summoning us to a meeting with him in the village of his birth, Mawmluh. On the agenda were "cromlechs and certain other matters".

Bling was hovering in wait by the Ka Nabon memorial. Scott parked the Ambassador on the grassy verge, and Bling led Desmond, Kynpham and me to a stretch of moorland strewn with cromlechs and monoliths. "These," our mentor explained, bringing the party to a halt, the better for us to shoulder the burden of his disclosure, "are cromlechs."

Aha . . .

"And in these cromlechs the Khasis place the ashes of their dead.

"You will see that there are flat stones and upright stones. The upright stones are buried some distance in the ground. If they were not, they would fall over."

Desmond and Kynpham would now and then attempt a refinement of Bling's exegesis. Kynpham, objecting to Bling's use of the term 'puja' to describe cromlech burial rites, simmered with amused indignation at the Presbyterian sage's efforts to construe the rituals of the orthodox Khasi faith that he, Kynpham, had been born to. But Bling, warming to the task of educating two young "university professors", as he called them, would let nothing stymie his lecture's flow, apart from an occasional photo-call among the stones.

But the unwelcome complications of the "professors'" contributions eventually prompted a change of subject. "Now," said Bling, "you will come with me, please, to my sister's house for further discussions."

"How are the elections going?" I asked him, as we ambled back to the village. "Are you confident of many votes?"

"Many, many votes," he smiled. "I am thinking of selling a forest to finance my campaign."

His sister turned out to be none other than Mrs. Nesidoh Roy Diengdoh, the cheery old schoolteacher who'd hugged me – and all the people of Wales – in the middle of Mawmluh's quiet main street the previous day. She greeted us with more hugs and *kwai*-red smiles, and sat us down in her cool, stone-built bungalow to take tea (from her best china), bread and butter, cakes and pastries.

The main body of the bungalow seemed to be one large, lofty space, with the living area divided from what I assumed was the kitchen by an eaves-level wooden partition. Bling, ready now to discuss "certain other matters", asked his sister to kindly leave the room. When she had disappeared behind the curtain that served as a door, he lowered his voice conspiratorially, and began to address himself to the next item on the agenda, from time to time casting an anxious eye towards the kitchen.

"You saw, Mr. Jenkins, the BBC film called *Monsoon*?"

"I did indeed."

"And you saw me on that film talking about UFOs? Well, I did not give the whole story on the BBC, but I will give it now to you. We are writing a book about it, and will be sending it to the defence department in Washington."

I unsheathed my Bic.

"I will give you the true history about the UFO that came down to earth in the small streamlet at Dympep Inspection Bungalow, Mawkdok village eighteen miles from Shillong towards Cherrapunji. It was about 3 p.m. in September 1967 or 1968, and the UFO came from the west towards the east."

"You saw it yourself?"

"My cousin U Purno, who was a *chowkidar* at the bungalow, and some other villagers saw the UFO. She, the UFO, came down and sucked up some very clean silverine water from the stream with a great sound. Everyone ran away. One man, who was repairing the road, was so afraid at the sight of it that he hid inside a culvert. He thought the whole world was being destroyed. The UFO stayed for fifteen to twenty minutes. And when it began to take off for the sky, in the same manner that present helicopters lift off, it made a big, big noise. It was like thunder, and fires burned small bushes in an area of sixty metres in diameter. Many people were very happy and clapped when it went away."

"What did it look like?"

"It was like a big basket about fifteen feet in diameter and about 25 feet high. A big basket surrounded by glittering electrics and clouds. We have taken photographs."

"Photographs? Of the UFO?"

"Photographs of the location. We will be sending them to the Washington defence department."

"You should send them to NASA as well," suggested Desmond, taking a mouthful of cake to stifle a giggle. "Some rocks in a stream – could be of crucial significance for the space programme."

"There is more," said Bling. "In 1983 in the month of July some pilots of the American defence forces, with their most powerful jets and after the greatest fight, brought two UFOs down from the sky."

"In Cherrapunji?"

"No, no. In Washington. The people in Washington asked what it was, but the pilots didn't speak a word. Then a judge came and spoke to the pilots. 'Please tell the people what it was you brought down from the sky,' said the judge. And the pilots said, 'Please give us sixty days, and after that we will explain to the people what we brought down from the skies.' But they never did explain."

"How did you hear about this?" asked Kynpham. "Was your cousin there?"

"Of course not. I read this in a magazine."

"What magazine?"

"It was an English magazine. Lent to me by an English man. I do not remember the magazine's name. As I was saying, the pilots never explained what was in the UFOs. But I believe," he lowered his voice and leaned forward, "I believe that inside these UFOs were four living creatures having the height of four feet and six inches."

"All four of them?"

"All four. And they were made –" he broke off to search for the word, his eyes lighting on some metal ornaments on a shelf. "They were made of – that material."

"Brass?"

"Brass. Exactly. They were made of brass and they had eyes like Chinese eyes. They were moving like robots. And I believe" – he paused, glancing edgily towards the kitchen, "I believe that two of the four were male sex, and two female. Now, in Brazil on or about 1946 or 1947 – and please say nothing of this to our friend Mrs. Richmond – in Brazil, when a certain father and his son were ploughing their field, a UFO came down to their field, and one of the creatures of female sex came out of the UFO to hide in a small bush."

"A brass female with Chinese eyes?"

"That is correct. Then the male creatures came out of the UFOs, and took hold of the son and led him to the female creature in the bush. Please, I repeat, say nothing of this to Mrs. Richmond. They put him together with her in the bush, and after half an hour he came out from the bush weeping and crying."

"A woman made of brass," said Desmond. "It must have been painful."

"His father too," added Bling, "had been very upset while this was going on."

"What father wouldn't?"

"Then the UFO took off," continued Bling, ignoring Desmond who, unable to stifle his laughter, had risen from the settee and was pacing the floor behind Bling's chair with a handkerchief stuffed in his mouth. "They came, I believe, from one of the planets, to learn who was living on this planet. And I believe that the offspring from that incident in the bush in Brazil was the pilot who came to the Khasi Hills in a UFO in 1967 or 1968 – because that pilot was about twenty years of age. And I believe that these UFOs coming from outer space to visit this planet were driven by living creatures, as written in the Old

242

Testament, who came down to earth and carried away the prophet Elijah to the heavens. These creatures, I believe, are descendants of Elijah."

"Does that mean God is a spaceman?" asked Desmond.

Bling gave a pained, impatient look.

"Were the creatures in the UFOs Presbyterians?" I wondered.

Ignoring yet another fatuous question, Bling took my notebook, saying he wanted to sign it. "Our pastors and the missionaries do not believe in this," he said as he penned an authentication at the end of my notes.

"This was expressed by me today in my home village of Mawmluh," read the signed and dated endorsement.

"I kindly request, Mr. Jenkins, that these two stories which have really happened in our Universe, here on planet Earth, as given by me, be included in your report on the Khasi Hills."

How, Bah Bling, could I leave them out?

79

When the Lewises left for home in December, 1860, exhausted after eighteen years of unremitting and often solitary labour, they took with them U Larsing Khongwir, their former houseboy turned evangelist. He was the first Khasi ever to visit Wales, and, for the home congregations, living proof of the Mission's success. His tour of the chapels was a sensation.

It was U Larsing's intention to return to Khasia having qualified himself to work among his compatriots as a teacher, but he would never see his Hills again.

Larsing Khongwir was born in about 1836 to one of the leading families of the village of Mawsmai. In Shillong I met Dr. Therlinda Khongwir who is descended from the same family, and who had herself recently converted from *Niam Khasi* to Presbterianism. She told me that after Larsing's father died, he was initiated by an uncle into the traditional beliefs and rituals of the tribe, but from the age of eleven, when he started attending the Mawsmai school, he became increasingly attracted to Christianity. This was unacceptable to his aunt, with whom

243

he was lodging while his mother was away in Calcutta, and he was ordered to give up his lessons.

In his distress, Larsing ran to the Mission Station, and tearfully described his plight to the Lewises. They decided to take him in. He became their servant and cook, until the time that he declared, soon after his baptism, that he wanted to give himself entirely to the work of the Lord. "I no longer want to serve at your table," he told the Lewises, "I have no love, any more, for cooking for the mortal body: I want to cook for the immortal spirit."

He was released from his domestic duties, and quickly distinguished himself as a winning evangelist and remarkably appealing preacher. A notable coup for him was his success in converting the *lyngdoh* (priest) of Jowai and his wife, but first he had to help the old fellow overcome his taste for the alcohol. "I have succeeded in weaning U Hat from strong drink by teaching him to smoke," he wrote in one of his letters. "On several occasions I have had to jump out of bed at night to fill the old man's pipe when his thirst would not be denied."

Larsing was twenty-four when he arrived in Wales. He had longed for that moment for so many years that it must have been the next best thing to striding over the threshold of heaven. "If I could fly as a bird," he had written from the Hills, "I would come to Wales straight away, and would kiss the boots of each one of you, I feel so grateful to you."

The Lewises took him first to Llandeilo where a spellbound congregation marvelled at the masterful delivery of the sermon he gave in Khasi and which William Lewis, standing beside him, translated into Welsh. "One of the most eloquent and talented preachers we have ever heard," was Llandeilo's verdict, according to *Y Drysorfa*.

They settled at Llandeilo for a while, then found a more permanent home at Wrecsam. These early months were a hectic blur of crowded and emotional missionary meetings such as Wales had never known.

"Here for you," William Lewis would declare, vindicated at last, and with the tears of his triumph streaming down his face,

"Here for you at last, sown in tears, brought forth in joy, is the promised sheaf of fruit from the Khasi Hills."

No less moved were the thousands of chapel-goers who for twenty years had loyally invested their pennies and prayers in the work of the Mission with little, until now, to show for their commitment. There had never before been a missionary who had returned to tell Methodist congregations about their labours in the 'pagan' world. It was therefore doubly spectacular for a missionary to have returned with a walking, talking convert in tow. "Those of us who saw him," wrote a contributor to *Trysorfa Y Plant*, "will never forget this short, slight, dark-skinned youth, with his natural humility, singing the old Welsh hymn-tunes in his mother tongue, and reducing thousands thereby to weeping the sweetest tears of love for the converted pagan."

He even lifted sad Eben Fardd to unwonted heights of doggerelising cheer, in his "On Occasion of Seeing the Cassian Native Evangelist, U Larsing":

> The distant Hills of Cassia
>   Now see the Gospel light;
> The rays of truth in India
>   Dispel the gloom of night;
> From Britain's coast have issued
>   A band of faithful men,
> To sound the name of Jesus
>   On every hill and glen.
>
> The Mission trumpet sounded,
>   The gospel banner waved;
> When forward rushed the Cassians
>   To be through Jesus saved;
> Among the youthful converts
>   U Larsing caught the sound,
> And to the Saviour Jesus
>   Himself for ever bound.

U Larsing came to Britain,
  The Mission's fountain head,
To see the springs in motion
  About which he had read;
He loves us, he enjoys us,
  Shall we not love him too?
For we are one in Jesus,
  Both Briton and Hindoo.

Ye Sons of British Christians,
  Take now U Larsing's hand,
To see our Preachers' College,
  To see our Gospel Band,
To see our Institutions,
  To see our Christian rule.
To see our 'Sociations,
  To see our Sunday School.

Then let him go to Cassia,
  Imbued with British taste,
And turn the skirts of India,
  From being a moral Waste,
To be henceforth a Vineyard,
  All sacred to the Lord;
That God may bless his mission,
  We pray with one accord.

Though the climate was too cold for him, and he was unable to undertake all the work that was expected of him by the enthusiastic congregations, Larsing's experience of the Welsh and their religion was like a dream fulfilled.

"I have been with Saheb and Mem Lewis for two months," he wrote to his uncle Luh. "We went from one town to the next, and I must have spoken to ten or fifteen thousand people in all, and two or three thousand in just one chapel! And I have heard ministers of great ability, and met deacons with burning spirits. But I cannot say I have had any clear idea of the meanings of the many sermons and addresses I have heard: I have sat somewhat like a stone in these gatherings with not one word penetrating my heart – because I do not understand Welsh. But to have been among these people has given me the greatest delight, for I know full well how much they love us, as we love them, for having sent the Word of God to us . . . You remember, uncle Luh, how we used to read in the *Confession of Faith* of the great quarterly Cymanfas, and the Monthly Meetings? You remember the Saheb describing them to us? Well, now I have seen them with my very own eyes. But I can't give you much detail about them. If I could only understand what was being said on these occasions, I'd feel as if I were in heaven, yes, here on earth – and my letters would be of greater use to you."

In addition to travelling widely in both Wales and England, he attended a school run by the Rev. Ebenezer Powell at Holt, near Wrecsam. But the climate wore him down, and in the summer of 1863 he caught a cold and suffered an attack of pleurisy.

"If I went back to the Hills and lived there for six weeks," he told his doctor, "I couldn't begin to describe to them the kindness I have received here, and the blessings that the Gospel has brought to England and Wales. O, how I should preach Jesus Christ to my compatriots there! I fear, though, that if I die here, that would be the end of the Mission. What would the Khasis say if I didn't go back?"

He was cared for in the homes of various leading Presbyterians, but his health steadily deteriorated. He died at Caergwrle on 24 August, 1863, and was buried in Chester Public Cemetery to the strains of "There is a happy land,/Far, far away . . . "

80

Though neither U Larsing nor the increasingly brittle Lewises ever went back to the Hills, it was not the end of the Mission. The Welsh incursion into the Hills never amounted to more than a trickle, but it was a steady and determined trickle, inspired by William Carey's famous missionary adjuration to "expect great things from God, attempt great things for God". From the missionaries' ranks there emerged in time many educators and doctors who are household names hardly less revered than the Mission's founder.

Thomas Jones is not indisputably "the father of Khasi literature". There are many who feel that this title belongs more properly to the Rev. Dr. John Roberts (1842-1908) whose literary achievements were considerably more diverse.

Born to a stonemason and his wife in Corris Uchaf, John Roberts was only nine when he went to work in the quarries, his father having died, and his mother and himself lacking any other means of support. Even as a child he harboured a fervent desire to become a missionary, and was an avid reader, hiding books in the stone stool on which he sat to split slates. Profoundly influenced by the Revival of 1859, he began preaching at the age of 21, and was accepted into Coleg y Bala in 1866. Before sailing to India in 1871 he married Sidney Margaret Jones, daughter of the minister and poet Glan Alun (Thomas Jones, 1811-66), who had been excommunicated by the Calvinistic Methodists for his boozy ways, but who eventually 'made good' as a preacher and ardent *eisteddfodwr*.

If the missionaries were dismissive of Khasi music, they were more responsive to Khasi oral word-craft, not least, of course, because the collection and publication of Khasi fables and gnomic *phawars* – epigrammatic couplets – helped popularise their Bible-centred literacy programme.

Like most missionaries, Roberts busied himself with religious texts, and wrote scores of hymns, but he also introduced Khasi readers to a wide range of poetry, folklore, oral tales, country proverbs and general knowledge which had little or no Christian intent, and he was the first to experiment with drama. His translations ranged from *Spectator* essays and snippets of Shakespeare to Longfellow's "The Psalm of Life" and the Felicia Hemans swashbuckler "Casabianca": "The boy stood on the burning deck,/Whence all but him had fled . . . "

The most famous of John Roberts's adaptations is his Khasi version of "Hen Wlad Fy Nhadau". As "Ri Khasi" (Khasi Land) it is the Khasi people's national anthem, although they've had to be choosy as to which of his occasionally imperialistic verses they sing today. Lines (roughly translated) such as

> The British have come, the Indians too;
> Khasi Land is refulgent with joy;
> Ignorance is banished, darkness is no more,
> Let the flowers of knowledge bloom.

have died a deserved death. These days only two of the original eight verses are sung:

> *Ri Khasi, Ri Khasi, nga ieit eh ia pha,*
> *Ka Ri kaba ieit uba rim uba jah;*
> *Ki tymmen mynhyndai la ngam iohi shuh,*
> *Jingkynmaw ia ki kan ym due*
>
> Chorus:
> *Ri, Ri, nga ieit thoin thoin la ka ri:*
> *Ngin kiew sha khlieh, shaphrano ngin mih,*
> *Umpohliew jingstad ngin iadih.*
>
> *Lum Khasi, Lum Khasi, kat phi ym ju don,*
> *Ka lyer basngewtynnad ngi bam katba mon;*
> *Ka um kaba shngiam ka tuid ha ki wah,*
> *Kam rngad myntlang ruh ka sah.*

["Ri Khasi, Ri Khasi, of all I love you,/Land beloved of those who are here no more;/Though lost to sight are the ancestors of old,/They will always be remembered. Chorus: Ri, Ri, truly truly I love you:/Upwards we'll march, ahead we'll emerge,/The water of wisdom will be ours. Khasi Hills, Khasi Hills, unique in all the world,/The air is cool, we lack for nothing;/The water is sweet that flows in our creeks,/Not even the winter can dry it up."]

Many youngsters I met were intrigued to learn that their national anthem, which is sung in all the schools before lessons begin, was also ours and the Bretons'. Every other young Khasi seems to play the guitar, and they'll launch into "Ri Khasi" at the flick of a plectrum.

But the missionaries' overriding literary preoccupation, until the end of the century, was the translation of the bible, and the propagation, through suitable texts, of Christian morality. The Lewises, the Robertses and their successors published Khasi versions of Christian standards such as *Rhodd Tad* (A Father's Gift), *Tyred at Iesu* (Come to Jesus), Watts's *Scripture History*, Bunyan's *Pilgrim's Progress* and *The Story of Mary Jones*.

These prolific *litterateurs* were assisted in their labours not only by their spouses but by native members of the Church whom they would call upon for advice. However, it was not until 1888 that the first ever book of Khasi poetry appeared, Sheikh Muhamad Amjad Ali's *Ka Myntoi* (Profit) – and that collection, as the author's name implies, was not by a native-born Khasi. Ali was born to a Muslim family in Sylhet, although he spent most of his life among the Khasis and identified strongly with their cause – sometimes, at any rate: in one poem he calls on the Khasis to revolt against their flirtation with an alien religion and their slavish dependence on the British; in another, he eulogises the Brits for painting much of the world pink, and invites them to carry on the good work. No doubt Ali, like Whitman, contained multitudes; he certainly perplexed the missionaries who, monopolising the literary scene, did their best to ignore him.

There was no ignoring the cultural revival, at the turn of the century, of which Ali was a precursor. Led by the erudite Jeebon Roy, pioneer of secular Khasi literature and founder of the Seng Khasi, it drew into its front ranks several writers, such as Rabon

Singh and Radhon Sing Berry, who had abandoned Presbyterianism and reverted to their native faith.

The proudly Khasi stance adopted by such authors encouraged Christian writers to be more celebratory of their own culture. Soso Tham, a Presbyterian by birth and a pupil of Dr. John Roberts, is accounted the greatest of all Khasi poets. A schoolteacher and lawyer, Soso Tham published two ground-breaking volumes of poetry in 1936 which, for the first time in Khasi verse, touch on erotic, social and political themes, and sing of everyday life. He attacks the self-forgetful materialism of the present and calls on his compatriots to remember a golden age when the Khasis were at one with each other and the natural world. He laments his contemporaries' ignorance of their own tribal religion, democracy, arts and customs. "We look for knowledge all round the world, but of our own we know nothing," he said, blaming British influence for the low esteem in which Khasis now held their traditional culture. Yet, in the preface to one of his books, he paid sincere tribute to the mission: "How grateful we are to the Welsh Mission for all it has done. The whole country must think about this. Whose kingdoms are ours? Whose citizens are we? What have the Syiems and the Khasi states done to drive away darkness? . . . The Mission has led the way; like a tusker, it has trampled down all difficulties without counting the cost; it has poured forth its own wealth and the best of its people for a hundred years . . . "

I say that Soso Tham is 'accounted' the greatest Khasi poet because there is no way that a non-Khasi speaker such as myself is able to arrive at an independent evaluation of these writers. They lack, so far, a Tony Conran to do for the translation of Khasi poetry what Conran did for Welsh in his pioneering *Penguin Book of Welsh Verse*. This brief and I hope not too wildly inaccurate survey of Khasi literature is based on discussions with Khasi writers, English-language articles in Khasi publications and the occasional university thesis. The academics' ploddingly inadequate pseudo-Victorian renditions of Khasi poetry merely becloud the treasures they labour to set before us. Fumbling towards Khasi poetry in this ripe old Oxbridge fog is rather like being marched up Shillong Peak, the

Khasis' highest mountain, and being persuaded that if it weren't for today's unfortunate low cloud there would be a spectacular view of the snow-tipped Himalayas far to the north. One can but hope for clearer weather, a translator who is in his bones a poet.

While the Welsh are often thanked for blazing the literary trail, their influence, which has yet to be analysed by someone familiar with both languages and both traditions, has not always been beneficial. The Welsh in the Khasi Hills wrote primarily to propagandise the Christian faith and way of life, setting an example in worthy moralising that has tainted much that has been written up to the present. The early missionaries were, after all, products of one of the least creative periods in Welsh literary history; this might account to some extent for the view of literature as 'moral uplift' that predominated for at least fifty years after their arrival.

Mary Lewis and, following her, Dr. John Roberts furnished the Khasis with an influential but narrow model of the novel in texts such as *The Pilgrim's Progress* and extended reworkings of the biblical stories of Moses and Joseph, with their characters reduced to uncomplicated, static 'types' engaged in simple plots based invariably on the ultimate triumph of bright-eyed probity and righteousness over the doomy machinations of evil. Christian writers, falling back on styles and themes pioneered by the missionaries, tended to dismiss native subjects as "dark knowledge".

Of the 120 books published between 1842 and 1930, about sixty were religious publications, and most of the remainder were text books. Soso Tham deplored the absence of 'the reading habit' among his contemporaries. "A modern Khasi does not read unless he is forced to in school and in church," he complained. "And Khasi youth will not read a Khasi book, however good it may be, unless it is a text book. Can there be a darker blindness than this?"

The showy respectability of Welsh Presbyterianism, seeping through to aspiring Khasi writers from the schools, the media and developing institutions, inhibited many authors from tackling some of the psychological and social difficulties of contemporary life. There were powerful voices raised against modern fiction, the evangelist Seint Singh, for instance, declaring in 1934: "We should not give [novels] to young people who are really young mentally, because these will doubtlessly spoil them. We have seen in the whole world that persons who delight in novels do not care anything about the preciousness of their life, and finally ruin themselves in immorality."

The Seng Khasi view was comparably prim. "To be good and righteous, and to reach the House of God in this age," wrote Sib Charan Roy, one of the association's founders, "we should not read or allow others to read any kind of 'Novel' (the story about sex), because such books do not improve upon the tranquil nature of man. On the contrary, they tempt their readers into bonding with evil." Hardly an encouragement to a questing young novelist, Christian or not, to take up her pen and write.

In the 1960s a new generation of writers shrugged off these stifling prescriptions and began to tackle contemporary social and sexual themes with an uncompromising directness. Chief among them is Desmond's novelist father, Leslie Hardinge Pde. His books, controversial at first, soon caught the popular imagination and were eventually deemed sufficiently 'respectable' to be the subject of a doctoral thesis at the university. They sell, as he says, "like hot cakes".

The Khasis, possibly half of whom are literate, have a deep-seated love of good story-telling; long, extemporised narrative poems, often with musical accompaniment, are still a vibrant part of their oral culture. A novelist of L.H. Pde's standing can expect to sell 2,000 copies of a new work within two months of publication; some of his titles are into fourth editions, and most of his books, passed eagerly from hand to hand, will have many readers.

The poet of the printed page, as even Soso Tham was obliged to acknowledge, has by contrast a much smaller readership. "This," Kynpham told me, "is because we are fundamentally a story-telling people, not a poetry-writing people." It may also have something to do with the neo-Victorian windiness of much that passes itself off as 'modern' verse, and routinely scoops the state literary awards. This tensionless whimsy, full of dancing daffodils and cuckoos afar, offers at best a chocolate box view of the tribal past and has virtually nothing to say about the agonising dilemmas of the present.

A sad consequence of Khasi poetry's apparent retreat into quaint irrelevance is that many of a talented younger generation, politically astute and steeped in the poetry of twentieth century modernists, have abandoned their native language as a creative medium and taken to English, contributing thereby to 'Anglo-Khasi literature' (yes, the Khasis too have a hyphenated offshoot of the native oak!). Their commitment to the survival of their language and culture is not in question; indeed, it was movingly in evidence at a packed and attentive poetry reading in which I was invited to participate in Shillong.

This was the first such gathering since the murderous communal violence of a few weeks earlier, and some of the poets were struggling hard to find words for complex emotions. In addition to powerful statements from more experienced poets such as Desmond, Kynpham and Robin, there were challenging contributions from a number of promising new writers. The young geographer Almond Dean Syiem, who is general secretary of the Meghalaya Post-Graduate Students' Union, wrote with anger about the continuing police brutality, and dingy cells where

> ... people are fettered and chained
> by men in iron hats
> whose favourite possessions are
> lathis and rifles.

> The sudden howl of street dogs
> opens the poet's ear
> to the screams of those
> who will not walk any more,
> whose skins will carry
> cigarette scars to the grave.

> When sentinels of the law
> mess your food with urine,
> and quench your thirst with
> water mixed with shave-lather . . .

Then, my people,
then even the winter skies might shed tears
for you this evening.

And Indari Syiem Warjri, though Khasi to the roots of her magnificent sheaf of black hair, twitted some of the hot-bloods with a compassionate and courageous mother's poem:

The God of revenge bloods the innocent child,
twisted faces dagger soft sleep.
"Kill the bastard before it grows up to fight,"
they chanted.
And a bloodied stone beside the unrecognisable
three-year-old face
are the dregs of last night's savagery.

Arms in slings, terrified eyes
below bandaged heads.
A child tugs her mother's skirts
"Ma, let's go home."
Shush, baby girl, unfeeling strangers
have ground beneath their iron heels
your dolls and your tea-set.
There are heated discussions over cups of
sweetened tea.
There are biased newspapers and impersonal
radio reports.
There is your soul splashed with blood.

I do not call you 'brother'
who wage war on children and watch as they
choke in silent anguish.

One reason given by these young poets for opting out of Khasi is that they wish to dissociate themselves from the daffs and cuckoos of "the old fogeys", and to appeal through newspapers, the radio and Indian publications to a wider public. Looking at this from a Welsh standpoint, it seemed, and still

255

seems, a slightly strange abdication, particularly as only 3% of Indians speak the country's supposed *lingua franca*; but perhaps in some cases 'the English phase' is temporary and amounts to a purging of clutter before a return to linguistic first positions.

Another reason for writing in English is hinted at in one of Desmond's poems:

> My burdensome English learning
> assails me, and the tomb it has become
> laughs and cackles without end.
> Hiding under dark cloaks of
> my alien patrons, I was
> taught to be ashamed
> of my own.

It is a painful fact of literary life for some of these writers that although Khasi is their everyday medium, they are not sufficiently confident in the language to make poems in it. This real or imagined incapacity is largely the fault of an education system which has Khasi as the sole medium of instruction at the primary level only. Secondary school pupils, abandoning their native tongue, are obliged to matriculate in English.

Dr. John Roberts, the 'other' father of Khasi literature, would not have approved. "He rebuked us always for not knowing our own language," Soso Tham once wrote of his old teacher.

81

The great Welsh Revival of 1904-5 leapt like a bolt of lightning to the Khasi Jaintia Hills, and John Roberts, with a little help no doubt from Headquarters, was its chief conductor.

As in Wales, periodic revivals have been vital to the growth of Presbyterianism, and none has made a more memorable impact than that sparked off by Wales's so-called Evan Roberts Revival.

Khasi Christians had been praying for a revival for at least three years. Then, in 1905, letters and eyewitness accounts, particularly those of Dr. John Roberts who had been home on furlough at the time, brought news of momentous revivalist happenings in Wales. It was the signal the Khasis had been waiting for. Within weeks revival fever took hold throughout the Hills, and soon reports were reaching Wales of "strange and indescribable meetings" in the Khasi Hills.

Huge prayer meetings, all-night singing festivals and, much to the alarm of the missionaries, exuberant dancing marked the Revival's triumphal passage through the Hills.

"Such singing!" enthused a breathless Mrs. John Roberts [sic] in *The Revival in the Khasia Hills* (Newport, 1907). "It is doubtful whether such singing can be heard anywhere outside Wales, even if in Wales itself. The people sing not only with their voices, but with all their bodies . . ."

As a main purpose of her little book was to elicit generous 'thank-offerings' from home congregations, she was at pains to emphasise the Khasis' undying gratitude to the Welsh for their spiritual salvation. "It was very beautiful to hear them speak of their 'parents' in Wales, and all that they had done for them. Before the Throne of Grace they constantly acknowledged their heavy debt to Wales, they pleaded for rich blessings upon the land, and we have even heard them thanking God that He had made such a spot as Wales. Yes, the tie between our Church in Wales and her Mission Field in India has been drawn very tightly now, and the outlook for the future is very cheering. The Christians have caught her spirit, and the genius of her administration is working in the Churches, Presbyteries, and Assemblies, making the Khasia Church a power in the country."

And, as in Wales, there were serious misgivings in certain quarters as to the unbridled hysteria of these revivalist gatherings and the 'pentecostal' disorder they called up. John Roberts was himself deeply uneasy about some of the Revival's manifestations; especially disturbing to him was the dancing that went on – men, women and children together – during church services.

The missionaries' disagreement among themselves about the effects of the Revival troubled some of the native elders. A deacon at Shangpung composed a prayer appealing to God to sort out the internal controversy: "O Lord, grant the missionaries wisdom to enable them to guide us in such a time as this. They might think that we are mad, but we are full of the new wine of the Holy Spirit."

The Revivalist vintage of 1905-6 certainly proved a heady wine, so much so that the doubts of John Roberts and other conservatives diminished with every fortifying intake of converts. In just two years, the Presbyterians, numbering about 22,500 at the beginning of 1905, added five thousand new Christians to their membership.

The Khasi Awakening spread revival not only to other parts of India but as far afield as Korea. It is hardly surprising, therefore, that the church historian J. Edwin Orr should have concluded in *Evangelical Awakening in India* (New Delhi, 1971) that "By far the most significant overseas event influencing the life of the Indian Church in the early twentieth century was the Welsh Revival of 1904."

Evan Roberts himself had a direct family stake in the Hills.

His sister Mary, married to Evan's fellow revivalist the Rev. Sidney Evans, of Casllwchwr, was a missionary in Khasia from 1920 until 1945, when she and her husband returned to Wales.

John Roberts never returned. His grave, with its iron fence and obelisk, is the most prominent in the Nongsawlia cemetery. Like that of the Rev. Daniel Jones a few feet away, it is also the grave of his child, Freddie Bach, who died aged seven months in 1874. Roberts himself was taken suddenly, and somewhat before his time, by the great cholera epidemic of 1908 which, says *The Dictionary of Welsh Biography*, "though far from well, he fought relentlessly and without mercy on himself."

82

If, as some young pastors fear, the Khasi Church is in danger of going the same wasting way as the *'mam eglwys'*, the likeliest cause of decline will be its conservatism. It may at present attract three or four thousand new members a year, but the failure to 'indigenise', together with the preponderance of 'biological' Christians over individually motivated believers, and a reluctance to engage with sometimes controversial socio-political issues, are factors that threaten to bring about a reversal in its fortunes.

The Church's radical tradition, epitomised by its founder, survives as a frowned-upon subculture. It manages, nevertheless, to throw up formidably intelligent and resourceful chips off the Jonesian block. One of Christ's most notorious activists in the Khasi Hills is the Rev. Prechard Basaiawmoit whom I met in the cool and musty tranquillity of Cherra Theological College, whither he'd been 'exiled' to keep him out of contention's way.

"I am nobody's friend, I am a real nuisance," beamed the goateed rebel. "Somebody said to me lately, 'No government likes you,' and I replied, 'Thank you very much'."

The college, founded by Dr. John Roberts in 1887 and rebuilt after the earthquake, is steeped in missionary history. The first theological institute in north-east India, it was built, possibly, on the site of Thomas Jones's house, and is sheltered from the sun by a great banyan tree planted, say the locals, by the Rev. Robert Jones about a hundred years ago.

It is north-east India's equivalent of Coleg y Bala. Ednyfed Thomas, who was principal here for many years, wrote in his history of the Mission that the College's courses, all taught through the medium of English, are of as high a standard as any arts university in India, and its Theology Licentiate compares favourably with the Diploma of the University of Wales.

The missionaries, by common consent, set exactingly high standards in both religious and secular affairs. Another missionary who has become something of a legend is the Rev. T. B. Phillips, who was also a principal here for some of his time. I took a note, one whisky-warmed evening in Shillong, of what Darwin Pugh had to say of him.

"We believe," said Darwin, putting down his glass and leaning forward in his chair, "that if T. Bevan Phillips had not come to the Khasi Hills and had stayed at home in Wales, he would have been a Labour Prime Minister of Britain. He started out as a coalminer but went on to take a tripos. As far as I am concerned, he was the greatest missionary. And the greatest orator. He would find a point of contact, and after that make three main points, and would be sure not to go on for more than fifteen minutes.

"T. B. Phillips was *it*, class AA. I realised this when he analysed Indian politics. A brilliant intellect, a first-class orator: sure-fire Prime Minister material. It was men of this calibre that the Welsh were sending us."

The biggest of the College's high, dark rooms is the William Lewis Hall whose 'SILENCE PLEASE' sign in letters two feet high seems a somewhat overstated injunction when all that is to be heard are a passing student's flip-flops and the shuffle of pages in the nearby John Roberts Library. Here, above the black-leaded cast-iron fireplace typical of all the old missionary buildings, hangs a sepia portrait of Georgian piety: "Mr. Arthur Jones, Tylorstown, Wales and the late Mrs. Jones, in memory of whom he gave £300 to form three scholarships at the C.M. Theological College, Cherrapunjee, Khasia, India. May 24th, 1924." A little mould has blotched the photograph's edges, but in other respects Mr. and Mrs. Jones have survived three quarters of a century in the world's wettest place remarkably well.

Running a library during the heaviest monsoon on earth, the librarian agrees, is not without its problems. There are the leeches to repel, the fires to stoke, the crumbling books to mend . . . But not for much longer: whether Cherrapunji likes it or not (and for the most part Cherrapunji hates it), the Theological College is to move to the city. I wonder how Mr. and Mrs. Jones will cope with the transfer from meditative Nongsawlia to the noisy stinks of Shillong – if, that is, they get as far as the removal van.

Prechard invites me into his office for an impromptu bowl of curry. Rebellion, it would seem, is in the Reverend's blood, for his forebears were among the warriors of Tirot Singh. The family, however, have been Christians for generations. His great grandfather was the Rev. Amirkha, one of the first Khasis to be ordained.

There seem to be more girls than boys in Khasi schools but, I put it to him, no women in the Theological College?

"Out of a total of seventy five students there are only three women doing their Bachelor of Theology degrees here at the moment," he replies. "Our church is very male-heavy as far as the ministry goes, but in other ways women play an important part. The women's wing is a semi-autonomous body with its own programme. They raise funds for the hospitals in Shillong and Jowai, organise the temperance movement and run the Bible Society and evangelistic committees. But if they are going to be more involved in the ministry, and I hope they are, they are going to have to campaign for it."

Prechard is a veteran of many campaigns. In addition to teaching at Cherra, he is pastor of Mawpat, a village on the outskirts of Shillong which had been waiting for years for a road and a water supply.

"Eventually," he said, "I got the villagers behind me to threaten the government with an ultimatum: give us the road and the water, or we'll go on hunger strike. You have to put yourself in the front line: I told my people that I would be the first to be beaten up, if it came to it, and the first to be arrested. Mawpat now has a road and water."

The Meghalaya branch of the People's Union for Civil Liberties, originally formed in 1982, has been stung into renewed action by the events of recent weeks. Prechard is its president.

"We are going to hold a public hearing regarding the atrocities and the state violence, and people's feelings about it. We will start the proceedings in two weeks' time, and eventually we will produce a report."

Which is likely to be 'controversial'?

"I expect disapproval from the Church – north-east Indian churches are famously fundamentalistic and conservative – but I invite that disapproval, so that I can explain my stand."

It will take more than threats of a hunger strike to win the latest campaign in which Prechard is playing a leading role, the struggle to stop what could develop into the biggest uranium mine in the world. At Domiasiat in the West Khasi Hills extraction of the Janus-headed mineral has already begun, in circumstances of semi-secrecy. According to Prechard, the deposit at Domiasiat amounts to 9.22 million tons – and it is part of a belt of uranium that is about 75 miles long.

"This," he says, "is bigger than the Australian uranium field, which is the biggest in the world. If we don't get this thing stopped, the human, cultural and environmental consequences will be devastating.

"I welcomed nuclear power when I first heard of it. I thought India and her poor people would become rich. Only recently have I begun to realise how dangerous it is, and how intimately it is bound up in the manufacture of nuclear weapons.

"Now, we Khasis are non-violent. We have not followed the ways of the Nagas and Mizos who have realised their political goals through violence. Non-violent direct action is how we managed to win our own state. But if India is allowed to mine uranium, we are going to contribute indirectly to nuclear war – our uranium could be responsible for destroying the world.

"There are also the more immediate health and environmental problems. The mining process is not dangerous in itself, it's the 'tailings' that arise from the milling process that are dangerous. For one kilogram of 'KO 308' there will be between one thousand and four thousand kilograms of waste. The fish in our streams are already dying because of uranium pollution. And our streams go to Bangladesh, although Bangladesh is not yet aware of what is happening."

The Government is attempting to bribe the West Khasis with schools, hospital and roads while keeping them in as much ignorance as possible about the consequences of uranium mining. But Prechard has been out preaching.

"It's the imperative duty of the Government to provide you with these essentials, uranium or no uranium, I have been telling the people. The Government is not fooling them as easily as it had hoped. They are learning fast. One of the landowners in the area got a State order to stop the Indian Government investigating on his land. I have a petition of 71 landowners who are against it, and the miners themselves have asked me to help them, because they are powerless against the State, the industry and the politicians."

Lately he has been to Germany, to meet politicans, Green activists and speakers from Chernobyl and Australia. "We learned that we are not isolated," he says. "It's a global problem."

But what about the isolation of his 'exile' to Cherra?

"Cherra's not a bad place to be," he smiles wickedly. "I can teach all the young pastors here. We have students from the whole of the north-east who are prepared to be involved, if and when we need people's power. My only real fear is that these terrorist groups that are springing up throughout the region will get the upper hand. We must be on our guard against that."

83

'The boys', as bemused citizens call the insurgents, are to be found in a bewildering array of movements, fronts, factions and cells throughout the north-eastern states, massacring perceived enemies of their ethnicity – women and children a speciality – under slogans such as "Nagaland for Christ".

Two students who often dropped in at the Prakash to discuss poetry and music over a bottle of Black Label, called by one afternoon to talk of sterner stuff: the struggle. They sat on my bed, in their spotless white shirts and designer trousers, and gave it to me straight.

"To understand these movements you have to look at what is happening," says Joe (not his real name: they asked me to use pseudonyms). "Outsiders are pouring into our Hills. They are taking our land and our jobs. They are marrying our women so they can steal Khasi property. They are trampling all over our language and culture, and abusing the rights of the Khasi people."

"Let me give you an example," says Wilson. "Non-tribals are not permitted to own land here. So what happens when a non-tribal wants to buy a shop in Iewduh [Shillong's market quarter]? He simply bribes a corrupt Khasi to be the owner of the shop on paper, while in actual fact he, the non-tribal, is the real owner.

"Armed groups like the Hynniewtrep Achik Liberation Council (HALC) or the Hynniewtrep Volunteers' Council (HVC) are committed to rooting out this kind of social evil, rooting out corrupt politicians who care only about their own seats and their own pockets."

"What do you mean by 'rooting out'?" I ask. "Shooting them?"

"If these wrong-doers persist in their ways, then, sadly and unfortunately, yes."

"The ultimate objective of both the HALC and the HVC is to liberate the Khasi people," says Joe. "We believe that sooner or later we may achieve independence – independence for all the north-east states. We in the north-east are culturally and socially similar, and we have enough resources to look after ourselves. We never wanted to be part of India. The upper classes and the rich don't mind belonging to India, but those who could have made it, and have been manipulated by the politicians, are fed up with the Marwaris from Rajasthan running all the businesses and controlling the politicians, they are fed up with protesters being tortured to the third degree by the police and army."

The discussion turns to other groups in the region – the Garos' Achik Liberation Matgrik Army, the Meghalaya Revolutionary Alliance (MRA), and the Indo-Burma Revolutionary Front which wants to forge a new nation out of north-east India and Burma. Some of these organisations are as ephemeral as a puff of gunsmoke, but others mean bloody business: we are not talking here of the rhetorical exhibitionism of Free Wales Army-style outfits, but of frustrated and invariably unemployed young men driven to desperate deeds by the conviction that the tribal cultures of the north-east are staring annihilation in the face.

"We are Khasi by blood, Indian by accident," says Wilson.

"India is the problem," adds Joe, "The HALC identifies India as enemy number one."

Are Wilson and Joe, I enquire, members of the HALC? Or some other group? On that question they are unwilling to be drawn. And anyway, it's time for them to be thinking of their next engagement, choir practice.

Yes, Wilson and Joe are good Presbyterian boys who go to church on Sundays, and view with some perplexity, I can tell, their Welsh drinking pal's bizarre lack of religion.

84

"The chapel was already full by the time we arrived, and as the hymn commenced the congregation rose to sing . . . Khasi were the words, but the feeling was altogether Welsh, and I shall never forget how they sang this wonderful old Welsh tune, until the chapel positively resounded . . . There was about this typical gathering much that intrigued and delighted us, so akin was it to the home associations; the congregation differed in language and dress, that is all . . . "

Little has changed in the century and more since J. Herbert Roberts wrote *Ymweliad â Bryniau Khasia*. If anything, the similarities are more pronounced, for the men, in their sober suits and shiny shoes, would pass muster in any chapel in contemporary Wales. Indeed, so strong is the church-going habit in Khasia, and so feeble has it grown in Gwalia, that the Khasi Sunday is by now considerably more Welsh than that of Wales.

The Pugh family, members of the big but crowded church at Mawkhar, have inclined lately to attend services at its 'overspill' church at Mawprem, which although only a couple of years old already has a membership of 1,200. Linda, her daughter Sharon and their driver Bari took me there in the jeep that she uses for her literacy crusades in the interior. The streets of Shillong were full of small groups of worshippers in their Sunday best, most of them clutching bibles, some holding umbrellas against the heat of the sun. The churches get so full that worshippers, especially from outlying villages, start arriving at least an hour before the service is due to start, to be sure of a seat.

I had hoped to glide with my friends unobtrusively to the rear. But the deacons on the door had other plans. The honoured guest from Wales would come forward, please, and sit with the elders at the front of the church. This being a new church, it was less than half full, and there was an acre or so of empty seats between the congregation and the deacons' pews facing across the church at the business end.

"In a few years' time," beamed the elder who showed me where to sit, "all these empty places will be full."

The deacons smelled of lunch. There was no mistaking the whiff of rice and boiled meats that clung to their clothes. Linda confirmed later that most people would have eaten lunch, at about ten or eleven, before coming to the main, one o'clock service.

Rather than run into quicksand with the deacons over my connections, or lack of, with the mother church, I busied myself with a hymn book as we waited for the service to begin. And here they all were: Cwm Rhondda, Aberystwyth, Llef, Blaenwern, Pennant, Gwalchmai, Pwllheli, Cyfamod – the great Welsh hymn tunes that have become so traditional a bulwark of Khasi Christianity that any move to 'indigenise' church services by introducing native instruments and compositions could expect to run into stiff opposition, especially among older Presbyterians.

The church, its bell clanging to hasten the stragglers, was broad, light and airy, its windowsills low enough to tempt an errant eye to go wandering through the trees and over the distant hills.

The opening hymn, "Kham jan, Ah Blei, ia Me . . . " ("Nearer my God to thee"), was sung to the tune of Clarach; then we sang what was possibly a translation of Ann Griffiths's "Yr Atgyfodiad a'r Bywyd" to John Roberts, Aberdare's Alexander, followed by what might have been "Gristion, gweithia" to the tune of Llantrisant – the attributions of the Khasi hymn book are vague, to say the least. The singing, interspersed with notices, prayers and readings (from *Acts*, I think, and *Romans*), was as impassioned and exuberantly harmonised as anything to be heard in Wales.

The service was conducted by Professor Pakem, vice-chancellor of the university, who also delivered the sermon, flanked left and right by vases of chrysanthemums. It is difficult to distinguish in such an address between the ardour of native oratory, still a feature of traditional village democracy, and the *hwyl* of Welsh preaching which the missionaries used to such persuasive effect. The two styles seem to have intermarried, breeding on the one hand a formidable line of Khasi pulpiteers, and on the other parliamentarians of renowned eloquence such as G.G. Swell.

An incidental quirk that Khasi elders and ministers have in common with the Welsh is that whereas the prayers are spoken in undiluted Khasi, odd words of English are often dropped into the sermon. But mother and daughter churches part company on the matter of a sermon's duration: in the Khasi Hills a 'good' sermon is expected to last for at least an hour and a half – although, as in Wales, every chapel has a large clock within a few feet of the pulpit, so that worshippers may be sure that ministers do neither more nor less than they're expected to.

Fortunately, the Professor proved a more succinct rhetorician than most, and we were shuffling back into the sunlight by about 2.30. Many of Shillong's other churches were still in deep session, their hymns and amplified sermons swelling into the streets through open doors and windows. Linda took me on a cruise of some of the city's dozen or so Presbyterian establishments. Several, with congregations of two or three thousand, were so packed that the lower panels of the rear walls had been removed, and benches had been set up outside to accommodate the overspill.

The Khasis love their hymns. But looking at their faces during the interminable announcements and seemingly humourless homiletics, I wondered if what might pass for attentiveness might not be disguising a less compliant emotion: bum-numbing, brain-dead boredom.

85

No one has thought longer and harder about 'indigenisation' than the Rev. Fortis Jyrwa. He has even written a doctoral thesis on the subject, but is afraid to publish it, in case his ideas engender an unholy theological earthquake.

"One of our major weaknesses as a church is that you don't see any significant differences between the church in Wales and the church in Shillong," he said, as we tucked into the roast beef, mashed potatoes, gravy and mint sauce his wife Mumtaz had prepared for the three of us.

"It's not that I want to do away with the Welsh hymns. Far from it. They have become part and parcel of my blood. But it disturbs me that when you go to any one of our churches you feel there is no difference between being here and being in Wales."

And Fortis, unlike most Khasis, has first-hand experience of Wales, having spent three months as a research student at the Theological College in Aberystwyth. A treasured memento of his stay is the rugby ball signed by the national XV: it has pride of place in his china cabinet.

"Please don't misunderstand me. If it were not for the Welsh sending the missionaries, I don't think I would be what I am today. They opened our eyes to the world, and the whole of society has benefitted, whether they are Christians or not. People to the south and north of us already had their own written language and literature, but we were still in the jungle. The missionaries' contribution to health and education has got to be recognised. And their influence on the development of Christianity in India in general.

"You see, the Government is against us, because we Christians have tended at the all-India level to address the 'low caste' people, the poor and uneducated – although we Khasis have no caste in our society, thank God, we have always been free and cordial with each other. But in India as a whole, the majority of Christians are lower caste people, and if it were not for Chistianity these people would be nowhere. The glory of the

Indian church is that it has done something to uplift the poor people – who are not even recognised by others as people.

"The missionaries are our fathers and mothers, I mean it. There are many, many plus points. But they were men and women of their age. For instance, they did not think equally in terms of the standard of living. They would pay their native teachers a salary of Rs. 25, and themselves Rs. 600. And the bungalows they built for themselves – huge! And the servants they had! They wanted to keep a distance from us. They would never come to our houses, and they were very strict that there should be no relationship or marriage with a Khasi. I would see the missionaries, in my village of Mawphlang, only on their evening stroll, when everyone would come out on the road and say *'Khublei'*, and then we would see them in church, and that is all. They didn't try to really understand our culture, they didn't try to help us understand the gospel in our own terms.

"They would tell us to develop a lifestyle akin to their own. For instance, a missionary told my sister when she was pregnant and cutting firewood in heavy rain, 'How dare you go to the field to collect firewood and get wet like this with a baby inside you. You should go home, warm yourself, drink milk, take two eggs, drink chicken broth, take a bath, put on warm clean clothes, see your hair is dry and go to bed and sleep.' My sister just said 'Yes, Miss', obediently after each of these instructions, and then she said to the missionary, 'You know, Miss, I can't afford to do even one of these things, because when I get home I will have to feed my cattle.' This may have been how a girl might have been expected to behave in Wales, if pregnant and caught in the rain, but such a view of things just didn't fit in with conditions of life here.

"But these are small things to us. Whenever we see people from Wales we realise that these people have made us what we are, sacrificing their lives – and the lives of their families – for the Khasi people."

Fortis is concerned that, in spite of a steady if slowing rate of growth, his church is in danger of losing its relevance, particularly among young people. Welsh ideas and practices have conditioned its development for too long. He and some of the younger ministers are concerned that native musical instruments, compositions and styles of singing should be introduced in churches alongside the Welsh hymns. And Khasi theologians should explore the correspondences between *Niam Khasi* and Christianity: the tradition of the cock as intercessor, for instance, has much in common with the image of Christ as mediator. Perhaps 'the Lamb of God' should be translated as 'the rooster of God'? Then there is the burdensome legacy of grandiose church buildings.

"We should stop building cathedral-style churches, it is beyond our ability," he said. "The missionaries favoured one form of building only, and their ideas have rooted themselves in the hearts and minds of the people, so that they can't think of any architecture or pattern or style that is not based on those that have existed since the missionaries came. We spend far too much money on the fabric of churches, when what we want is many churches in a simplified form."

In recent weeks the church had, tentatively, published some of the thoughts of Fortis in a pamphlet, but he dared not publish the thesis.

"It would upset people," he explained, "It's far too controversial. But we have got to grasp this nettle, we have to find ways of indigenising the church, so that it doesn't lose its relevance in the Khasi Jaintia Hills. When you visit a church in Mizoram and listen to their drums and the lyrics they have written themselves, you really feel you are in Mizoram. But our wonderful instruments are never heard in the churches here. Even today, sometimes, you hear what used to be said in former times when people were asked 'Are you a Christian?' 'No, I'm not a Christian, I am a Khasi.'"

Fortis admitted that the Seng Khasi, as the only organisation in the north-east committed to halting the march of Christianity, had done much to retard the Church's development. But the Seng Khasi would have had less to complain about if the missionaries had been more responsive to the indigenous culture. He hoped now that a *rapprochement* with the Seng Khasi was possible.

"There is a widespread movement these days to go back to the roots," he said. "Most of the young educated people will not accept unquestioningly what the church does and says. In the days of the missionaries, their word was law, and anyone who questioned them had to get out of the church. These days we have the maturity as a church to look at ourselves and, when necessary, to be self-critical."

As Fortis drove me back to the Prakash in his jeep, he spoke of his admiration for Thomas Jones – "a real champion of the Khasi people" – and his frustration at not being able to understand Welsh, the better to comprehend the history of his church. A full history, from a Khasi standpoint, has yet to be written.

"Don't imagine," he said as we glided through Shillong's early-to-bed streets, "that the whole thing was done by missionaries. There was no more, at any one time, than one missionary in about six or ten centres. There were many Khasi and Jaintia heroes of whom we know little or nothing – they never came into the official picture. And I would like to bring them to light – people like the Khasi missionary who did so much to start things in the Mizo Hills."

The Prakash was in darkness when Fortis dropped me off, so, not for the first time, I had to scale the chained and bolted iron gates, and wake the lad who always slept in the lobby in order to obtain my key. Blearily, he handed me a couple of notes from callers, one of which, from the university's Centre for Creative Arts, had promoted me from a mere Mr. to Dr. and raised me to the status of a great river: 'Dr. Niger Jenkins' was asked to be speaker and guest of honour at a demonstration of bamboo arts and crafts. "We shall greatly appreciate and thank you very much," read the invitation, "if you will kindly participate and benefit us with your esteemed experience . . ."

As my esteemed experience in this field went no further than knocking up a bow and arrow for a game of cowboys and Indians, I thought it wise, after my quackery in the pulpit, to refrain from adding the skills of instant bamboozler to an increasingly mythological C.V. Besides, I had already committed myself on that day to the quest for Khasi music.

86

The Khasis, declares *The Dictionary of Welsh Biography* in an entry on Dr. John Roberts, "had no music of their own". It is a grotesque lie, symptomatic of the way in which the missionaries, sweepingly dismissive of 'backward' custom, encouraged their converts to look with shame and contempt on traditional Khasi culture.

To the Rev. Jacob Tomlin, who first pointed the Welsh down the path to India, Khasi singing amounted to little more than "screaming".

It has long been recognised, even among Christians, that the powerful strictures of expansionist Presbyterianism did no small damage to Khasi folk culture – as of course they did, from the eighteenth century onwards, to the folk culture of Wales. Converts were obliged to dissociate themselves from all manifestations of 'erroneous' former ways and adopt not only a new religion but a new culture. The hymns of Pantycelyn and Ann Griffiths were to supplant the hypnotic drums and raucous *tangmuri* of the ancient rituals.

The drums and pipes of the big dance festivals, which are attended by thousands of people, represent the most confident public manifestation of Khasi folk music. But Khasi music has a quieter, lyrical side which, thanks to its more domestic expression, has suffered considerable neglect.

A leading exponent of this kind of music is Brek Wanswett, who, paradoxically, composed the song that rallied the peoples of Meghalaya behind the successful and bloodless campaign for full statehood. The exuberant "U Piad Khasi Baiar" has become a new national anthem, as popular as the Khasi version of "Hen Wlad Fy Nhadau".

Brek is master of the *duitara*, which is often referred to as 'the queen of Khasi instruments'. Vaguely akin to the guitar, the *duitara* has four silk strings, and is made of a single piece of hollowed-out papaya wood, with deerskin stretched over the soundbox. Its slightly muffled chatter is the perfect foil to his daughter Jurimon Risaw's blue sky of a voice.

It was the playing of these two fine musicians, in the *Monsoon* documentary, that first got me excited about the Khasis:

> *Hei ho u lapbah Sohra mynta u la wan.*
> *Pangah dieng ki siej ba svmpat u Kyllan.*
> *Her kynting lyoh khyndew na ki them sha ki lum . . .*

[Hey! Here at last the torrential rains of Cherra./See the whirlwind flay the swagger of trees and bamboos./Up fly the clouds from earth to sky . . .]

Lakyntiew, a friend of the musicians, took me to meet them.

After *kwai* and tea, they performed a short selection of songs for us – Brek, in woollen hat, immobile apart from the flurry of his fingers about the neck and bridge of his *duitara*, Jurimon swaying cheerfully on a seat beside him, her voice soaring and diving above the ground her father's music builds for her. Orchids, waterfalls, festivals, stones and sacred groves – Brek's songs are hymns of praise to the beauty and endangered customs of his treasured *Ri Khasi*.

Here, surely, was someone whose musical genius could help the church to 'Khasify' its services. I put the 'indigenisation' idea to him, but even he, being a Presbyterian, would have none of what plainly struck him as a most unnatural proposition.

"Christ said, 'I build my church on rock, not on sand,'" he declared. And that was an end to the matter.

Brek, who is from the War foothills near Cherra, is acknowledged, by the few who take any serious interest in the *duitara*, as one of the instrument's four or five leading players.

"It was in 1960 that I started to play, in response to a music competition. It was easier for me, because we attend the church and we sing tonic sol-fa – although in those days, of course, the church discouraged the playing of traditional instruments. We weren't even allowed to see the dance – if you did, you were thrown out of the church. And if you listened to a gramophone, there would be people who'd ask 'Are these words polite or impolite?' The words 'I love you' on a gramophone record were

273

considered very bad. But in the late sixties the church started relaxing its attitude."

If congregations remain conservatively attached to the Welsh hymns, official disapproval of indigenous music has now evaporated. The Presbyterian church has recently decided to establish a cultural department which may be in a position to give Brek and others the support that has been sadly lacking.

Meghalaya's state radio seems to be the only organisation in the Khasi Hills promoting Khasi music, although the paltry two rupees (four pence) royalty paid for a new piece of music is not enough to keep a musician in *duitara* strings. In Brek Wanswett, Jurimon Risaw and musicians like them, Khasi culture (not to mention the authorities responsible for promoting tourism) has assets which it is wastefully squandering. Church and classical music, Hindi and western pop have deafened people's ears to the sounds of their own culture. During the entire twelve months prior to our meeting, this Dafydd Iwan of the Khasis had received only one invitation to perform. He spends four hours a day practising and composing, but has to make his living as a peripatetic music teacher. This neglect of someone who should be a major cultural presence seems both reckless and unjust.

"Traditionally," said Brek, "the public expectation of playing and enjoying Khasi music is bound up only with the dance. The *duitara*, though, is used in little story-telling gatherings around the hearth. And the flute is used by the shepherds in the fields. There's no regular appreciation, no professional connection in the application of our music. It's just for our own satisfaction, a little bit of recreation after a hard day's work.

"You'll find that a lot of Khasi stories are tales – often told to music – about how to grow up, because the parents, busy all day in the fields, don't always have time to teach their children in any other way.

"Why do youngsters lose interest and get attracted to Indian or Western music? Because, until now, there have been no artists among us playing their own instruments to international standards. If there was somebody to play our own music and cross the barrier of the Khasi Hills and Meghalaya, our people would be attracted to their own music.

"Another problem is that all educated and learned musicians live in Shillong, and Shillong is steeped in classical, church, jazz and pop music. Those people who know our traditional music can't write it down, they are village people. And the town people, who could write it down, don't go to the villages, they tend to ignore traditional music."

As the author of the only Khasi musical text book in existence, Brek hopes that more tonic sol-fa transcriptions will help popularise the music, but the breakthrough he hopes for is unlikely to happen until someone with vision, and a modest amount of money, begins to make discs and tapes of this music.

"There is a need to get our music recognised," he said. "The idea of playing our music and celebrating our culture in case it goes away has not entered the public mind."

No recording of traditional Khasi music is publicly available, although before I left Shillong, Brek kindly presented me with a one-off compilation of bits and pieces he had recorded either in the home or in the studio, for the state radio station. He described them too modestly as "recorded in raw stage": most are recorded to a high standard, and are crying out for the wider distribution that is secured only by commercial publication.

He also handed me a brief shopping list, for a metronome, two pitch pipes and a conducting stick, items available only from the West. It was reminiscent of an order sent to headquarters by the Rev. Robert Evans, the former Aberffraw farm-worker who introduced the tonic sol-fa system to the Hills between the late 1880s and early 1900s. The Mission Board in Liverpool received from 'Saheb tonic sol-fa', as the Khasis called him, an urgent request for some vital pieces of equipment: fifty tuning forks.

87

We were supposed to rendezvous with a tiger-man in the jungle near Nongpoh, but we ended up instead with a shamanistic poet.

The tiger-man, a figure to be found in several of the villages of the interior, is born with the ability to turn himself – literally, they say – into a tiger. He will take himself off into a cave to effect this metamorphosis, but even in day-to-day life he is distinctly tigerish. Desmond showed me some photographs of one: the man was rather short of stripes, but in his claw-like nails and the piercing intensity of his eyes there was certainly something of a big, if ferociously pixilated, cat.

We have sent him word to expect us. Desmond and Scott, our driver, know the area well, having travelled hereabouts on many occasions collecting songs and stories. The rough stone and mud track out of Nongpoh is dry, and we make steady progress along a lushly tropical, broad valley until, within a couple of miles of the tiger man's village, we are brought to a sudden halt by a work-party building a bridge over what used to be a ford. We abandon the jeep and head off down a footpath to the nearest village.

Pahambir, about half a mile into the jungle, is a typical Bhoi country settlement. Situated in a hillocky clearing, it consists of twenty or thirty huts with mop-top thatches and wattle-and-mud walls. The village is more or less self-sufficient: in every direction there is food – lime-green acres of lilting paddy, pineapple plantations, hairy black porkers dozing in bamboo pens, cows with clunking neck-bells drifting in and out of the bushes, banana trees flashing their green scimitars in the golden light.

Desmond sends a messenger to the tiger-man's village. We wait for him sitting under the thatched overhang of a hut where Desmond sometimes lodges on his field trips. The daughters of the house, one with a baby in a shawl, eye us timidly from the opposite end of the overhang, while Desmond chats to their father in Khasi and I listen to the relentless jet-like whine of the cicadas. Scott plies everyone with dripping slithers of the juiciest pineapple I have ever tasted. The sun in Pahambir seems the village's hardest worker, drying out sticks of firewood on the baked earth yard, and desiccating swathes of finely chopped pork raised on a hurdle five feet above the ground, to keep it from the dogs.

The hut is a simple two-room windowless box, almost devoid of furniture and belongings. There's a rack for the gleaming cooking utensils, a calendar, a few tiny squatting stools, and a stick placed horizontally across one corner to serve as a clothes horse. There are no beds: the family sleep on straw which they spread every night on the earthen floor. On a shelf overhead there's a chunky family bible, seemingly raddled with antiquity, but published, I note, as recently as 1977.

The tiger-man, it appears, cannot be found. But the village story-teller, too old to climb our hillock, would like us to visit his compound.

We find him squatting in the shade of his overhang, surrounded by younger generations of his family and a few neighbours. The sun is busy here too, drying out lengths of cotton which have just been spun and bleached on a pair of looms. The storyteller is very old indeed, perhaps in his nineties; I wonder as he stands to greet us if his perilously thin legs will support his few pounds, but there's more sinew and inner strength to Mr. Dorbar Jaid Doloi Nongkymm than at first meets the eye.

After a short discussion with Desmond, who hasn't met the man before, he agrees to tell us a story.

There is a ritual to be observed. First his daughter, slim and sassy with her broken-toothed smile, wraps a turban round his head which she has woven herself. Then, squatting on a stool in the middle of the yard, he places on the ground in front of him the traditional egg-breaking board, the *dieng shat pylleng*; alongside it he puts a metal cup full of water and a small basket containing rice and an egg. He slops some water over the black wood of the board to clean it, then deposits some rice at its centre and a pinch of five or six grains at each corner.

Chanting, he places the egg on the nest of rice in the middle of the *dieng*. Then he picks it up, spits on it, rolls it round in his hand and launches into the story, his voice rising and falling as if in the throes of some oriental blues. He is clearly in a trance, oblivious to what is going on around him.

"This is truly marvellous," whispers Desmond. "The flow of his language is beautiful – he's saying things now that he would never be able to say in normal everyday circumstances."

Although I understand not a word of his story, its music and the sacramental atavism of the occasion send all the rivers of Khasia coursing down my spine. This is poetry, the marrow, bone and flesh of it; here, in all his knobbly, bardic majesty, is the kind of poet that we in Wales can only write history books about, a functioning remembrancer of the tribe. What are all those Shillong-bound poets doing writing theses about Wordsworth and Larkin, when they should be out here among the palms and whining cicadas, learning all they can, for their culture's sake, from this distinguished bardic elder?

His performance lasts about twenty minutes, with brief pauses and tailings off – to emit a groan or cough, or to replace the egg on the board before, once again, picking it up, spitting on it, and rolling it in the hand. Then he takes off again, with sky-bound swoopings of his freshly inspired incantation.

Desmond summarizes the story. The Sun, lusted after as ever by her brother the Moon, fled in shame from her sibling's advances and hid in a cave, thereby plunging the world into darkness. The creatures of the earth, unable to find food, grew increasingly desperate for the Sun to return to the sky. The stronger animals, the Elephant, the Horse, the Rhino and the Buffalo, volunteered to go in search of her, but they failed in their quest. The Hornbill also offered to help, but when he reached the Sun's hideout he tried to make love to her, and she, contemptuous of his advances, threw her stool at him and broke his beak – which is crooked to this day. Finally the Cock agreed to go and plead with the Sun to come out of her cave. "Give me a sign," said the Sun to the Cock. "I will crow three times," said the Cock. "Very well," said the Sun, "after you do that I will come out, and the world will be happy once more." So the Cock crowed thrice, and the Sun returned to the sky.

At the end of the story, the old man sweeps the rice from the board, stands with the egg in his upraised hand and flings it violently at the *dieng*. Shell shrapnel goes flying across the yard, and splatterd yolk drips down the sides of the board. Then he squats back down to read us a brief message from the way in which the bits of egg-shell are scattered. All manner of fortunes can be told by egg-breaking, from whether or not one should invest in a new rickshaw, to matters of health and affairs of the heart. To simplify a complex procedure, fragments lying with their insides downwards generally betoken a favourable sign, and vice versa. What no-one wants to see is a number of fragments lying in a line: this is the road to the funeral pyre.

On this occasion, the omens appear to be good. A bottle of rice beer is produced and poured into a tin mug, from which we all take regular sips.

The old man tells me, through Desmond, that he is largely deaf and partly blind. It's not often, these days, that he is called upon tell a story, and none of the younger people in the village are interested in following in his footsteps. "When I crumble," he says, "there will be no-one any more."

With the warmth of the rice beer blooming inside me, I'm tempted to learn Khasi, build a hut in Pahambir and stay here forever. But perhaps it's not wholly the Garden of Eden imagined by the fleeting visitor, who may be in need of the reality cadences of an R.S. Thomas. Too far for me, no doubt, to see the T.B. and the tooth-rot and the diarrhoea draining the babies of the stuff of life; too far for me to see the kraits and the leeches and the thatch-rotting endless monsoon rain . . .

88

"Two monsoons are the life of a man," the old colonialists used to lament as they succumbed in their hundreds of thousands to cholera, T.B., dysentery, malaria.

The sanatoria and medical services they established were invariably for Saheb's benefit only; the natives, with whose traditional ways (and traditional deaths) they believed there should be no interference, were left to fend for themselves. The Welsh, however, saw things differently.

After the missionaries had started clearing a doorway to the soul with their education and literacy programmes, they began to address the body's needs. The medical mission they established, with its dispensaries, rural health centres and health education schemes, saved countless thousands of Khasi lives. When they opened the first of several hospitals in 1883, they set out to serve both Europeans and natives alike.

The first doctors in the Hills were greeted with dread and suspicion, and there was uproar when the Welsh tried to halt the march of killer diseases such as smallpox – which the Khasis believed to betoken the visitation of spirits. But such was the success of the medical mission that many Welsh doctors are remembered today as people's heroes.

Discounting the brief service of the unfortunate Dr. Richards, the Mission had to wait thirty-seven years before appointing its first doctor and inaugurating a medical programme.

Most missionaries attended a short medical course and were packed off to India with a stethoscope, a thermometer, a case of instruments and a copy of Culpeper's herbal remedies. Their training was rudimentary, but there was much they could do to help the sick and educate the poor about some of the causes of ill-health. That hoary old slogan of 'muscular Christianity', "Cleanliness is next to godliness", which is still seen all over India, probably saved as many lives as penicillin.

Thomas Jones, who apparently had no formal training, nevertheless ministered to the sick to the best of his ability. He is held to be the first to attempt to disabuse the Khasis of their belief that a sick person should not be treated for fear of further aggravating the angry spirits who had inflicted the illness in the first place.

The medical mission proper began in 1879 with the arrival of Dr. Griffith Griffiths (1852-1932) who opened a dispensary and a four-bed hospital at Mawphlang.

His grandson, the Pontypridd writer and former police inspector Basil Griffiths, told me about him. Born in 1851 at Tŷ Mawr Farm near Aberdaron, he was the stern, puritanical son of an even sterner seafaring father, Captain Richard Griffiths who was master of his own sailing ship, the *Carmel*, which carried slate as far afield as South America. Captain Griffiths, it was said, ran his ship with the bible in one hand and a whip in the other (and is buried in the graveyard of R.S. Thomas's old church at Aberdaron).

The Captain and his son fell out over the boy's disinclination to follow him as a seafarer. Young Griffith stormed off to Scotland – on foot, according to family legend – in the company of his cousin Robert Evans ('Saheb tonic sol-fa'), and took a degree in medicine at Glasgow University.

When, eventually, the two cousins 'saw the light' they decided to enter the ministry and become missionaries. But before sailing to India they thought it proper to equip themselves with wives. Conveniently to hand were the two daughters of the late Rev. John Phillips, the founder and first principal of Bangor Normal College. "Accordingly Annie Phillips married my grandfather," Basil Griffiths told me. "There seems to have been little courtship involved in this arrangement, and according to my mother the two sisters were more or less directed to their Christian duty." The four newly-weds sailed together for India in October, 1878.

Dr. Griffith Griffiths was only twenty-six when he arrived in the Hills. Various tales of his exploits have come down to his grandson. "There seems to have been a recurring problem of water-borne diseases, and it fell to my grandfather to persuade some Khasis to remove themselves to healthier parts. Meeting with opposition from the headman, he set about using chloroform on a boy whom he then miraculously brought back to life, thus proving his magical powers and getting the people to remove themselves. It was also said that in similar circumstances he obtained the agreement of the headman by holding him over a fire!"

The Griffithses, who spent a quarter of a century in the mission field, produced no less than sixteen children, all but five of whom died in infancy, mostly of tuberculosis.

Dr. Griffiths could be as hard on members of his own family as he was on the Khasis. Basil's father, who was born at

Cherrapunji in 1886, would speak of the time when his father removed his tonsils simply by ordering him to 'open wide' and then snipping out the offending organs without any form of anaesthetic. "In later life when my grandmother was unwell my father purchased some patent medicine for her which she felt was beneficial, but when my grandfather, despite his medical training, discovered it contained the sinful substance of alcohol, he poured the potion away and forbade her to obtain a replacement. No cooking would be allowed to take place in the home on the Sabbath, Sunday newspapers were an unheard of wickedness, and even travel on that day was avoided."

The Griffiths family left the Hills in 1904 after the doctor was poisoned by a leech on one of his jungle expeditions. "Griffiths, Khasia", as he was known among the chapels, spent the rest of his life as a minister in various parts of Wales; he died in Cardiff, aged 81.

The doctor's children were raised speaking Welsh and Khasi. "My father always spoke with great affection of the native people who, it seems, virtually brought him up. He attended a mission school as a boarder, and as the journey from the village in which he lived was considerable, he was carried in a basket on the back of a native for a day or more. On one such journey he was attacked by a snake which was killed by the Khasi bearer at great risk to himself."

At school one evening the boy heard what he thought was the sound of pye-dogs pattering outside – but it was the preliminary shuffling of 1897's devastating earthquake. Running outside, he beheld great fissures opening up in the ground, into one of which he saw a man fall, to be pulled out just before the earth closed up again.

Dr. Griffiths, based in Cherra at the time, lost his hospital, his house and his furniture. "Everything that could be broken is lost," he wrote home. "Today I found an ink bottle among the debris, and it is, I suppose, the only one now in Cherra, for I have been trying to buy one . . . from the ruins of the shops here, but could not find any . . . The catastrophe has been appalling . . ., and it is enough to make one's blood freeze to think of the villages of Shella, Sohbar and Nongwar sliding down the hills and burying their inhabitants . . . The part of Cherra called Nongrim is going down the ravine with a sickening thud-thud with every shake and with every shower we get . . ."

Equally at home in Welsh and Khasi, Basil's father knew little English when he left the Hills, aged 11, and was sent to a public school for the children of middle ranking civil servants and others in the colonial service.

"Here he suffered the most barbaric humiliations," Basil told me. "One of his earliest experiences was of a master who conceived of my father's lack of understanding of what was said to him as a perverse and deliberate stupidity. Calling him out in front of the class and taking hold of a large book, the master brought the volume down with full force on my father's head, knocking him unconscious to the floor."

By the time he had completed his education the Welsh boy from Cherrapunji had lost entirely his ability to speak Welsh.

89

A medical missionary, the Welsh soon realised, could wield greater influence among the Khasis than any other kind of missionary.

An early observer of Dr. Griffiths' work at Mawphlang was J. Herbert Roberts who noted that during the rainy season up to forty people a day would attend his little hospital. While the doctor saw to their bodily needs, his assistant, the evangelist U Kypa Ka Hen, would sidle through a gap in the patients' 'pagan' defences and attend to their spiritual wants.

"The evangelist," wrote Roberts in *Ymweliad â Bryniau Khasia*, "is well suited to this work, being an unrivalled conversationalist, full of stories, and able to speak on any subject under the sun. Of necessity, many of the patients are pagans, and with some of these the evangelist gets talking first of all about some ordinary, everyday topic; then, having won a patient's attention and trust, he leads the discussion on to matters of faith and the meaning of life. Dr. Griffiths assured us that important work was done in this manner. When he asked people where first the Light entered their souls, often enough he received the reply, "It was in the waiting-room of the Medical Centre with U Kypa Ka Hen."

The first history of the Mission, the Rev. Griffith Hughes' *Bryniau Cassia* (?1889/90), makes explicit the usefulness of the medical mission in the task of evangelisation. "Giving medicine to [the Khasis] and making them better not only won their respect and good will, and opened a path to them, it also shook their faith in demonism, and tended to make them think favourably of Christianity," he wrote.

Word rapidly spread to remote parts of the Hills about the famous Dr. Griffiths with his hospital and his chapel. Increasing numbers of patients, often with family and friends to keep them company, came over great distances to seek the missionary's wondrous cures.

The clinic at Mawphlang continues to do important work. It is one of three rural health centres supported by the Women's Auxiliaries of the Presbyterian Church of Wales, who are also raising £25,000 of the £1m needed to finance the new building programme of the hospital in Shillong.

The Khasi Hills Presbyterian Hospital, Shillong, which opened in 1922, is one of the most impressive legacies of the Welsh. Nobody calls it by its cumbersome official title: it's known by everyone, still, as the Roberts (after its founder) or the Welsh Mission Hospital, and folk memory is likely to keep it that way.

This 250-bed establishment in the intensely Khasi district of Jaiaw is today one of about a dozen hospitals dotted around the city, but its reputation throughout the whole of north-east India is legendary, and two of its former superintendents, Dr. John Roberts and Dr. Arthur Hughes, are people's heroes all over the Hills. Time and again I met older Khasis who wanted to talk about Dr. Hughes: "Dr. Hughes saved my life in 1964"; "Dr. Hughes cured my son's cancer"; "Dr. Hughes was a saint – if poor people couldn't pay, he'd cut their bill in half"; "Dr Hughes worked so hard that he'd take his breakfast and lunch in the operating theatre . . ."

On the day of my visit the hospital was untypically quiet. The current medical superintendent, the cheery Dr. Pherlok Lamare, explained that both patients and some staff, particularly nontribals, were still afraid to venture into Jaiaw after the recent troubles. "It's almost like being on holiday," he laughed – the notion of a holiday, I imagine, being foreign to a man whose commitment to this hospital, like that of his illustrious predecessors, seems total.

First we visit the out-patients' waiting room, formerly an operating theatre, which is a kind of shrine to the founders. Photographs of Dr. Gordon Roberts and his wife Katie straddle the fireplace, above which sits a tablet commemorating their work and, hanging at a jaunty angle, a portrait of Dr. Hughes.

Dr. and Mrs. Roberts arrived in Shillong in 1913, but his ambitious plans for a hospital were destined to remain a dream until after World War One. On leave in Wales after the war, he raised £30,000 towards the project, and donated thousands of pounds of his own earnings as an Indian Government civil surgeon. Opposed initially by the authorities on the grounds that the sick in India would not submit to becoming in-patients, the hospital began as a two-roomed cottage. As the contributions from Wales flooded in, usually in the form of endowments of beds and cots, the hospital started to take its somewhat piecemeal shape. Many of the early nurses were women labourers who had worked on the construction of the hospital – it was the job of the first matron, Margaret Buckley, to turn them into passable health workers.

Within a few years it became the leading hospital of northeast India, attracting patients from well beyond the borders of Assam. One such was the Senior Maharani of Gwalior in Uttar Pradesh who had travelled the length and breadth of India seeking relief from a serious illness. This wealthy and highly orthodox Hindu princess and her entourage hit Shillong in style, taking over an entire boarding house for the summer.

After lengthy consultations between her senior physician, senior Government doctors and Dr. Roberts, the Welshman was eventually allowed to examine the Maharini. Diagnosis was difficult, because she refused to expose more than a small

285

portion of her anatomy, and she consented to surgery only under certain conditions. Most of the private wards had to be set aside for the Maharini's use, and accommodation had to be provided for the royal grandmother, her senior physicians, ladies in waiting and minister of state. The summer house on the lawn had to be made over to the royal astrologer who would predict when things were to take place.

The astrologer finally decided that the auspicious time for the operation would be when Dr. Roberts said he was ready to perform it. A hen was killed and hung up in the Maharini's room, the operation took place, and the princess made a good recovery. She was so impressed by Dr. Roberts and his Khasi nurses that she endowed the hospital with a major benefaction which enabled it to develop as an institution equipped to deal with surgical problems that few others in the region dared handle.

The private or 'European' wards, with their spacious individual rooms and magnificent views over the northern ridges, are still an important source of income, although it's mainly professional Khasi families who fill the private beds today. The daily tariff is Rs. 100 (£2), at least double the charge for a bed on the open wards – which to a considerable extent they subsidise.

"All patients have to pay," said Dr. Lamare, "but if very poor people have an operation which costs Rs. 1000 (£20) and they only have Rs. 700, we will do it anyway and ask them to bring the money later. Of course, many do not, so we simply register the money as an outstanding debt – such debts total thousands of *lakhs*. We never send collectors after the poor people, but in the private ward if they don't pay up we are after them within hours!"

India is full of time-capsules of the glory days of the Raj, and the little gazebo-like reading room at the end of the ward is one of them. Nothing here has changed since colonial times, when the main clientele were Assam tea planters, army wallahs and government top-brass and their families. The books they read as they recuperated in their silk dressing gowns are still here, gently crumbling witnesses to literary tastes long since out of time and place.

In contrast to the sedate ambience of the 'private' wing, the 'public' wards are normally severely overcrowded, with patients and their families jostling for floor space in the corridors, and often two children to one small cot. But today, because of the communal tensions outside, everyone has a place and the beds lining the corridors stand idle, their straw mattresses holed and gaping but good for a few patients more before they are thrown to the flames. There are dozens of plaques on the walls acknowledging the endowment of beds and equipment by individuals and chapels all over Wales.

The chief illnesses these days are T.B., gastro enteritis, heart disease and diabetes. Smallpox has been eradicated, but an old killer that medical science almost vanquished, malaria, is now making a wolfish come-back. The mosquito-borne parasite responsible for the disease is becoming increasingly resistant to drugs, and there is the spectre of untreatable malaria appearing before the end of the century. Another rising menace is AIDS.

I wondered if, in response to India's rampant birth-rate, the hospital did many vasectomies.

Dr. Lamare. "They are not encouraged here – we Khasis are too few! Sometimes men in their fifties come to us, whose wives are about to have, say, their fifteenth child. We ask them if they want to do anything about it, but as often as not the woman say they'll go on having babies until the equipment wears out!"

There is no fear of any 'equipment' wearing out in the hospital's nursing school which is as briskly protective of its starch-bright trainees as a five-star nunnery. Khasis comprise about a third of the seventy-five students, and even girls whose homes are only a few streets away are obliged to board in the student hostel whose regulations permit no more than one brief excursion a week beyond the hospital gates. After three years' training they are committed to three years' service in the hospital before, invariably, flitting off to America, southern India or the Arab countries. It's a demanding regime, but ever since the school was established in the 1920s as the first in the

287

north-east it has produced nurses of exceptional skill and commitment.

Confined as they are to their cloisters, the trainees have to make their own entertainment. A tradition started by the Welsh and continued to this day is the annual Christmas pageant. Hanging in the students' common room is a hand-tinted photograph of a pageant in the 1950s, showing the matron, Margaret Owen, surrounded by nurses dressed in all kinds of fancy outfits, including, piously, the Welsh national costume.

As pungent as the down-draughts from the hospital's smokestack that swirl around its low red roofs is the legend of Dr. Arthur Hughes. He and his wife Nancy left Shillong in 1969 after thirty-one years' service, but his legacy as a surgeon, administrator and wizard of improvisation is everywhere apparent.

Beneath that belching smokestack, whose emissions in pre-electricity days used to be the signal to the whole of Shillong that Dr. Roberts was getting up the power to perform an operation, are two gargantuan Cochran boilers. Sledged, rollered and inched into place with all the sweat and craft once employed by the Khasis to erect their giant monoliths, they ensure a constant supply of hot water and steam to power the many remarkable installations of Dr. Hughes. There's the central heating system, the first in north-east India, which he cobbled together from the pipes and radiators he found in an old ship in Calcutta. There are the two huge washing machines he acquired from the American army in World War II. There's the Arthur Hughes patent steam drier and the Arthur Hughes steam cooking range.

Then there was our Arthur Hughes three-course lunch, and the Arthur Hughes afternoon tea that Dr. Lamare and I shared in his office (which had been, of course, Dr. Hughes's office): dainty sandwiches and delicious golden teacakes such as you might find in a Bala teashop. All was prepared for us Welsh-style by Mr. Ajit Barua, an exiled Bangladeshi Buddhist, who had cooked for Dr. Hughes for thirty years.

"Somebody should write a book about Dr. Hughes," said Dr. Lamare, passing the scones. "He was a pioneering surgeon who performed several operations which had not been performed before. He knew all the flowers and grasses by name, and had a brilliant mind for technological problems. He would never stop reading. When he got interested in steam, he used to sit until two or three in the morning reading about its applications. He was a major figure here, yet when I worked for a year at the Royal Liverpool Hospital and visited his local church and various chapels in north Wales, nobody seemed to know of his achievements. I had to tell them."

Dr. Lamare and his family live next door to the hospital, in one of three voluminous bungalows (Dr. Hughes's, as it happens) built by the Mission for its medical supremos. The living room alone could swallow in its entirety the kind of seaside maisonette many of the missionaries retired to. Here, in addition to bulky items of Hughesian furniture, are one or two mementos of Dr. Lamare's travels in Wales, such as the *Gaeaf, Gwanwyn, Haf, Hydref*' teacloth that graces his coffee table.

"My visit to Wales simply confirmed my feeling that the Welsh influence here is so pervasive that it's difficult to tell what is 'traditional Khasi' and what is Welsh," he said. "The Khasis think of themselves as fine orators, but when I heard the Rev. Ednyfed Thomas preaching at the Jubilee celebrations last year, I realized precisely where this – how do you say it? – *hwyl* came from. It's unusual, isn't it, to find two peoples so far apart geographically with so much in common?"

We'd spent much of the day talking of the two medical heroes, Roberts and Hughes. At the end of it, I had little doubt – although he'd sink the suggestion with a gale of laughter – that in Pherlok Lamare I had met a third.

90

Shullai is a name almost as common among the Khasi Jaintias as is Jones among the Welsh. So the likelihood of locating a certain Jubilee Shullai, with little more to go on than a faded photograph from a vestry in Caersws, might be considered remote. But, with help from Dr. Arthur Hughes, Bill Price of

Newtown Comprehensive School succeeded in making contact with that very Shullai, by letter, in 1989. It was time for me to brave the pot-holes and coaltrucks of the Jowai road to meet in person an old teacher who has never forgotten that she owes her own education to the children of Caersws.

Bill Price knew nothing of 'the matter of Khasia' until, idly nosing around the vestry at Caersws as he waited for his son to emerge from Sunday school, he came upon a large brown envelope containing about twenty sepia photographs and half a dozen letters, sent from India in the 1930s. The letters, several of which began "To all my kind friends in the Primary Sunday School at Caersws and at Greenlands", were from or about a young boarder at the Welsh Mission High School for Girls in Shillong. Her name was Jubilee Shullai. It appeared from the contents of her letters and those of her teacher, Hilda Jones, that the girl's education was being funded by a 'gift scholarship' collected by local Sunday school children.

"She is nearly 12 now, and a bright-faced pleasant little girl as you will see from the photograph," Hilda Jones had written to her friends in Caersws. "She is wonderfully gentle and rather subdued . . . Her quiet gentle ways are perhaps due to the fact that her mother has been a widow since Jubilee was a wee girl, and she has suffered great persecution since becoming a Christian . . ."

The Caersws children sent money regularly for little Jubilee, as did young collectors all over Wales for many Khasis and Jaintias who would otherwise have been unable to afford an education. The system had been established by Mary Lewis in Cherrapunji in the early 1850s. Jubilee's progress reports to her benefactors were effervescent with gratitude.

"I am glad to tell you that now I am in Class VII," she wrote in February, 1935. "I have a great deal of needlework to do in this class. I am very happy that I have been promoted to this class and it is by your great kindness in helping me that I have been able to stay in school until now. My dear friends, every day I remember you in love and my spirit longs to meet you. I feel you are all like my own brothers and sisters with our own mother. So often when I am in school I think of you."

290

What, Bill wondered, was this Welsh Mission? Although a somewhat disconnected Baptist himself, he went so far as to join the Presbyterians, for a time, in order to learn more about the Mission and to re-establish neglected links – by, for instance, raising £1500 to send a badly needed incubator to the Welsh Mission Hospital in Jowai. But he found the Presbyterians careless of their own past, and tight-fistedly indifferent to the plight of the Third World.

"I was disappointed, to put it mildly," Bill told me. "I tried to get the local churches to raise this money as a Thomas Jones memorial, but they made it quite clear they did not want to know. One of the ministers said the work of the Mission Board was of no concern to him: his job was to look after four churches in mid-Wales, not bothering about India, Africa, Timbuctoo and the moon.

"Presbyterians," he sighed. "They believe nothing, say nothing, do nothing, care for no-one. A Welsh chapel these days is a religious knacker's yard."

Exceptions to this dispiriting rule, he found, were the old missionaries themselves. When he heard that Dr. Arthur Hughes was to visit the Hills in 1989 he asked him to try to look up a woman called Jubilee Shullai, aged about 70, and give her a letter. Mission more or less impossible, warned Dr. Hughes. Far too many Shullais. But he agreed to try.

In the hubbub of a reunion of medical workers in Shillong Dr. Hughes asked a church elder if he didn't by the remotest chance happen to know of a Jubilee Shullai.

"That's her over there," said the elder – and the letter that Bill had waited nearly four years to deliver found its recipient at last.

Although Bill had given me Jubilee Shullai's address, I didn't need it. She turned out to be Dr. Lamare's mother-in-law: his son Gavin would take me to her.

Jowai, chief town of the Jaintia Hills, is only forty miles from Shillong but the journey, on Meghalaya's roughest and busiest road, took us two and a half hours, and would probably have taken longer had it not been for Mohammed's expert weaving and tacking between the smoke-belching coal-trucks.

Driving in these conditions is hard mental and physical labour, particularly for the truck-drivers, many of whom die broken and exhausted before they reach middle age. They overload their vehicles to such an extent that the trucks are only just able to crawl up the winding roads, and brake-failure while coasting downhill is common. Every driver employs one or two helpers, so that whenever a truck comes to a standstill on a slope, the helpers leap from the cab to chock its rear wheels with wooden wedges or rocks; if the truck can manage to surge forward a foot or two, the helpers will chock the wheels again, until, after perhaps ten or fifteen increasingly purposeful surges, the truck manages to regain, unassisted, its snailish momentum.

The chock-stones abandoned in its wake present subsequent road-users with a rigorous test of swerving skills.

Near the end of our journey we passed Thadlaskein Lake which, according to legend, was dug out by the anti-British leader Sajar Nangli and his followers using nothing more than the tips of their arrows. Nearby was a shut-up government hotel called the Orchid, its faded pinkwash streaked with monsoon mould. It looked decades old, but had been opened – briefly – only a few years earlier. Thadlaskein is described routinely as 'a beauty spot'; take away the trucks, and, sure, everywhere in the entire Shillong-Jowai corridor is 'a beauty spot'; but that road and its thunderous coal cavalcades are the blight of the region's tourist aspirations.

Before entering Jowai the road descends to cross a broad valley of rice paddies then rises steeply into the town itself which has grown up around a tight cluster of pine-topped hills. This being market day, the town centre was an almost impenetrable scrum of porters, packhorses, taxis, carts, stalls, cages and dozens of buses so crammed with green produce that the only space for passengers was on the roof with the goats and chickens. Jowai in the 1850s scandalised William Lewis. He found the people of this place obsessed with gambling, and more drunken and depraved than almost anywhere in the Hills. Arson was a local speciality: to finance their gambling, thieves would torch perhaps a dozen houses a month, and help themselves to the contents as the householders fled.

"Your loving Jaintia girl", as Jubilee used to style herself in her letters to Caersws, lives with her husband in a solid oak bungalow in the Mission Compound's peaceful backstreets. Having phoned before leaving Shillong, we found a large contingent of her family assembled to greet us.

The master of domestic ceremonies was her son-in-law, the Rev. Heipormi Khonglah, who has the raffish good looks of an MOR pop crooner (which, indeed, he turned out to be). He led us round the edges of the flagstone yard, where a harvest of paddy had been spread to dry, and into the cool bungalow.

As we sat talking, the children of the family gathered shyly in the doorway. They had never seen a white man before.

"Come on, children," said the Rev. Khonglah, "come and greet our friend from Wales."

"I thank God," said Jubilee at the mention of Wales, "I thank God that he gave Wales and the Welsh people the gift to help others. We have all been so blessed."

The children timidly shook hands with me. "Go on," laughed the Rev. Khonglah, "give him a kiss." And each landed a kiss on my cheek before scurrying with a giggle back to the safety of the doorway.

Jubilee's big shy smile, much remarked on by Hilda Jones, creased close to tearfulness as she remembered her mother and the persecution she suffered. It was a story to compare with Ka Nabon's.

"Very soon after I was born, my mother told my father she was going to follow Jesus Christ. My father was very angry, as he was a non-Christian. He and all of her own family, who were also non-Christians, persecuted her very bitterly. But she stood by him.

"Then my father left my mother, and her own family refused to have anything to do with her, and took the older children away from her. My grandmother burned my mother's bible and chased us out of the house – we had no money at all.

"Then my mother went with me to Shillong – on foot, there was no road then. Just the two of us. She was not afraid of anything, because she knew that Jesus was with her."

"She earned her living by sewing and we were very poor. It was when I was in the High School that Miss Hilda Jones asked her to come and work in the school as a matron.

"Years passed by. Then in 1938 when I was in Class X my grandmother was sick, and asked my mother to come and look after her – the very grandmother who had chased us out from our home confessed then that she wanted to turn to Jesus Christ. One month after becoming a Christian, my grandmother passed away, saying to my mother – because we did not have men at home to guide and lead us – 'I will go to Jesus and he will be your shepherd'."

Her husband, Mr. Gondrickson Passah, had his own memories of the twelve hours it used to take to walk to Shillong.

"That old path could be dangerous," said Mr. Passah, a retired lawyer who resembles a tubby Enoch Powell. "When I was a youngster I was chased along it by Thlen murderers who had been waiting behind a bush to attack us. There were two of them and two of us. We were teenagers – we could really run. And thank goodness we did, because those murderers would have had us."

But wasn't the Thlen these days simply a metaphor?

"It certainly is not," said Mr. Passah. "Just two or three months ago, at Mookympat, 42 kilometres away from here, there was a Thlen atrocity. A man had been told by Thlen keepers to get Khasi blood. He wasn't able to find anyone to get blood from, so he killed his own children – four of them – when his wife was out of the house. The villagers were outraged. They took the man into the forest and killed him straight away."

Some metaphor . . .

Lunch – soup, chicken, rice, fish, boiled vegetables – had been prepared for us next door, in the home of the Rev. Khonglah and his wife Dr. Joannietta Shullai. The Rev.'s electric guitar was propped against a speaker-stack in the living room. He uses it for gospel-singing in his church, Jowai's third, and newest, Presbyterian establishment which already has a membership of 1,000. He has also recorded an album of evangelical pop on which he croons like a cross between Lionel Richie and Dafydd Iwan.

There was time after lunch for a brief tour of Jowai.

First, history: the memorial tower near the Myntdu river to the Jaintias' own rebel hero, Kiang Nongbah, whom the British hanged in 1862. Swap this valley's green waves of rice for whiskered ears of barley, and you could almost be on the banks of the Tywi between Carmarthen and Llandeilo: it even has a graceful suspension bridge for pedestrians, beside which two anglers were patiently awaiting their supper.

The Jaintia Rebellion was one of the most serious tribal challenges to British rule in north-east India. It seems to have been provoked by the Bengal Government's imposition of an income tax, hard on the heels of an explosively unpopular house tax: income tax was a levy incomprehensible to a people whose trade was conducted largely by barter.

An apparent reduction in strength of the Sylhet Light Infantry encouraged the Jaintias – or the Pnars, as they more commonly call themselves – to strike while the oppressor's guard seemed to be down. On the night of 23 January, 1862 Kiang Nongbah led 600 rebel patriots into Jowai where they set fire to the police station, the Welsh Mission school and the houses of some Christians. Within days, a full-scale military operation to crush the rebellion was under way. The rebels held out for several months, retreating to stockades bristling with bamboo spikes, and launching guerilla attacks on the government forces. But their rocks and arrows were no match, ultimately, for the elephant batteries, musketry and cannon of the 6,000 soldiers the British fielded against them.

Kiang Nongbah was finally captured on 27 December, 1862, although his rebellion was to sputter on for another eleven months. He was 'tried' three days later, and three hours after his conviction he was hanged in Jowai market place. Every Pnar is familiar with U Kiang's famous dying words. As the British slipped the noose around his neck, he told his people that if, as he hung there, his face should turn towards the west, his country would remain forever captive; but if his face turned eastward, his country would one day be free. To the joy of his compatriots, Kiang Nongbah died facing east.

But is there not a mischievous ambiguity in that dying message? To Indian nationalists, who encouraged the erection of monuments to freedom-fighters all over India after 1947, there can be no question that the 'country' Kiang refers to is ultimately India, and the freedom he aspires to is freedom from the British. But in today's increasingly centrifugal political climate, a Khasi-Jaintia nationalist might interpret Kiang's words as a call to freedom from India. And a Jaintia nationalist might look to Kiang for an endorsement of his desire to stand apart from the Khasis. For although the Khasis and Jaintias are ethnically one, and the Jaintias' language, Pnar, is a dialect of Khasi, there is mounting impatience among the Jaintias that their cultural distinctiveness is being overshadowed by the Khasis, and some are advocating Jaintia separatism.

Kiang's torching of the Mission school and the homes of Christians shows clearly that the Jaintia patriots identified the Welsh and their religion with the colonialist oppression. At the beginning of the nineteenth century the architects of Empire were intractably hostile to missionaries, but they soon came to value the role played by a successful mission in reconciling disgruntled natives to the imperial plan. It did not go unnoticed that not a single adherent of the Mission joined the rebels. Nor did it go unrewarded. A few months after the 'pacification', the Lieutenant Governor visited the Hills and expressed great satisfaction with the work and influence of the Mission; by the end of the year the Government had more than trebled the Mission's education grant. It was now official policy "not to leave [the Jaintias] in their old state, but . . . to extend our intercourse with them, and endeavour to introduce among them civilization and order". The Mission was perceived, by both ruled and rulers, as a vital instrument of that policy.

It is often said of Khasi churches that no sooner is one built than it's full to capacity, and it's time to start planning a new one. The same can be said of hospitals.

The one and only hospital in the Jaintia Hills is the Welsh Mission Hospital in Jowai. Built in the tin-roofed, Assam bungalow style and situated on a spur of pine-fringed land at the edge of town, it was opened in 1953. As a plaque at the entrance states, it was the gift of the Presbyterian Church of Wales to the Church of the Hills, and most of the £35,000 spent on building it came from the pockets of people in Wales.

"This hospital," said the Rev. Khonglah, as we stepped into the gloom of the entrance hall, "has been a wonderful thing for these Hills. It has saved thousands of our people from an early death."

The Mission's first hospital in Jowai was opened in 1889, but it was destroyed, like all the Mission's buildings, in the 1897 earthquake. Its replacement was opened in 1914 by Dr. Edward Williams (1866-1925), a native of Corwen, who was for many years the only medical missionary in the Khasi Jaintia Hills. His work, he wrote home, was continually impeded by the superstitions of the people, particularly "their steadfast belief that devils are the cause of every illness." There were some amusing misunderstandings. "Lately," he reported, "I examined a man's foot then wrote out a prescription on a piece of paper for him to take to the compounder to have it made up. But instead of doing that, he took the paper on which I'd written the prescription, and rubbed his foot with it!"

The need for a bigger, more modern hospital was felt before World War II, but its construction was held up until the war ended. By today the hospital that was new in 1953 is overcrowded and chronically run-down. Five doctors and 140 beds for the whole of the Jaintia Hills, a region about the size of Dyfed, is woefully poor provision. No equipment has been replaced since the missionaries left in 1969. The electricity cuts out for ten or fifteen minutes about four times a day. The washing and drying machines broke down years ago – dirty sheets are scrubbed 'clean' on the washing shed floor. Dozens of patients, some of them dying of malaria, have to lie on mattresses on the ground.

This severely stressed hospital survives, just, on much less aid than the hospital in Shillong. But in spite of the dinginess of their surroundings, the staff, immaculate in their starched whites, are cheerful beyond reason, and determined not to be beaten by worn-out equipment and soaring patient rolls.

"The missionaries have left us, but the missionary spirit lives on," said Dr. S. Rani, the medical superintendent. "We couldn't run the hospital without it."

As in Shillong, the missionaries and their supporters in Wales are memorialised throughout the hospital. In the entrance hall, photographs of Dr. Norman and Mrs. Phyllis Tunnel smile down from an illuminated "EXPRESSION OF APPRECIATION : GRATITUDE : RESPECTFULNESS" presented by the people of Jowai. And above each bed there's a plaque acknowledging endowers in Wales.

"*Gwely* Marian Pritchard" honours a much-loved matron who served at Jowai from 1946 until 1968. The Rev. Khonglah pointed to a scar on his cheek. "See this? I cut myself badly when I was a child, and it was Marian Pritchard who stitched me up."

Miss Pritchard, some believe, also gave her name to a local school. "This came about," said Khonglah, "because a Roman Catholic father very nearly married her, but it didn't work out because of their different faiths, so he built a school and named it after her, the Marian High School."

At the heart of the Mission Compound is a flat-topped hillock on which repose the church and Mission house. To the Jaintias of old the hillock was cursed: they watched and waited as the Welsh built, gleefully confident that the aliens' walls would collapse and their Mission founder. But it was human rather than demonic agency that wreaked occasional havoc on the Mission's buildings. In the 1880s, for instance, when the missionary was away on tour, the villagers decided that the Christians were to blame for the outbreak of a serious epidemic; so they set fire to the Mission house, completely destroying it, and coming close to killing the missionary's wife and children.

In 1883 Jowai's 218 Christians opened their first church. Built of stone, it was designed to seat a congregation of 400, and was the only chapel in the Hills ever to boast a gallery. This architectural wonder, which the locals described as "a double chapel" or "two chapels, one on top of the other", was destroyed, of course, in the great earthquake.

It was replaced by the present substantial building whose interior, with its polished balustrading and imposing central pulpit, is the most Welsh of any of the chapels I visited. Two relics from the rubble of the first church are embedded in the wall behind the pulpit.

One is a marble tablet, broken in half by the earthquake, to the memory of Sarah Ellen Jones who died here in 1887; the mother of six small children, she was married to the Rev. John Jones (1847-1909) of Holywell, who had been inspired to become a missionary when, at the age of fifteen, he heard U Larsing preach on his tour of Wales.

The other is a stone to the memory of Elizabeth Jerman Jones, who died of jungle fever in 1873. She was the wife of the Rev. Jerman Jones (1833-1890), one of the most prominent of the missionaries. Born at Llangristiolus, Ynys Môn, Jones worked initially as a farm labourer and quarryman. Then he began to study for the ministry at Clynnog Fawr, under Eben Fardd, the renowned poet, schoolmaster and grocer. Completing his studies at Bala, Jones started his missionary career at Jowai in 1870. He is remembered to this day as the man whose forceful personality and sheer physical strength put the fear of God into the sinners of Shillong and 'persuaded' them to do away with the town's weekly 'gambling holiday'. He is also famous for the courage he showed during the devastating cholera epidemic of 1879, the "six weeks of death" during which he threw himself into relieving the people's suffering, heedless of the mortal danger to which he was continually exposed. By 1890 he had, as the Khasis say, "burned himself out for God." Ill and feeble, he sailed for home, but died within two miles of Dungeness.

The Mission house next door to the church is another time capsule. All is much as it was when the last of the missionaries walked out of the front door in December 1969. The present pastor, the Rev. Challam and his wife seem almost to be camping in rather than inhabiting this bungaloid mansion, which could be carried block, grate and flagstone to the Folk Museum at St. Fagans to illustrate how a Welsh farm-boy or slate-splitter could, if he heard the Call, win himself a handsome slice of the colonial good life.

Here, still, are the missionary wardrobes, washstands, cane loungers and bureau. Here too, unread for nearly a quarter of a century, is a case full of Welsh books: the poems of I.D. Hooson, Emrys ap Iwan's *Homiliau*, hymn collections, theological studies and a copy of *Y Beibl*, on the flyleaf of which is written *"I Marian Pritchard, gyda dymuniadau gorau oddi wrth Mr. a Mrs. Griffiths a Grace ..."*

"They left us so much," said the Rev. Khonglah, "but the strange thing is they told us so little about themselves. Who were the missionaries, as men and women? What was this country Wales that they came from?"

I asked what use these days were the cavernous chambers of the Mission house?

"We use them for meetings," he replied. "The Khasi Jaintia people have committees for everything – another legacy of the missionaries. When Jesus comes again, we will have to have a committee to decide whether it is true!"

The missionaries' meals were prepared not in a kitchen but in a cookhouse at the rear of the building which could – and today does – house an entire family of Jaintias in relative comfort. The servants' quarters, in contrast to those of the Saheb and Memsaheb, were a pokey little attic under the hot tin roof, with barely enough headroom for even the Gwenallt-sized Rev. Challam to stand up straight. It can't have been easy trying to sleep with the heaviest rains in the world thundering down on these corrugated sheets.

As we talked on the verandah, I could imagine the missionary and his wife perched up here of an evening, the Lord's masters of all they surveyed – she, perhaps, knitting, he jerking the pipe from his mouth to yell to a player on the soccer pitch below, "Kick the ball, not the man!" . . . as the houseboy served their postprandial tea.

No wonder the missionaries were loth to leave the Hills and give up their palatial dwellings for a pebble-dash Barratt-box in Rhyl or Barmouth.

91

Why did the missionaries leave?

It is generally believed that they were expelled by central government in accordance with an official determination to rid the country of destabilising foreign influences. 'Proof' – never substantiated – that the missionaries were up to no good in Assam was the revolt against central government of the increasingly Christian Naga and Mizo tribes. Had not the Mizos launched their revolt on March the First? Was this not conclusive evidence, bayed the newspapers, that the Welsh missionaries were using their patron Saint's day to promote tribal separatism? Out with foreign missionaries! They would be given until midnight on December 31, 1969 to pack their bibles.

The reasons for their departure seem to have been more complex than this.

When I visited the Catholics' Sacred Heart College in Shillong, an airy Italianate seminary complete with cuppola'd mini-basilica, I was surprised to meet several Italian fathers in their eighties and nineties who had spent most of their lives in the Hills and were resigned, happily, to dying there. I heard also of Irish missionaries still at large decades past the supposed deadline. Why, I asked the Khasi scholar Father Sngi, had the Presbyterian missionaries been expelled while the Catholics had been allowed to stay?

"The Welsh missionaries were not exactly expelled," explained the rotund Father Sngi who, in his *dhoti*, goatee and turban, is 'indigenisation' personified. "They left, really, of their own accord, partly because the Presbyterian Church was mature enough in the 'sixties to want to go it alone, and partly because the Welsh, unlike the Catholic missionaries, were not prepared to take Indian citizenship as a condition for remaining in the Hills."

There was, then, no dramatic ejection of the missionaries, rather a gradual squeezing out. In the 1950s the Government made it clear that only missionaries involved in educational or medical work were welcome in India; if they were there to evangelise, they could go home, the sooner the better. The Welsh Mission was not much affected until about 1966 when the Government started to impose severe restrictions on the entry of Commonwealth missionaries, and to impede the free movement of those already inside the country – particularly in sensitive border regions like Assam. Missionaries on furlough in Wales – such as Margaret Owen, matron of the hospital in Shillong – suddenly found the doors closed to them when they tried to return to the Hills.

In April 1969 thousands of Christians marched through Shillong to demonstrate against the Government's anti-missionary policies. "We pray for retention of foreign missionaries", read the placards; "Foreign Missionaries: Harbingers of Literacy and Education", "We are naked, who will clothe us?", "We are sick, who will take care of us?"

But the Government's campaign of attrition coincided with, and probably accelerated, a process of disengagement between mother and daughter churches which had been under way since the early 1930s.

"There was a constructive policy on the part of the Mission – long before Independence – to withdraw and relinquish authority to the Khasi Church," Dr. Arthur Hughes told me. "This would naturally have tended to the departure of Mission staff members progressively, and in 1969 it could be said that the whole process had reached its intended culmination. Many, or most, of the Roman Catholic missionaries never expected to return home under the terms of their community. Their vocation was to serve to the end in India. Had we, on the other hand, determined to follow that course, we would perhaps have come under more criticism on the ground that this demonstrated that we were determined to hold on to power for ever!"

Dr. and Mrs. Hughes were among the last to leave. Their final years were a period of irksome uncertainty: they got on with their work at the hospital, while the authorities consistently failed to renew their annual 'residence permit'.

"This was always described as subordinate ineptitude, that we were alright, not to worry," he explained. "When we did finally leave the Chief Secretary to the Government came down to our house in person and told us that it was the Government's wish that we should stay – there was no intention to send us out. But by this time we had secured a young Bengali surgeon who had worked in Rhyl, and we thought that it was wiser to leave as soon as he arrived. By this time I was physically near to exhaustion, and had already had one coronary."

The missionaries returned to a Wales cutting herself adrift remorselessly from the Christianity that had sustained her for a millenium and a half. In the halcyon days of sex 'n' drugs 'n' rock 'n' roll, when imperialism was about as fashionable as Queen Victoria's bloomers, these uncool Methodistical dudes must have stood out – if noticed at all – as bizarre relics of Britain's ill-gotten, late unlamented Empire. Even in the chapels, there was little to remind the dwindling congregations of the Khasi Jaintias, now that the Mission collection boxes no longer did the rounds.

Bryniau Casia, once a fabled name throughout the land, was poised to drop into the great dark sack of national forgetting.

92

After a meal in Desmond's marital home, prepared for us with grace and panache by his heavily pregnant wife Lisa, we drift next door to meet the rest of Lisa's family.

I take a few snaps of the gathering, but Lisa herself declines to be in them – the Khasi Jaintias believe it's bad luck for a pregnant woman to have her photograph taken. Then we settle down to a little religion and philosophy with her jovial father, who has just come in from an evening out.

"Now tell me," he says, "what do you as a Christian . . ."

"I'm afraid I'm not a Christian," I feel obliged to confess.

Lisa's father, who, like us, has had a few beers, blinks. This, I am aware, is a Presbyterian household.

"Not a Presbyterian, maybe," he soldiers on, "but Church of Wales or whatever . . .?"

"No, I'm not a Christian of any kind."

"Not even a Catholic?"

"No."

Incredulous silence.

"You believe in God, surely?"

"Not really, but . . . I'm very interested in cosmology."

"You, a Welshman, are not a Christian? I don't believe this, how could it possibly be?" He rubs his face in his palms, and blinks again. "A Welshman who doesn't believe in God?"

"I think most people in Wales today don't believe much in God."

"Impossible, I can't accept it . . . Surely not? Something's gone wrong here, something's gone terribly wrong . . ."

"Anyone for a beer?" asks Desmond . . .

93

The Nongkrem Dance, five days of dancing, goat sacrifice and revelry, is the most ancient and renowned festival of the Khasis.

The tourist-bereft Government of Meghalaya would no doubt like it to become a tourist attraction, but the festival has proudly resisted any move to turn it into some folksy cultural peepshow. What is done at the Nongkrem Dance has been done, with little alteration in the protracted and complex rituals, for perhaps hundreds of years. It is exuberant ceremonial art, with high religious purpose and deep social meaning.

The missionaries, of course, hated it – or, at best, affected disdain. Khasi dances in general, opined the Rev. Griffith Hughes in 1890, were characterised by "plenty of sound, but not a lot of music . . . These dances, together with the archery competitions, represent the Khasis at their most barbarian. The language used by the boy dancers is lewd in the extreme." Until the missionaries left, it was an offence meriting instant banishment from the Church even to witness a traditional dance. Such anathemas are fading history by now, and there is considerable regret among Christians that so many families were persuaded to sell or melt down the crowns of silver and lariats of bobbled gold that were handed down over generations for their daughters to wear in the dance.

The *Pomblang bad Shad Khyrim* (goat-killing dance of Khyrim), to give the Nongkrem festival its full name, is held every autumn not in the boulder-strewn village of Nongkrem itself but a mile down the road in Smit, whither it transferred in 1830. Smit, about ten miles south-east of Shillong, is approached through rolling fields of cabbages, cauliflowers, lettuces, potatoes: the orangey earth of the Hills, which looks as if it has been stained by countless centuries of *kwai*-juice gobbed upon it, is so fertile that it could probably turn a row of broomsticks into an orchard overnight.

The village of Smit is a ramshackle clutter of concrete boxes built down two sides of a scrubby triangle of grass. There is nothing to prepare one for the breath-catching magnificence of what heaves into view at the far end of the village green: the great bow-backed palace of the Syiemship of Khyrim, the very hub of Khasidom, and inspiriting powerhouse of today's cultural reawakening. Presiding over a pristine gritsand arena, and freshly thatched with sun-grass, the *Iing Sad*, as it is called, looks like an upturned boat or a huge turtle. This style of building – or small, family-sized versions of it – used to be found all over the Hills, but few are seen today.

The *Iing Sad* at Smit, the last of its kind, is in essence a *llys* comparable to the court of a medieval Welsh prince. It is the home of the ruling family of Khyrim, which is one of the twenty-five Khasi states; it is the seat of government and justice; it is a place for artistic patronage and the telling of stories. It is also a building of religious significance: at its dark centre is a sacred oak pillar swathed in bamboo matting, with a picket fence around its base. It represents the golden ladder or tree linking heaven and earth, and no one except the *soh-blei* (high priest) – not even the Syiem himself – is allowed to touch it.

Long before the Europeans arrived in the Hills, the Khasis had evolved a distinct and elaborate form of democracy which still subsists beneath the overlay of Indian national and state authority. The Syiem, therefore, is in no sense a potentate: he is appointed through a democratic procedure, and remains accountable to the people. It used to be said that to be elected Syiem, a man had to be both mature and personable, and could abandon all hope of becoming Syiem if he was blind, deaf or lacking a moustache. The present incumbent, the affable – and moustached – Dr. Balajied (chosen one) Singh Syiem, who is also a medical practitioner in Shillong, would seem to be handsomely qualified for the job.

Thanks to an introduction from Desmond, I was privileged during the festival to be invited inside the *Iing Sad*, where I took tea and biscuits with the *Syiem Sad* (queen mother).

The palace is raised about five feet above the ground, and fronted by a deep verandah with huge oak-trunk supports. Not a single nail was used in the building's construction, the use of metal – particularly iron – being considered taboo. Nor is the palace supplied with electricity: the only light in the large central chamber comes from a small square of glass in the thatch overhead. Most of the *Syiem Sad's* furniture had been removed: for the past three weeks the palace had been home to the Syiem's musicians whose every waking hour had been devoted to intense rehearsal. There were just a few benches and, immovable in the centre of the room, the sacred hearthstone, around which food is prepared and eaten, stories are told and tribal lore is imparted by the maternal uncle. There was no fire that warm day, although the cosy savour of woodsmoke hung everywhere. The only competing smell was a sharp punge of goat wafting from a side-room where the sacrificial bleaters awaited their fate.

The three-week Nongkrem observances, only the last few days of which are a public celebration, begin when the Syiem sends to every corner of Khyrim a small chaplet of cane, each with a distinct arrangement of knots which can be 'read', informing the various localities about the tributes that are expected from them: goats, roosters, hurdles of thatch and free labour. The first formal function is the ritual re-roofing of the *Iing Sad*. The Syiem's priest initiates the proceedings by climbing to the apex of the roof, where he prays to God for a successful re-roofing and a prosperous new year. Then he cuts away the first wad of old thatch. The whole community turns out to share in the work of stripping the roof, cleaning and washing the exposed interior, and re-thatching. The job must be finished by nightfall.

The *Iing Sad* is then ready for the musicians. As the Twenty-four Metres are to Welsh poetry, so are the Thirty-two Rhythms to Khasi music. The Syiem's musicians, particularly the drummers, have to familiarise themselves thoroughly with the Thirty-two Rhythms, each of which has a specific role to play in the Nongkrem Dance. Their weeks of rehearsal are necessary not only to hone their musical skills but to bring their bodies up to pitch: they are required to beat and blow for hours on end, and need to be in good physical shape for nearly a week's hard labour with little rest.

The drums, cymbals and ramping pipes of these half dozen musicians are the Nongkrem festival's musical turbine, accompanying not only the dances but the chicken eviscerations and goat sacrifices. There's plenty of whooping and yelling by both dancers and onlookers (some of it, no doubt, 'lewd'), but in all other respects the music is non-vocal. R.T. Rymbai, a Seng Khasi leader, explains: "A Khasi believes in a God who is good and kind and who would not fail him. He also believes that gratitude is the highest form of virtue, and that God desires him to live his life fully. Hence the festivals. When a Khasi is happy, he shouts, he laughs, he dances. When he is sad he sings mournful songs. And so in his festivals, you find him laughing and dancing, but do not find him singing."

The snaking stridor of the oboe-like *tangmuri* has about it the blood-thrilling earthiness of vintage Beefheart. It makes hair-raising, narcotically beguiling music: no wonder it had the missionaries worried.

If Irish dancers are motionless above the waist and frenetic below, and the arm-jiving Bretons are wild on top and cataleptic about the legs, the Khasi dancer could be considered a combination of the two: her top half Irish, her lower half Breton . . . as still as a statue. But look at her bare feet, just visible beneath the hem of her layers of velvet and silk: they may never break contact with the ground, but those feet are on the move, no doubt of it, inch by inch their busy toes are edging them forward. Why, in half an hour or so she and her co-virgins – the dancers must be virgins – will probably have completed a circuit of the Smit arena. And look again at her body, that "perfect parallelogram", as Henry Yule put it: there is, yes, the breath of a pulse radiating from the region of her lower torso, and the hint of a lilt in the plumes that rear from her silver crown . . . suggesting that in her unstill depths she is by no means immune to the music's earthy proposals.

The girls, laden with gold and red-coral bead necklaces, chains, bracelets and ear-rings, seem to wheel as slowly in their anti-clockwise course as a spiral galaxy. At the motive core of this gyre is the Syiem's sister, the 'queen', who is protected from the sun by a pink parasol held by a gentleman in a dark suit.

The men dancers, by contrast, are a red-silk blur of busyness, cavorting round the outside of the circle with a sword erect in the right hand, a whisk of silk twitching flamboyantly in the left. Plumes of rooster or peacock feathers sway from their turbans, and silver quivers and arrows rattle at their waists. The only sartorially discordant note is the footwear: plimsols here, clumping boots there, and cost-accountant's socks.

The dance is an enactment of the social relationships in Khasi society – and a reminder, according to Kynpham, of traditional roles.

"The men are always on the outside of the women," he said. "It is to teach people that we men are protectors of the home, the women and the land. The dance, now that many Khasi men are drunkards and mistreat women, reminds the men of their responsibilities. They need to be reminded, because women are deserting Khasi men for non-tribals because of the way men treat them, especially the rich and the drunks."

Of the dozens of goats sacrificed during the festival, only one is a 'sanctified' goat. His sacrifice is therefore of particular significance. But it is not, Kynpham stressed, a sacrifice to God. "That would be the greatest sin," he said. "God has given it to man to rule over the earth, over every other creature. In our religious ceremonies we offer our sacrifices only to a trinity that we find everywhere – *Thawlang* (the first ancestor), *Iawbei* (the first ancestress), and *Suidnia* (the first maternal uncle)."

The first ancestor in this case is U Shillong, founder of the state of Khyrim which, until the British started to divide and rule, also embraced the rich and powerful state of Mylliem. U Shillong, who has an almost God-like status among the Khasis, was believed to dwell in a sacred grove near the summit of the 6,000 feet high Shillong Peak. Imagine, then, the outrage felt throughout the land when the Ministry of Defence uprooted the entire grove to build a sprawling communications base for the Eastern Air Command. Where once there towered the holiest oaks of Ri Khasi, there bristles now a metal scrubland of satellite dishes, antennae and masts rooted in acres of concrete, all fenced against intruders with twee mottoes like "Vigilance is the price of freedom" or "Know your limitations – then exceed them". Desmond gives voice to "U Lei Shyllong,/Lord Protector of this land", in one of his poems:

> Men no longer call me
> these days, and without
> shame or consideration
> strip me bare
> of my green raiments . . .
> . . . now I stand guard
> with a monstrosity planted
> deep within me
> to watch over this land
> like a single evil eye.

But men do still call U Shillong, at least during the Nongkrem Dance. The rooster sacrifice to the first ancestor takes place on the same afternoon as the sacrifice of the sanctified goat. The toothless (and today, shoeless) old *soh-blei*, who is master of the sacrificial ceremonies, explained to me beforehand that he would be examining the entrails for a red or black blemish; he hoped not to find one because this would be a bad omen not only for the Syiem but the state of Khyrim in general. A few years ago he had detected such a mark, and there had followed a bad year for the farmers, with excessive wind, rain and hail.

As his breath indicated, he had already been slaking his sacramental thirst, the consumption of rice liquor being required priestly practice. Padding around in his nylon socks was also, he smiled, part of the job.

When a crowd of perhaps a thousand had assembled, the Syiem and the *soh-blei* led the sacrificial party slowly through the village, flanked by a dozen musketeers letting out high-pitched whoops as they fired their flintlocks heavenward, showering the musicians behind them with a confetti of blasted newspaper tamping. Behind the band glided the queen under her pink umbrella, and a phalanx of lesser dignitories. Bringing up the rear was the sanctified billy, nudging and butting his harassed minder.

The procession made its way to a plateau half way up a grassy hillock on the outskirts of the village. The crowd, now grown to two or three thousand, took up positions around the edge of the killing and dancing pitch, and the priest and two assistants sat down on a large rectangular stone. Behind them, on chairs, sat the turbanned Syiem and company, including his besuited secretary of state – a portly Presbyterian, who had explained to me earlier that there were no theological difficulties with his being an onlooker, as long as he didn't participate.

The first to feel the sacrificial blade was the rooster. To the tireless battery of the pipes and drums, the *soh-blei* splashed liquor and powdered rice over the quizzical-looking bird, not forgetting to help himself to copious libations. Then he took a knife and sawed rapidly at the rooster's throat, leaving the bird to bleed to death before voyaging into its interior. Within a few minutes he was hauling festoons of intestine from the rooster's corpse, scrutinising every steaming inch for the stigmata of doom. Judging by his boozy smiles, all seemed to be well in that department.

The goat, meanwhile, had been getting restless, and was making increasingly determined efforts to butt its minder in the balls, much to the spectators' loud amusement. As the goat's moment approached, the flustered minder and some helpers dragged the unmanageable beast to the middle of the pitch, and the Syiem stepped forward with an armful of fresh banana leaves to calm him down. The drums and *tangmuri* had reached a feverish intensity, but the goat, now munching serenely, was oblivious at last to the antics of humankind. And as the goat stood there, head down, savouring his cud, a man in ceremonial robes danced to his side, raised a scimitar high with both hands, and swept the blade down – down and clean through the animal's neck, instantaneously severing the head.

There was widespread relief, as the head was delivered to the *soh-blei*, that the cut had been a clean one: to have botched the job, to have had to use more than one blow is held to be a very bad omen indeed. But what of the guts and, above all, the lungs? The animal's torso was carried at a trot to a grassy slope behind the altar-stone, where it was lost beneath a huddle of experts, all shouting advice and banter at a drunken old fumble-thumbs wielding the carving knife. He had managed to unravel the intestines which were piled up near the genitals, but he was making no headway with the lungs.

"Oh, come on, boys," joked one of the younger men, "let's all go and have a drink, we can come back later and finish this."

They all, except fumble-thumbs, burst out laughing. Then suddenly he stood, sweating and triumphant, brandishing the lungs. They were radiantly pink and, yes, U Shillong be praised - he put the severed wind-pipe to his lips and blew them up like balloons – yes, pink and blemish-free. The signs were propitious: Khyrim was in for a good year.

The disembowelling party hastened to the *soh-blei* and the Syiem with the news. The lungs were handed to the Syiem who inflated them for all to see, then gave the signal for the dancing to commence.

The dances that followed were male-only. Two teams of six dancers came forward in pairs. They placed their swords on the altar stone, made obeisance to the Syiem and *soh-blei*, then, taking up their swords, initiated the protracted *shad mastieh* (dance of the men). This was a sequence of war dances involving cock-like scuffings of the turf, boastful prancing with swords and whisks, and stylised feints and lunges. In one dance, small boys in full tasselled regalia attempted to imitate the movements of the men, drawing laughter and warm applause

311

from the spectators. They also enjoyed the Syiem dancing with an assistant priest, particularly when a little dog started yapping at their chieftain's heels, and he had to chase it from the pitch at sword-point.

As I watched the dancing an exuberant Father Sngi, in turban and billowing *dhoti*, bounded up to shake my hand. "A wonderful sacrifice," he beamed. "A tremendous day for Khyrim and all the Khasis. What it shows is that these people still believe that Iewduh market in Shillong belongs to them, in spite of the British giving it to Mylliem for help in the war against Tirot Singh. Yes, oh yes, a thrilling sacrifice! Everyone is so happy."

The dancing ceased at sunset, although the musicians, now visibly tired, continued to play, *rallentando*, as the sacrificial meats were loaded into a conical basket and carried downhill by a female bearer. We all then followed her, as slowly as we had come, back through the village, the children shouting and laughing, the men and women smiling their *kwai*-red smiles, as the muskets blattered flames at the gibbous moon.

High in the electric blue ahead of us stood Venus; beneath her loomed the hump-backed silhouette of the *Iing sad*. And into that celestial darkness, one after another – Catholic, Presbyterian, orthodox Khasi and parasol pink as the lungs of a goat – the *tangmuri* drew them.

94

Was it worth it? What did 'the biggest overseas venture ever sustained by the Welsh people' do for the Khasis? What did it do for the Welsh?

Outside civilisation would have bulldozed into the self-contained world of the Khasis with or without the Welsh. Most Khasis seem relieved if not thankful, however, that it was the Welsh rather than the Bengalis or the English who played the decisive role in the modernisation of their society. Christians and non-Christians alike may be justifiably critical of certain consequences of bossy Methodistical paternalism, but most seem to acknowledge that the distinct historical experience of the Welsh equipped them with an unusually sympathetic understanding of Khasi aspirations.

We in Wales, the very first of England's colonies, might like to imagine that all the pomp and rapacious circumstance of Empire was nothing to do with us, an egalitarian and democratic people with a deep-seated affinity for the underdog. But Wales, whether we like it or not, played her part – and not always a dishonourable one – in her neighbour's 'absent minded' frenzy to paint the planet pink.

The Welsh in the Khasi Jaintia Hills were part of that classic imperialist chronology succinctly defined by General Sir Charles Napier, the conqueror of Sindh: "a good thrashing first and great kindness afterwards".

No one can deny that as the Welsh, in their kindness, built they also destroyed. Even Christians acknowledge the harm that was done to the Khasi way of life by boxing converts away in mission compounds and attacking every manifestation of tribal culture – from musical instruments and rice beer to traditional sports and personal names. What perhaps the Khasis do not realise is that the Welsh, in the name of Reformed Christianity, had recently subjected their own civilisation to almost identical prohibitions. In the ensuing upheavals, both societies re-made themselves. What survived the cultural attrition was, in both cases, the one tool that was vital to the negotiation of a future: the native language.

The mid-nineteenth century, when the Mission to the Hills began, was a dispiriting and threatening period for Wales. Having suffered the ruthless suppression of a series of popular movements such as the Merthyr Rising and the Charter, the Welsh had then to endure a protracted campaign by the ideologues of the British State to persuade them of the anachronistic barbarity of their language and culture. In both crude and sophisticated ways, they, like their Celtic brethren in these islands, were treated as an inferior race, debarred from the imperial comity for as long as they clung to their ignorant ways and outmoded language. Some, cowed by the advertised 'superiority' of Englishness, obediently locked into postures of cultural cringe; more stood their ground and resisted the anglicising fever.

The missionaries, almost without exception, recognised in the Khasis a small people with an ancient language who were confronted, whether they realised it or not, with powerful new forces that threatened to sweep their culture away. If the missionaries were themselves part of the Khasis' problem, they also represented something of an imperfect solution. They taught the Khasis to read, as their forebears had taught the ungodly Welsh to read, largely for religious reasons. But, conscious of how translation of the bible had saved the Welsh language from extinction, they would have been fully aware of the wider cultural consequences of giving back to the Khasis their long lost book. John Cowper Powys once wrote of the Welsh, "A Book saved the culture of this bookish people." The same might be said of the Khasis.

This is why, in spite of the long shadow that once fell on him from Wales, you never hear a Khasi, Christian or non-Christian, speak ill of Thomas Jones. "The debt we owe him cannot be measured," wrote Duari Ropemay in 1975. "This man from overseas has redeemed the Khasi race from the shame of not having their own written language, and he has pulled it from the deep pit of ignorance to the sunshine outside, enabling it to be at par with other civilised races."

The Khasis too were "a people taut for war". They continue to excel with the bow and arrow: archery to them is as much a tribal obsession as is rugby to the Welsh. But the target these days is a straw man, and there are those who complain that Christianity has made the Khasis soft, incapable of firing a shot in anger. The modern world of bursting populations, violent disorder and scarce resources is shoving hard at the Khasis' green door, and frequently lurching destructively over the threshold. Since British rule brought an end to internecine war and murder, the Khasis have managed to achieve their political objectives through peaceful means. But in the increasingly anarchic climate of the north-east, where the machete and the Kalashnikov are a disenchanted boy's best friend, it remains to be seen whether the Khasis, in the treacherous times that lie

314

ahead, can resist getting sucked into the bloody maelstrom that is swirling around them. Is their book and the wisdoms inscribed therein enough of a guide and defence?

A quarter of a century after the last of the missionaries left the Hills, the Welsh legacy there is like the bloom of *cawl cennin* drifting from the missionary kitchen through the whole of the Khasi house. While the Khasis remember the Welsh – more with affection, I think, for the good the missionaries did them, than regret for any Puritanical heavy-handedness – it is curious and sad that we have largely forgotten them.

"And what did the Mission do for Wales?" It was David Syiemlieh who asked that question, as my friend Dafydd Rowlands, the twice-crowned bard from Pontardawe, drove the three of us up to Aberriw to visit Thomas Jones's mill. For the Christian, it is a question that can be answered only in Christian terms. Today's Presbyterians look on the Mission, in the words of Dr. Arthur Hughes, as "the most significant work ever of the Welsh Calvinistic Methodists." 'Gallant little Wales', in an extraordinary burst of generosity and commitment, did what she perceived to be her evangelical duty and delivered into the benighted depths of the 'heathen' world a gleaming shard of what she held to be the Truth. For the missionaries and the congregations that supported their work, it must have been sufficient in itself "To labour and not ask for any reward, save that of knowing that we do Thy will."

Beyond this intangible 'benefit', the Mission's legacy in Wales has yet, perhaps, to be realised. Many Khasis, alarmed at the rapid decline of the 'Mother Church', think it's high time an old favour was returned. When I was in Shillong the Presbyterians were rehearsing a choir to send west in 1993 with no less an ambition than the reconversion of the Welsh. I warned them that this might take some time; they smiled and sang on. It certainly seems that 'mother' is looking to 'daughter' for help: the Presbyterian Church of Wales is so short of ministers that it is now canvassing for recruits in the Khasi Hills. Soon, perhaps, there'll be a Rev. Mania Lyngdoh or Crankshaft Khongwir struggling to learn Welsh (and patience) among the lightless heathen of Blaenau Ffestiniog.

But it is surely time that the relationship between the two peoples developed on a more secular level. As a resourceful people with a state government of their own and a far better record than us for hanging on to their language and the lineaments of an ancient culture, the Khasis could certainly teach the Welsh a thing or two. There could be active town twinnings; educational and medical exchanges; courses in each others' language and culture; collaborations in music and drama; joint publishing ventures; ecology forums based on the Khasis' age-old 'green thinking'.

As some of these things start to happen, and Wales begins to reacquaint herself with a significant part of her story, we may look forward to the old 'mother/daughter' relationship changing into something less parental and hierarchical, a relationship of sisters.

SELECTED BIBLIOGRAPHY

In addition to the publications listed below, I am indebted to the writings of many Khasi and Indian authors whose works are scattered through a variety of theses, journals and commemorative volumes, few of which are available in this country. Chief among these writers are the late Professor R.S. Lyngdoh, Professor Imdad Hussein, L.H. Pde, Professor H.W. Sten, Dr. I.M. Simon, Professor Hamlet Bareh, Gilbert Shullai, the Rev. J. Fortis Jyrwa, R.T. Rymbai, Rita Dorothy Dkar and Dr. David Syiemlieh.

W.J. Allen, *Report on the administration of the Cossyah and Jynteah Hills Territory*, 1858.

N.K. Barooah, *David Scott in North-East India: a Study in British Paternalism*, 1970.

Y Drysorfa Ysbrydol, journal of the Calvinistic Methodists, from 1799 onwards.

Griffith Ellis, *William Lewis, Khasia*, 1903.

Robert Evans, *Y Ddaeargryn yn Khasia a'i Heffeithiau*, 1903.

Alexander Frater, *Chasing the Monsoon*, 1990.

P.R.T. Gurdon, *The Khasis*, 1907.

Joseph Dalton Hooker, *Himalayan Journals*, 1855.

Griffith Hughes, *Bryniau Cassia*, ?1889/90.

W.M. Jenkins, *Life and Work in Khasia*, ?1900.

Merfyn Jones, *Ar Fryniau'r Glaw*, 1980.

J. Fortis Jyrwa, *The Wondrous Works of God*, 1980, and "The missionaries and the Khasi Jaintia people", *New Welsh Review*, No. 21, 1993.

V.G. Kiernan, *The Lords of Human Kind*, 1972.

Robert Lindsay, *Anecdotes of an Indian Life*, 18??

J. Meirion Lloyd (ed.), *Nine Missionary Pioneers*, 1989.

A.J.M. Mills, *Report on the Khasi and Jaintia Hills*, 1853.

James Morris, *Pax Britannica*, 1968, *Heaven's Command*, 1974, and *Farewell the Trumpets*, 1978.

John Hughes Morris, *Hanes Cenhadaeth Dramor y Methodistiaid Calfinaidd*, 1907.

Nalini Natarajan, *The Missionary among the Khasis* (1977).

Stephen Neill, *A History of Christian Missions*, 1990.

Pauline Phillips, *A View of Montgomeryshire*, 1977.

Marian Prichard, *The House of Vision*, 1976.

William Pryse, *Introduction to the Khasi Language*, 1855.

Raymond K. Renford, *The Non-Official British in India*, 1987.

J. Herbert Roberts, *Ymweliad â Bryniau Khasia*, 1888.

Jai Prakash Singh (ed.), *Archaeology of North Eastern India*, 1991.

H.W. Sten (ed.), *Khasi Studies* (a quarterly journal), 1987- .

David R. Syiemlieh, *British Administration in Meghalaya: Policy and Pattern*, 1989.

Ednyfed Thomas, *Bryniau Glaw*, 1988.

J. Tomlin, *Missionary Journals and Letters*, 1844.

Henry Yule, "Notes on the Khasi Hills and People" in the *Journal of the Bengal Asiatic Society*, Vol. XIII, 1844.

ACKNOWLEDGMENTS

This book could not have been written without the financial support, practical assistance and encouragement of many individuals and organisations, both in 'Gwalia' and 'Khasia'.

My first debt of gratitude is owed to the Welsh Writers' Trust, an off-shoot of the Welsh Union of Writers, for the 1991 John Morgan Writing Award, a sum of money which enabled me to spend a month in the Khasi Hills. I am grateful too for the dogged determination of Michele Ryan and Carmel Gahan of Teliesyn to make a film about the Welsh in the Khasi Hills: in 1993 I returned to the Hills with a Teliesyn crew, and the resulting documentaries, *Gwalia yng Nhasia* and *Gwalia in Khasia* were broadcast by S4C and BBC Wales in March/April 1994 and September 1996 respectively. I thank Teliesyn's thoroughly professional team (Michele Ryan, Roland Denning, Will Jacob, Ray Parker, Non Eleri Hughes, Dafydd Rowlands, Douglas Thorpe) for the patience and good-humour with which they indulged their fumbling novice of a presenter. Thanks are due also to my mother Gloria for generous financial help during the writing of this book.

For their advice, practical assistance and, in many cases, hospitality I would like to thank the following: Alexander Frater, Robin Reeves, Kevin Thomas, Hywel Francis, Dafydd Rowlands, Basil Griffiths, Alun Bannister, the late Rev. Ednyfed and Mrs. Gwladys Thomas, the Rev. Merfyn and Mrs. Dilys Jones, Bill and Georgina Price, Graham Allen and Sian Rhisiart, Dr. Arthur Hughes, the Rev. Dafydd Andrew Jones and the Presbyterian Church of Wales, John Whitehead, Nickie Charles, Felicia Hughes-Freeland, Professor Audrey Cantlie, Sheenagh Pugh, Ken Cockburn, Jan and Mike Harris Edge, Glenys James and the staff of Mumbles library, the late Les Holland and the staff of the library of the University College of Wales, Swansea, and Sam Davidson who kindly gave permission for us to reproduce the picture of a barque from his book *Samuel Walters—Marine Artist, Fifty Years of Sea, Sail and Steam* (Jones-Sands Publishing, 1943). Warm thanks, for their enthusiasm and diligence in the production of this book, are due to the staff at Gwasg Gomer, particularly Dyfed Elis-Gruffydd and Mairwen Prys Jones.

I am indebted, above all, to the following people of the Khasi Jaintia Hills for their warm welcome, unbounded hospitality and all kinds of help: Robin Ngangom, Kynpham Singh Nongkynrih, Desmond Kharmawphlang and his entire family, particularly his father Leslie Hardinge Pde, Willis Knight and family, Ananya Guha, Dr. Ivan M. Simon, Dr. Pherlok Lamare, Gavin Shullai, Dr. Balajied Singh Syiem of Khyrim, Manik Laborious Syiem of Mylliem, Esther and Darwin Pugh, Linda Pugh Lyngdoh, Millionora Lyngdoh, Sela Khathing and family, Dr. Orlando Lyngdoh and family, U Hipshon Roy, Hamlet Bareh, Fathers George Kottuppallil and Sngi, Prof. Noorul Hasan and family, Rev. Fortis Jyrwa and his wife Mumtaz, Webster Davies Jyrwa, Jubilee Shullai and family, Rev. Wellburn Manners, Dr. B. Pakem, Rev. Dr. H.M. Rapthap, Prof. H.W. Sten, Gilbert Shullai, Dr. David Syiemlieh and family, Kong Rani Shullai, Almond Dean Syiem, Brek Wanswett and family, Col. Yusuf Ali, Celestine Lamin, Mr. D. Chaudhury, Bah Harvey Diengdoh, Rev. Prechard Basaiawmoit, Prof. Imdad Hussein, Ka Mable Lucy Tariang, V.S. Narasimhan, M.R. Pattanaik, all at the Prakash, Lakyntiew Richmond Lyngdoh and Prof. G.G. Swell M.P. without whose kind assistance I would never have obtained permission to enter the Hills. To all these friends in the Khasi Jaintia Hills I dedicate this book.

No less a debt of gratitude is owed to my long-suffering family who have tolerated my being away in the Hills, if not physically then mentally, for the best part of three years. Diolch yn fawr, Delyth, Angharad a Branwen am eich calondid haelionus a rhadlon.